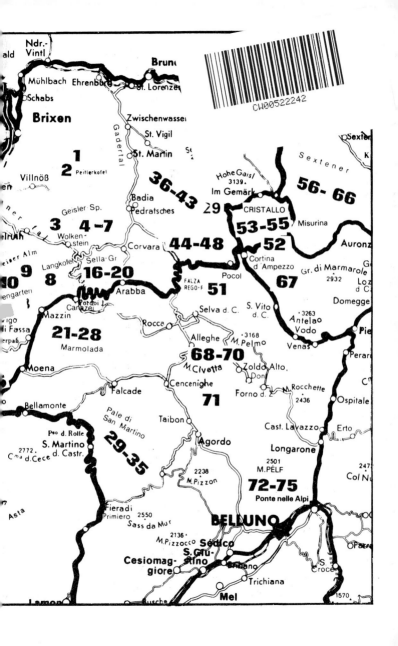

VIA FERRATA
SCRAMBLES IN THE DOLOMITES

Front Cover: The Nose on the Via Tomaselli, Punta Sud, Fanis Group.
Photo: G. Sellers
Back Cover: Paternkofel, De Luca-Innerkofler protected wartime path.
A tunnel at the start of the path.
Photo: G. Sellers

Senterio delle Bochette Alte - crossing a snow gully
Route 77 Photo: G. Sellers

VIA FERRATA
SCRAMBLES IN THE DOLOMITES

Translated
by
CECIL DAVIES

From
KLETTERSTEIGFÜHRER DOLOMITEN
by
Höfler/Werner
(Bergverlag Rudolf Rother, München)

SECOND EDITION
Revised and Enlarged

CICERONE PRESS
MILNTHORPE, CUMBRIA

© Translation: Cicerone Press 1992
ISBN 1 85284 089 7

First published 1982
Reprinted 1986
Second Edition 1992
Reprinted 2001

*The publishers wish to thank Mr Tom Phillips for
additional notes used in preparing this edition.*

Route sketches by R.B.Evans

CONTENTS

THE EASTERN DOLOMITES

TRANSLATOR'S NOTE

This guidebook is translated from the German work **Klettersteigführer: Dolomiten** published by Rother of Munich. Outlying areas not popular with British climbers have been excluded, as have the Julians. All the major areas, however, are comprehensively covered.

The area covered by this guidebook is politically Italian but culturally and historically is closely connected with German-speaking Austria. Many of the inhabitants are bi-lingual and most public notices appear in at least the two languages, Italian and German, often in three to include the local language Rhaeto-Romanic. Maps print names of places, huts, mountains etc. sometimes in German, sometimes Italian, often in both. In this guidebook, which is translated from German, both German and Italian names are given as far as possible - but no consistency is attempted. German names are often given first.

The type of route described here is known in German as a 'Klettersteig' (climbing-path) and in Italian as a 'Via Ferrata' (iron way). (Plural: vie ferrate.)

The German word 'Karren' is translated throughout as 'limestone pavement', though in fact the German word covers a wide variety of more or less horizontal and/or fissured limestone formations: do not expect always or even frequently to find limestone pavement of the classic Malham kind!

The German word 'Latschen' is often left untranslated, as this kind of dwarf pine quickly becomes familiar to all walkers in the eastern and southern alps.

C.D.

NOTE TO SECOND EDITION

About forty new routes have been added and the descriptions of those in the First Edition revised where necessary. While the translator cannot be held responsible for any errors in the original German publication, a few apparent mistakes have been noted. The routes have been re-numbered.

The flowery style of some of the opening paragraphs of route-descriptions may not appeal to some British climbers but is a characteristic of the original.

C.D

VIE FERRATE IN GENERAL

Even before the turn of the century, when the opening up of the Eastern Alps to tourist was completed and the number of mountaineers increased by leaps and bounds, a start was made on reducing the difficulty of specific hard sections of popular climbs by means of wire ropes and iron rungs. The first protection in the gap between the summits of the Grossglockner (1869!), the Heilbron Way in the Allgau (1899) and the Eggersteig in the Wilder Kaiser (1903) originated thus. The advance into acknowledged climbing-grounds followed, with the building of the Pössnecker Path on the west flank of the Sella. After the First World War, military routes with fixtures, such as the Alpini Way in the Sexten Dolomites, were also put at the service of the mountaineer.

However, the real development of protected climbing routes did not begin until the thirties, when the S.A.T. (Societá Alpinistica Trentina), an independent mountaineering club from Trent, together with the C.A.I. (Club Alpino Italiano), shortened and made easier the time-consuming approaches to popular climbing routes in the Brenta, by installing artificial aids. This was the beginning of the Bochette Way, which was continued after the Second World War in work covering many years, and which soon achieved great celebrity. The boldness of the route and its alpine beauty were discovered by numerous mountain walkers, although, following its builders' intention, it does not touch any summits. The Bochette Way became the model for further installations of the same kind, although the original principle - not to build such artificial routes to summits - was soon broken. Recently opinions have been expressed in the C.A.I. that all new installation of 'iron ways' should be forbidden, which understandably has led to vigorous and continuing debate.

The climbing aids (wire ropes, rungs, pegs, ladders) which have been fixed with great effort and skill on difficult, sometimes vertical, and even overhanging rock, enable even non-climbers to do routes which formerly were Grades III, IV and V. So theoretically any plain-dweller in reasonable physical training and active in sports could successfully tackle a via ferrata without further ado. But two conditions must be fulfilled without qualification: absolute freedom from dizziness, and a certain degree of mountain experience, including not only sure-footedness but also an awareness of alpine dangers. Mountain experience is acquired almost automatically through a series of trips, but feelings of dizziness are constitutional and cannot always be overcome by slow habituation of looking steeply down. So anyone who is not completely certain on this point should go only with a guide or a reliable companion.

Even though the artificial protection on such routes in the Dolomites is usually in good condition (in many other East Alpine mountain groups protection, fixed umpteen years ago, is often neglected, because no one bothers about it any longer), nevertheless one must test each rung etc. for firmness before putting weight on it, just as the climber tests his hold, for naturally its security in the rock can be damaged by the weather. Further - a fixed rope should always be used by one person at a time, because the unequal pull on the rope can jerk one off one's balance.

SAFETY ON VIA FERRATA ROUTES

Vie ferrate are frequently demanding undertakings requiring experience in many aspects of mountaineering. These, reduced to essentials, are:
*   Fitness
*   Experience of almost every type of alpine terrain
*   Rock-climbing ability at least to Grade III

At all events it is certain that on not a few Dolomite vie ferrate one must really *climb!*

Routes like the Via Bolver-Luigi on the Cimone della Pala or the Via Fiamme Gialle on the Palazza Alta in the Civetta Group are not just short gymnastic exercises but make big demands on supposedly experienced mountaineers. Therefore fitness and experience in almost every kind of terrain, such as a broken rock, snow, ice, steep grass etc., are recommended.

In addition there are also some objective dangers which threaten via ferrata climbing. Experienced mountaineers, used to climbing, and physically resilient, are not really at risk on 'iron ways'. But things which nevertheless can make a via ferrata really hairy are:
*   Damaged wire ropes (the danger of being injured by torn strands)
*   Protection that has gone missing (that means free climbing)
*   Icing (demands experience of coping with bad conditions)
*   Danger from lightning.

It is obvious that one simply does not start on a via ferrata on a day when one thinks a thunderstorm likely! And what if you get into a mess of that kind in spite of careful planning? The guidebook recommendation for this has long been: "In a thunderstorm get away from iron ladders and wire

Fig. 2

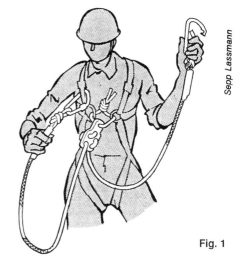

Sepp Lassmann

Fig. 1

ropes". All very fine - but once more that means free climbing. How many people who go on vie ferrate are capable of that?

SAFETY EQUIPMENT
In the early 1970s self-belay by means of a sling and karabiner was advised. In recent years safety equipment for via ferrata climbing has been progressively improved:
*   Helmet - for protection from rock-fall
*   Chest - or seat-harness - or complete harness
*   About $3^{1}/_{2}$ metres of 11mm rope
*   Two special via ferrata self-locking karabiners, with rope-blocks
*   Kinetic impact shock absorber
[Note: The special krabs, rope-blocks (clips to stabilise the rope on the krab) and the kinetic impact shock absorber (KISA) are all made by 'Camp' and are easilly obtainable in shops in the Dolomite area. C.D.]

SELF-BELAYING ON VIE FERRATE

Tie the rope to the harness so as to form two armlength pieces. At the end of each make a loop in which the karabiners are hung. These in turn are clipped on to the steel rope. Thus, at least on traverses or ropes that do not run very steeply, one is completely protected. Two karabiners are used because with only one you would be unprotected at the moment when you have to re-clip where the rope passes an anchorage. Using two of them, one is still in place before the anchor during the re-clipping and thus provides self-belay.

If the wire rope runs vertically or diagonally this form of self-belay can no longer be used. A fall along a vertical or diagonal rope can generate an impact in the order of two tonnes. The safety committee of the German Alpine Club has established through research into falls that a load like this can cause the self-belay (rope, double or single), the via ferrata karabiner, the wire rope and even the anchorage(!) to break.

This danger can be counteracted by means of a kinetic impact shock absorber (KISA). The principle and application of this are extremely simple (see Fig.1). The KISA is so constructed that when one part of the rope is put under stress because of a fall it slips through continuously with a definite braking power as far as the knot or karabiner of the second part. Even though the falling climber admittedly falls about a metre further in consequence, the maximum strain of possibly two tonnes is reduced to one third (see Fig.2). *(According to the German Guidebook not all shock absorbers available on the market conform to technical standards. It is important that the shock absorber is sold and purchased only with the rope threaded in by the manufacturer as other ropes can have too low or high a braking power and thus nullify the gain in safety.)*

From the safety angle an idea from an Italian mountaineering equipment firm appears interesting: a clearly designed plastic plaque shows in words (multi-lingually) and diagrams the correct methods and possible dangers of using vie ferrate (see Fig.3). Since the summer of 1986 these plaques are gradually being placed at the starts of Italian vie ferrate.

Experienced mountain walkers can be assumed to know about normal equipment, the Alpine distress signal and the like. Important in addition: tough *gloves*. For one thing they can protect you from being hurt by torn strands of wire rope; for another, you can hold on to the ropes better with gloves that grip well. This is especially true when the ropes are wet. Peculiarities pertaining to particular routes are indicated in the text.

On longer routes and those leading to great heights a bivvy-bag should be carried.

Fig. 3

GLOSSARY

Italian	German	English
Ago	nadel	needle, pinnacle
Aiuto!	hilfe!	help!
Appiglio	griff	hold
Baita	unterstand	dug-out (military)
Biforcazino	wegteilung	path junction
Bivacco fisso	biwakschachtel	bivouac-box
Bocca	sattel, pass	saddle, pass
Bocchetta	kleine scharte	small pass, gap
Caduta di Sassi	steinschlag	stone-fall
Casera	almhütte	alm hut
Cengia	band	ledge
Cima	spitze, gipfel	summit
Col	hügel	hill (N.B.!)
Conca	kar, kessel	corrie, basin, combe
Corda	seil, kabel	rope
Cresta	grat	ridge, arête
Croda	felswand	cliff, wall
Destra	rechts	(to the) right
Diedro	verschneidung	dièdre
Difficile	schwierig	difficult
Dosso(n)	rücken	ridge
Forcella	scharte	small pass, gap
Ghiaio	schutt, geröll	scree
Ghiacciao	gletscher	glacier
Ghiaccio	eis	ice
Gola	schlucht	gorge, ravine
Gradini	klammern	iron rungs
Lago	see	lake
Malga	alpe, almhütte	alp, alm-hut
Marcia	tritt	foothold
Monte	berg	mountain
Parete	wand	wall, cliff
Passo	pass, joch	pass
Pericolo	gefahr	danger

Italian	German	English
Pericoloso	gefährlich	dangerous
Pian, Piano	ebene, hochfläche	level tract, plateau
Punta	gipfel, spitze	summit
Rifugio	hütte	mountain hut
Sasso	fels, stein	rock, stone
Scala	leiter	ladder
Segnalazione	bezeichnung	way-marking
Sella	sattel	saddle
Sinistra	links	(to the) left
Soccorso alpino	bergrettung	mountain rescue
Val	tal	valley
Van. Vant	kar, kessel	corrie, basin, combe
Vedretta	gletscher	glacier
Zoccolo	vorbau, sockel	base, plinth

ABBREVIATIONS

B	Beds		
hr(s)	hour(s)	min	minutes
km	kilometres	m	metres
M	Matratzen (communal mattress sleeping-places)		

MAPS

Tabacco Wanderkarte	1:50,000	Sheets 1, 2 and 4
Kompass Carta Turistica	1:50,000	Sheet 55
		(Cortina d'Ampezzo)
		Sheet 73
		(Gruppo di Brenta)
	1:30,000	Sheet 073
		(Dolomiti di Brenta)
Also useful for general orientation:		
Freytag/Berndt: Wanderkarten	1:100,000	Sheets 16 and 17
(Western and Eastern Dolomites		

CLASSIFICATION OF VIE FERRATE
ACCORDING TO DIFFICULTY

There seems to be no sense in trying to apply free-climbing grades to vie ferrate. The following comparisons are based on the impressions of via ferrata users who are also rock-climbers. It would be useless to assign a grade of difficulty derived from rock-climbing to every via ferrata. No one would use it. The following may give some help as criteria:

Pisciadù Via Ferrata
   Makes demands equivalent to Grade I

Via Ferrata Zacchi
   Makes demands equivalent to Grade II

Via Tomaselli
   Makes demands equivalent to Grade III

Via Ferrata Piazzetta
   Makes demands equivalent to Grade IV

The following broad classifications may be of help but are not infallible and can change with conditions. The group classification is repeated at the heading of each climb.

a) For footsure mountain-walkers, also for children (on a short rope) and beginners; easy and without problems

5	Grosse Tschierspitze, protected path
7	Sass Songher, protected path
19	Piz Boè, Lichtenfelser Steig
23	Sasso Bianco, Sentiero attrezzato dedicato a Lino Pederiva
40	Monte del Vallon Bianco, Via della Pace
43	Kleiner Lagazuoi, Rock Tunnel
51	Averau and Nuvolao, protected paths

b) Easy for experienced mountain-walkers free of vertigo

1	Peitlerkofel, South Ridge
2	Tullen, Günther-Messner-Steig
4	Piz Duledes, protected path
9	Rosszähne and Maximilian Way
12	Kesselkogel, traverse
13	Passo di Lausa, Scalette Way
14	Grosse Latemarturm, Sentiero attrezzato Campanili del Latemar

c) **Some experience, sure-footedness and freedom from vertigo necessary**

d) **Absolute sure-footedness and freedom from vertigo necessary**

61   Paternkofel, Schartenweg (Wind-gap path)
62   Toblinger Knoten, reconstructed wartime path
66   Alpiniweg, Strada degli Alpini
73   Via Ferrata Sperti
76   Sentiero Alfredo Benini
78   Sentiero delle Bocchette Centrale
79   Via delle Bocchette (Sentiero SOSAT)
82   Sentiero Ettore Castiglioni

e) **Additional mountain experience and climbing ability necessary**
8   Plattkofel, Oscar Schuster Way
22   Collàc, Finanzieri Way
25   Marmolata, Westgrat
33   Croda Grande, Via Ferrata Fiamme Gialle
38   Cunturinesspitze, protected path
44   Col Rosà, Via Ettore Bovero
45   Tofana di Rozes, Via Giovanni Lipella
64   Sextener Rotwand, Via Ferrata Mario Zandonella
65   Via Ferrata Aldo Roghel - Cengia Gabriella
67   Circuit of the Sorapis Group
68   Civetta, Via Ferrata degli Alleghesi
69   Civetta, Via Ferrata Attilio Tissi
72   Via Ferrata Zacchi
74   Via Ferrata Berti
75   Via Ferrata Marmòl
77   Sentiero Bocchette Alte
81   Sentiero Brentari and Sentiero dell'Ideale
89   Sentiero Gustavo Vidi, Sentiero Claudio Costanzi

f) **Good climbing technique on very steep rock required**
16   Piz Selva, Pössnecker Steig
24   Bec de Mesdi, Via delle Trincèe
29   Via Ferrata Bolver-Lugli, Cimone della Pala
35   Monte Agnèr, Via Ferrata Stella Alpina
42   Southern Fanisspitze, Via Cesco Tomaselli
46   Tofana di Mezzo, Via Ferrata Giuseppe Olivieri
70   Palazza Alta, Via Ferrata Fiamme Gialle

g) **Perfect climbing technique on vertical rock required**
20   Piz Boè, Via Ferrata Cesare Piazzetta
71   Cresta delle Masenade, Cima Moiazza Sud, Via Ferrata Gianni
     Costantini

19

Climbing stemples on the Via Ferrata Dino Buzzati, Pala Group

The Western Dolomites

The Western Dolomites, a great group of independent mountain massifs, comprise the area between the Etsch and the Eisack in the west and the line Gaberbach - Andrazbach - Cordevole in the east.

The Schlern (Sciliar) and Rosengarten, whose connected Dolomite massifs embrace the Tschamin Tal (Val Camin) and the Purgametsch Tal in the bristly bow of rock, are not only a climber's paradise of the first rank, but also attract users of climbing-paths with three rewarding goals which offer excellent insight into the western corner-stone of the Dolomite world. The approach - from Bolzano (Bozen) into the Eggen Tal and over the Karer Pass (Passo Costalunga) into the Fassa Tal (Val di Fassa) - is near and without problems for the motorised mountaineer from the German-speaking area of Germany and Austria.

The Schlern (Sciliar), the principal western pillar of the Dolomites, towers over the Seiser Alm (Alpe di Siusi) and the lesser mountains of Völs (Fie) and Kastelruth (Castelrotto) with the mighty structure of its massive plateau. The Burgstall (Monte Castello) forms the northern edge of the Schlern (Sciliar) Plateau, from whose mighty north-west precipice a pair of slim, free-standing rock towers has broken off: the Euringerspitze and the Santnerspitze - alpine landmarks of the Schlern, with all its weight of history. The heart of the neighbouring Rosengarten offers an even grander showpiece: the Vajolet Tower.

The Tschierspitzen (Pizzes da Cir) and Sass Songher, striking masses of rock in the northern wing of the Grödner Joch (Passo Gardena) road, hang over the limestone plateau of the Gardenaccia (Gardenatscha Hochfläche) and the Puezspitzen (Punte del Puez), together with the Geisler Group (Gruppo Odle). The small, isolated rock massif of the Peitlerkofel (Sass de Putia) is only very loosely joined to the massif north of the Grödner Joch via the Kreuzjoch, Sobatsch (Sobuccio) and the Kreuzkofel Joch (Passo Poma).

Anyone who wants to attempt a climbing-path for the first time is well advised to take the problem-free goals north of the Grödner Joch: Sass Songher and the Tschierspitzen may threaten the ignorant with their forbidding series of walls - they offer the mountaineer problem-free normal routes, and the easy ledges and friendly ridges with their modest iron additions will certainly urge many a climbing-path beginner to greater deeds. As such in their turn Sass Rigais and the Peitlerkofel offer themselves - here the more modest mountain walker can enrich himself with a genuine climbing-path experience. For experienced 'ferratists' both routes are problem free, rich in views and most enjoyable. While the isolated Peitlerkofel is best reached from the fastnesses of the Vilnöss Tal (Val di Funes), the Tschierspitze and Sass Songher lie on the central east-west route over the passes through the Dolomites. Here too the Grödner suggests itself as the ideal starting-point.

The Langkofel (Sasso Lungo), first climbed in 1896 by Paul Grohmann and companions, has fascinated all generations of mountaineers since then with its extremely bold towers and peaks and the invited comparison with a gothic cathedral. The summits of this rock group, which surround the Lanfgkofel and Plattkofel combes in a semi-circle, can - with exception of the Plattkofel - only be reached on altogether difficult routes. The Oskar-Schuster route through the forbidding Plattkofel north wall uses a natural groove and ravine system and is only sparsely protected - to climb it is a vast climbing experience.

The Sella, a plateau of mountains on an almost rectangular base, puts its stamp with its sharp contours on the sky-line silhouettes of four main valleys of the area. A mighty, undivided, pillar-shaped, clefted Dolomite block forms a broad, jutting scree-terrace all round, which in places is reduced to a narrow rock ledge. Above this terrace-ledge a second, higher reef of Dolomite rears up with steep, threatening walls, out of which in turn some pyramid-shaped rock summits rise to dominating heights. The contrast between the massive lower rock plinth and the thousand-fold ledged and clefted upper massif gives the Sella its unalterable character. The Pisciadu Path, a monument of climbing-path building-art, offers with its calculated measure of technical perfection the greatest degree of unalloyed enjoyment of rock. The demanding Pössnecker Path also, whose protection was finally set in order in 1981, is one of the 'plums'; while the via ferrata Cesare Piazzetta on Piz Boè must be regarded as one of the 'rare flowers'.

Finally, the Marmolata leads the user of climbing-paths into the highest, glaciated region of the Dolomites and demands from him the strength, endurance and self-possession for a long route on rock and ice. With the Via delle Trincèe, a technical counterpart of the famous Tomaselli climbing-path in the Eastern Dolomites is now created in the Marmolata area as well.

Collàc, Cima Dodici/Sass Aut and Cima dell'Auta orientale are likewise summits in the Marmolata Group, mountains which, of course, are overshadowed by the Dolomite Queen - the first lying south-west from her, the Cima dell'Auta south-east. None the less the climbing-paths on these 'Nameless Ones' are rewarding and still relatively little visited.

There are also now vie ferrate in the Southern Marmolata area, until recently very lonely: on the unfamiliar Three-thousander Cima del Uomo and on Costabella, sadly renowned through the mountain war of 1915-1917, on which the author Karl Springenschmid has set a literary monument with his book of the same title.

The Pala Group, rising between Cismon and Cordevole is distinguished by slim summit forms and a great wealth of fantastic rock sculptures. The famous Cimone della Pala is considered to be the archetype of the boldest rock sculpture. The extensive rocky high-plateau (Pala Hochfläche) which is stretched out behind the series of summits of the main ridge at an altitude of 2500m to 2600m is characteristic. The glaciation is also worthy of notice. The Pala Group, formerly only a paradise for good rock climbers, has now become a dream-goal for experienced 'Ferratists' also, through the establishment of several climbing-paths. The two climbing-paths at the north and south ends of the main chain, linked by walkers' paths, offer the highest degree of excitement, variety and wealth of experience. The central starting-point is San Martino di Castrozza.

The vie ferrate on Croda Grande and Monte Agnèr are in the southern range of the Pala. The Iron Way on M.Agnèr, which dominates this part of the wild Pala, is worth mentioning here. It must be counted among the great goals of via ferrata users.

1. Peitlerkofel (Sass de Putia) 2874m, South Ridge
Peitlerkofel Massif (Group b)

Up the south ridge a well protected climbing-path, free of problems and very much used, leads to the summit, which has become famous on account of its comprehensive view: in clear weather the view all round includes the Glockner group, the Rieserferner group, the Zillertal, Stubai and Ötztal Alps, the Ortler group, and even the great peaks of eastern Switzerland. To the south the nearby teeth and ridges, rock-walls and

23

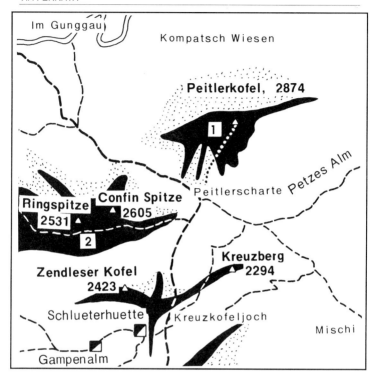

towers of the Dolomites rear up from the valleys with special impressiveness.

Approach: From St Peter (S.Pietro) in the Villnöss Tal (Val di Funes) it is best to go by car via St Magdalena on a narrow motor-road to the Zannser Alm (Malga Zannes) 1680m, guest house and mountain hotel. From the alm the road follows the Tschantschenön-bach (St Zeno-Bach) southeastwards, and crosses it after 10mins. Now fork left on the Adolf-Munkel Weg (No.33) and drive somewhat more steeply through the forest to the Gampen Alm (Malga Gampi) with a small refreshment house: up to here by car. Further north-eastwards, crossing a ridge coming down from Sass Bronsoi, to the Schlüter Hut (Refugio Genova) 2301m, in 1-1½hrs.

Ascent: From the hut eastwards on a wide path in 5mins to the Kreuzkofeljoch (Passo di Poma) 2344m; here bear left on the upper path, and finally northwards in the direction of the Peitlerkofel, which is already visible, almost on the level, in ¹/₂hr into the Peitlerscharte (Forcella Putia) 2361m; paths cross here.

Bear right obliquely up the slope into a broad depression divided by the gully of a mountain stream. In steep curves further to the parting of the paths: to the right steeply and in places with easy scrambling up on safe rocky terrain; to the left, wholly without difficulty, but on the other hand longer - to where the two alternative paths re-unite. Further to the gap between the Gr. Peitlerkofel and the Kl. Peitlerkofel; from here the rocky south ridge climbs steeply up to the main summit.

Firm wire ropes and steps cut in the rock lead excitingly and fascinatingly further; only one short interruption in the rope calls for easy scrambling (Grade I). Further, well protected, and finally over a stretch of scree presenting no problems to the stony summit with its iron cross.

This route climbs 500m from a start at over 2300m, and may sometimes hold snow well into July. Basically the route is an obvious line beside a stream for most of its length. The protected sections are short and almost all avoidable if one takes the leftward branch path that traverses at about 2800m, joining the more direct line a few score metres below the summit itself. The rest is direct, steep and a bit loose underfoot. This is not a three star route, and except as a venture into otherwise untrodden territory, is not really to be recommended to the regular ferrata climber.

Descent: As for Ascent. Anyone who has not to get back to a car can descend from the Peitlerscharte eastwards to Untermoi (Antermoia) or Campill (Longiarú), or westwards to Halsl (Passo Rodella).

Altitude Difference: Zannser Alm 1680m - Peitlerkofel 2874m, Schlütler Hut 2301m - Peitlerkofel 2874m.

Time Required: Zannser Alm - Schlüter Hut 1-1¹/₂hrs; Schlüter Hut - Peitlerkofel 2hrs.

Difficulty: Sure-footedness and freedom from dizziness required; technically without difficulty.

Base: Schlüter (Peitlerkofel) Hut, (Rifugio Genova) 2301m. Built in 1898 at the instigation of the celebrated Bozen mountaineer, Johann Santner and at the expense of Franz Schlüter of Dresden. The fine hut stands 5mins below the Kreuzkofeljoch (Passo Poma). Wardened from 1st June to 1st October. 65B, 20M.   25

2. Tullen 2653m, Günther-Messner-Path
Peitlerkofel Massif   (Group b)

This circuit of the Aferer Geiseln has no huge rock scenery to offer, but instead a pleasantly romantic rock-garden on the home ground of the Messner family of mountaineers. The Aferer Geiseln, a rock ridge which runs along like an observation terrace parallel with the north wall of the Geislerspitzen can now be traversed, chiefly on the south side, just below the crest. The northern section of the round-route, which reaches its highest point at the Peitlerscharte, makes a complete circuit of the northern part of the Aferer Geiseln possible. Moving quickly, fit climbers with stamina can combine the traverse with an ascent of the Peitlerkofel. In the route described below, the Schlüter Hut is recommended as the starting-point, because it is convenient to have the same valley- and mountain-bases from which the two routes (both fairly easy) can be managed in one day. As the valley-crossing north of the Aferer Geiseln does not include any *via ferrata* at all no further details of this alternative descent are given here.

Approach: As for the Peitlerkofel (Sass de Putia) South Ridge as far as the Schlüter Hut, 2301m (Peitlerkofel Hut; Rif. Genova).

Ascent: About half-way along the gentle path from the hut to the Peitlerscharte the Günther-Messner-Path branches left at a sign-post. The path leads across steep grass up the ridge and then right to a small, flat, grassy col where you turn west. Now almost level, north of the ridge, below a vertical cliff-face, to a small col through which the south side is reached again. Up a ledge with fine views, with the Geisler Group in sight all the time, up to the crest of the ridge. A short fixed rope leads to a vertical ladder, which is descended. [A path from below joins the route here.] The path now goes right again and runs along the grassy south flank in easy switch-backs, with steeper re-ascents here and there as well. There is a further view of the north side from a short section of the route along the crest. After descending alongside several pinnacles you go down through a steep, wild ravine on the north flank, where some lying snow lasts until early summer. Then once more on the south side of the crest. You follow the ridge and descend again on to the north flank, along which you traverse on fixed ropes. Soon the high summit-cross on the Tullen comes into sight; but before that is reached there is yet another steep descent in a long groove protected by wire-rope, down as far as the corrie. Now you can climb the Tullen on a track in a mere 20mins and enjoy the splendid panorama from the summit.

Descent: The rest of the route is in part visible from the top. First you stroll comfortably through a high, vegetated valley. Below the rocks *Auf den Kofeln* at a sign reading [Caseril, 32A], turn down sharp left. After regaining height easily you reach a fine viewpoint. A descent with splendid views introduces the *finale* of this route with a *cresendo* of alpine flora. At the first fork on the steep south flank you keep left, and after another, last, re-ascent and yet another fine descent, finish up in a dry stream-bed that joins the rippling Kasserill stream. The paths on both sides of this stream lead to your starting-point, the Zannser Alm.

Altitude Difference: Zannser Alm 1680m - Schlüter Hut 3201m - Tullen 2653m. Re-ascents c.400m.

Time Required: Zannser Alm - Schlüter Hut 2^{1}/2hrs; Schlüter Hut - Tullen c.3-4hrs; descent from summit to Zannser Alm c.2^{1}/₂-3hrs.

Difficulty: No difficulties in normal conditions.

Base: Schlüter Hut 3201m. (For details see Peitlerkofel, South Ridge.)

Tip: Anyone wanting to do the Peitlerkofel and the Günther-Messner-Path comfortably in one day should stay the night at the Schlüter Hut, climb the Peitlerkofel first and use the Günther-Messner-Path as an alternative descent. A complete circuit of the Aferer Geiseln demands a day to itself anyway. Only the so-called *Russiskreuz* (1729m) is to be recommended as the starting-point; this stands 500m west of the junction of the road through the Villnöss Valley and the "Brixner Dolomiten Strasse".

3. Sass Rigais 3025m, Traverse
Geisler Group (Gruppo Odle)   (Group d)

The main peak of the Geisler Group has two faces: the north flank, which falls into the Vollnöss Tal (Val di Funes) is extremely forbidding, while the side facing the Grödner Tal (Val Gardena) is, as it were, comfortably plump and fairly steep. Up this the normal ascent-route, partly protected, and improved in the summer of 1973, conquers the 1000m of height astonishingly easily.

Not having fashionable climbing-routes to recommend it, Sass Rigais is hardly a magnet for ambitious rock-virtuosi. But for foot-sure baggers

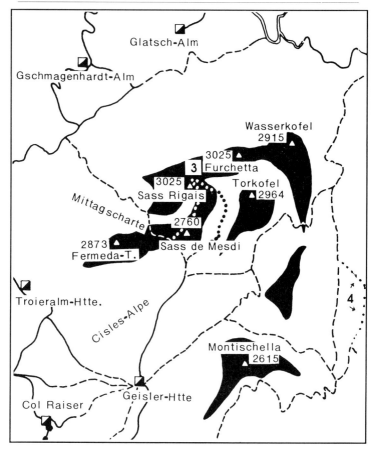

of 3000-ers and those who love peaceful adventures in the Dolomite landscape, the biggest rock massif in the Geisler Group needs no further recommendation. The view alone over the pine-covered Alp de Cisles (Tschisla Alpe) to the Langkofel standing *contre jour,* is worth the ride into the Grödental and up the Col Raiser.

Sass Rigais is moreover a renowned viewpoint and the outer horizon is filled with the Marmolata, Pelmo, Antelao, Tofane, Pala, Rosengarten, Schlern, Brenta, Adamello, Presanella, and the Ortler, Ötztal, Stubai, Zillertal, Venediger and Grossglockener groups, and in front of these an impressive close-up view of the Sella, Langkofel and Plattkofel, as well as of neighbouring Geisler peaks.

Approach: From St Christina, 1427m, drive on a good little road along the eastern bank of the Rio Cisles to the valley station of the Tele Cabina. Now, most conveniently, with the cable lift up to the Col de Raiser, 2107m: the lift shortens the footpath No.1 (road for cars, lorries prohibited) through the Cistes Tal by a good hour. You reach the Geisler Hut, 2037m, in 20mins on Path No.4, gently downwards across flowery meadows. A signposted path also leads directly north-east from the Col de Raiser in the direction of Sass Rigais, so that there is no need to descend to the Geisler Hut. Follow these signs to where the path branches off to the Mittagscharte (Forcella Mesdi).

Ascent A) The waymarked Path No.13 leads northwards from the Geisler Hut across humpy alpine terrain. After about 10mins, at 2123m, use the lower path towards the east, that crosses the slope pleasantly and reaches the boulder-strewn pasture of the Plan Ciantier, about 2300m, from which Sass Rigais rises. Do not follow Path No.13 any further, but the red marker-pegs which curve left into the steep scree groove of Forcella Mesdi (Mittagscharte). Up through this, until an unmistakable fork in the path under yellow crags leads right to a water-eroded rib and the first wire rope, which removes the difficulty from a slabby step up a wall. After the crags of the first rocky top, with goods holds and protected, you climb on a narrow path in many serpentine curves over the stony middle section - cushioned with isolated patches of grass - to a shallow ravine. On its upper side the red paint-marks point obliquely upward to the right, to the ranged rocks of the south-east ridge. A fixed wire rope points the continuation to the forward summit, from which in easy switchback over the knife-edge ridge (which is somewhat exposed, but composed of sound rock) the summit is attained.

Ascent B) First as *Ascent* A to the Forcella di Mesdi/Wasserinnental (Val Salières) fork. Here keep to the right and, through the wide, ever-steepening combe, reach the craggy rock-terrain under the Furchetta. In steep curves up to the gloomy Salièresscharte 2696m which divides the upper part of Sass Rigais from that of the Furchetta. Here via a broad groove up to the actual cliff-foot. A smooth 10 metre high step - the most demanding place on the route - is surmounted with some iron pegs and wire rope. The rest of the ascent leads, without difficulty and always well marked, partly via well protected ledges, via the shabby, scree-covered and steep east flank, to the summit.

Descent: As ascent A) or B).

Altitude Difference: Geisler Hut 2037m - Sass Rigais 3025m. Altitude difference of the climbing-path: Ascent A) about 450m, Ascent B) about 320m.

Time Required: Col de Raiser - Geisler Hut 20mins, Geisler Hut - Sass Rigais 3-3$\frac{1}{2}$hrs; descent 2hrs.

Difficulties: For the pretty sure-footed, a climb to enjoy.

Bases: Geisler Hut (Regensburger Hut) Rifugio Firenze in Cisles) 2037m, CAI, wardened from May to mid-October. 52B, 40M; Col Raiser Refuge, 2106m, at the mountain station of the cable lift, newly opened in 1978, wardened June to the end of September, 25B.

4. Piz Duledes (Piz Duleda) 2909m, Protected Path
   ## Puez Group   (Group b)

Piz Duledes stands almost exactly between Sass Rigais, a favourite mountain with climbers, and the well-known Puez Hut. As a peak it is impressive only from the north, where its steep rock walls fall into the highest part of the Villnöss Valley. While a walk up its easy south side is admittedly not an exciting climbing adventure, it is not merely a 'bad weather alternative' either - for instance, if Sass Rigais is too risky. Piz Duledes is ideal for beginners and for children. Everyone can enjoy the long descent via the Col da la Pieres with its exceptionally fine scenery. The path from the rough, dry limestone plateau to the flowery meadows, where edelweiss grows, below the rock cirque, then again the abrupt change in the alpine scenery when you enter the gloomy ravine below the Forcella di Pizza, eroded into uncanny shapes - all this is impressive and memorable.

Approach: As for Sass Rigais Traverse. (Route 3)

Ascent: From the Geisler Hut (Rif. Firenze) follow the sign for Col Roa. First, the path (No.2/3) leads down to the stream-bed, crosses it and goes up the romantic mountain valley, keeping all the time along the wide, dried-up, sandy stream-bed. Shortly before the valley-head, at the big waymarked rock, take the path to the right and climb leisurely in the gradually narrowing valley to the fork: Forcella Roa (No.3)/Forcella di Sielles (No.2). Go left there into the scree-filled basin surrounded by rocks: this now widens again. The route leads at first through a gently rising grassy hollow, then somewhat more steeply over the highest grass, now interspersed with boulders, and finally into the corrie under the summit cirque. To the left the path leads to the Forcella della Roa, 2617m, and to the right directly to the Forcella Nives, 2740m. On an almost level connecting-path you easily reach the rocks under the Forcella Nives. From the distance this looks really dark and off-putting, especially if you notice the steep snow-gully on its southern edge. But the climb through it proves surprisingly simple. Ropes lead out of a groove on the northern side of the ravine up to the saddle. A marked screepath leads to the summit.

Descent: A) From the Forcella Nives directly south over the flat scree-field about the size of a football pitch (waymarks on stones), then more steeply downhill on the Siellesgrat (ridge) - now narrower and fissured - and immediately after the first slope turn down to the left (waymarks: no route on the rest of the ridge). Down left on a flat-topped ridge on to Path 2 leading up from the Puez Hut, and here to the right. At first easily downhill, then up for a short distance on the west flank of the broad ridge. You go over on to the east side and there walk along an entertaining rocky path, with wire-rope rails in places, to the Forcella Sielles, 2505m. From there a leisurely descent to the Geisler Hut (Regensburger Hut).

B) From the Forcella Sielles up to the south through boulders with some assistance from fixed ropes, but finally in weary bends up the wide range of scree interspersed with grass, to the Col de la Pieres 2759m, an enormous plateau falling gently towards the south. Go for a short distance along by the steep drop on the north until a cairn marks the descent into the west flank. Via steep bends (scree) to about half-way down into the south-east flank; then the path goes west horizontally. Past a bizarre rock-formation and to the right (fixed rope) out of the rocks. First, in wide curves on scree, then over the grassy slopes of the wide cwm; a surprisingly beautiful section - the Sella and Langkofel Groups are in sight all the time! At the penultimate col there is a splendid view straight down to the Geisler Hut, and at the Forcella di Pizza, 2489m, you are in for yet another surprise: a rugged, eccentrically eroded rock tower stands right in the middle of the gorge. The descent that follows is not difficult although it is very steep and has fallen into disrepair in many places. Unfortunately you cannot avoid going uphill again a little to the Geisler Hut, which you have already seen from above.

Altitude Difference: Geisler Hut 2037m - Piz Duledes 2909m - Forcella Sielles 2505m - Col de la Pieres 2747m - Forcella di Pizza 2489m.

Time Required: Geisler Hut - Piz Duledes c.3hrs. Shortest way back 2$^{1/2}$-3hrs. Way back via the Col de la Pieres 4-4$^{1/2}$hrs.

Difficulty: A simple, protected path.

Base: Geisler Hut 2037m. (For details see Sass Rigais Traverse Route 3.)

5. Grosse Tschierspitze (Cirspitze) (Pizzes da Cir) 2597m, Protected path Puez Group   (Group a)

This beautiful, massive rock pyramid overtops all the summits in the jagged rock chain which forms the Grödner Joch (Passo Gardena) on the north side. Formerly this much visited viewpoint often used to be climbed through the famous Adang Chimney; because of a huge landslip in 1962 this route, once a very difficult climb, is no longer possible. The short climbing-path to the summit - completely without difficulty - is nowadays a favourite half-day expedition from the Grödner Joch; the views of the neighbouring Sella, the Puez and Geisler Groups and of the east flank of the Langkofel (Sasso Lungo) are magnificent. In clear weather the distant view reaches as far as the Ortler, Ötztal, Stubai and Zillertal Alps, and the Glockner and Venediger Groups.

Starting Point: Grödner Joch (Passo Gardena) 212lm.

Ascent: From the Grödner Joch first on a cart-track, then on waymarked paths across broad meadow-lands towards the rocky ravine on the left, west of the summit. Via a steep scree slope up in curves into the ravine until the first wire rope leads out of a broad, slabby rock ledge towards the right, on the west flank of the summit massif. Now you follow the good waymarks which lead in zig-zags via broad ledges, small rock steps and

---

Pisciadu climbing path - at the top of a bulge climbed on stemples.
Photo: A.H.Pilkington

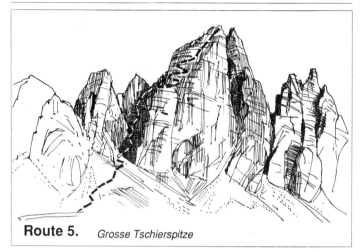

Route 5. *Grosse Tschierspitze*

shallow chimneys, protected in some sections, on to the gently sloping slab of the summit crag, which falls away precipitously to the north.

Descent: As Ascent only!

Altitude Difference: Grödner Joch 2121m - Tschierspitze 2597m.

Time Required: Grödner Joch - Tschierspitze 1 ¹/₂-1 ³/₄hrs. Descent 50mins.

Difficulty: Technically without difficulty; sure-footedness necessary.

Tip: Still rewarding in late afternoon, too!

6. Tschierspitze V (Pizzes da Cir) 2520m, Via Ferrata
   ## Puez Group   (Group c)

The well known and much frequented Grosse Tschierspitze (Cirspitze), which can be climbed without difficulty on a protected path, has gained a serious rival in one of its western neighbours. Via ferrata enthusiasts would prefer the lower summit with the considerably more exciting ascent every time, if they could choose. But both summits can easily be climbed

A steep reachy stretch on the Via della Trincee.
Photo: A.H.Pilkington

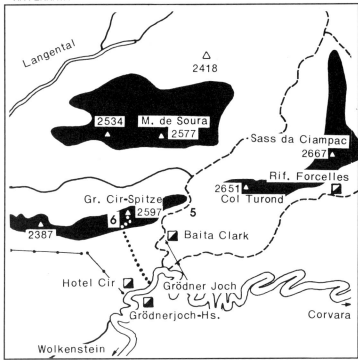

even when only half a day - whether early or late - is available. The bottoms of the climbs are linked by a convenient path.

Starting Point: Grödner Joch (Passo Gardena) 2121m.

Ascent: Directly opposite the old "Grödner-Joch-Hospiz" some 200m below the top of the pass to the west, a former vehicular track turns off to the left by the "Cartoleria". After about 15mins this path ends at a small private hut. From there, to the left over the stream and on a path for about 100m to the ridge, with good views, where the top station of the Danterceppies Gondola Lift, 2298m, with its conspicuous directional-radio aerial and restaurant signpost, is quickly reached along old wheel-tracks. (This point can also be reached on a rather monotonous and longer metalled road (traffic forbidden), which leads up north in many hairpin bends directly from the top of the Pass at the modern "Cir" inn.) Up the grassy ridge, gaining about 80m height, then over steep crags to the first red waymark on the rock. Up a gorge-like gully on the left edge and up the first small ladder to the right at its upper end. On a fixed rope up the first rib to a small platform, then up a moderately steep wall to a small cleft. A really demanding, airy section of cliff, which finishes on an earthy platform, is the real 'plum' of this mini-ferrata. A short rope leads on to a flat section of ridge from which the summit block rises. Go round it to the right; a last rope leads from the back through a gap to the summit - a small area!

Descent: A) As ascent.

B) On a rope down through the fissure on the east of the summit-block - about 15m loss of height. From there a small band of scree (fixed rope) leads down to the col. In the very steep gorge-like gully on a narrow path to the exit from the climb.

Altitude Difference: Grödner Joch 2121m - Tschierspitze V 2520m.

Time Required: Grödner Joch - Tschierspitze V 1¼-1½hrs. Descent ¾hr.

Difficulty: Moderately difficult, really airy in places, but very short. Considerably more demanding than the principal summit.

Base: None.

Tip: The path that links the Danterceppies Top-station 2298m and the Baita Clark 2222m makes it possible to walk easily to the protected path on the Grosse Tschierspitze; both summits can easily be climbed in one half-day.

7. Sass Songher 2665m, Protected Path
Puez Group (Group a)

Towards Corvara and Colfuschg (Colfosco) Sass Songher - the characteristic landmark of this winter-sport centre, falls away in precipitous walls and wildly fissured pinnacles, spurs and ribs.

Luis Trenker is said to have climbed this south flank on his father's rope when he was only five years old. Today a very simple made route leads from the far side via the broad, benign north ridge, to the summit, which is rewarding for the magnificent view alone: the neighbouring Sella is seen splendidly, while the glaciers of the Zilliertal, the Rieserferner Group and the Hohe Tauern gleam from the far north. The valley-view

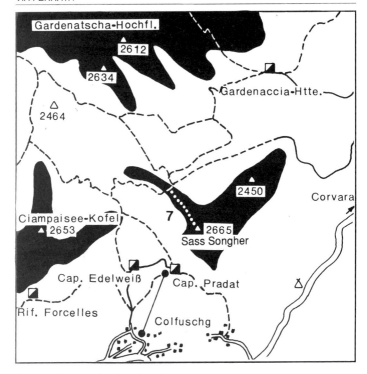

down to Corvara is all-embracing.

Approach: From Corvara to Colfuschg (Colfosco), 1615m. Parking by the church-yard, by the valley station of the chair-lift or, after a steep climb up the narrow village street, at the end of the village by the meadow fence.

Ascent: From Colfuschg northwards steeply up over the smooth, gently rising meadows of Tal Pradat (Val Stella Alpina). On past the Edelweiss Hut and further on Path No.4 into the boulder-strewn valley basin in the direction of the Tschampatsch Joch (Forcella Giampa) as far as the baroque shrine dating from 1730; 200m beyond this, Path No.7 forks off right. You get here most quickly by using the Pradat chair-lift, which swings you up in a few minutes to the Capanna Pradat, 2039m; from here

Sass Songher **Route 7**

an almost level path leads to the fork. Now across up steep grass and scree slopes, in places under rock buttresses and high yellow walls of Upper Triassic dolomite. To the right on broad ledges to steep grass slopes; here up in curves, finally under lines of cliffs to the right to the Sass Songher Scharte in 1¼hrs. South-east on Path No.7 up the broad scree slope to below the summit rocks. Here left and via easy rock terrain, protected with wire rope where necessary, in curves to the upper summit slopes and the summit cross.

Descent: As Ascent. Anyone not needing to return to base can descend east from the Sass Songher Scharte towards La Villa or extend the relatively short expedition by walking round to the Puez Hut or the Gardenaccia Hut.

Altitude Difference: Colfuschg (Colfosco) 1615m - Sass Songher 2665m.

Time Required: Colfuschg - Sass Songher 3hrs; using the chair-lift 2¼hrs.

37

Difficulty: Technically without problems. Can also be recommended for children and beginners (take a short rope).

8. Plattkofel (Sasso Piatto) 2964m, Oskar-Schuster Way Langkofel (Sasso Lungo) Group (Group e)

The gigantic, triangular, uniformly sloping rock plateau of the Plattkofel (Sasso Piatto), surrounded by velvety meadows, belongs - together with the gothic Langkofel (Sasso Lungo) and the Schlern (Sciliar) massif - to the familiar panorama of the Seiser Alm. Altogether different - forbidding - is the north flank, which is cut up by bewildering ice-ravines and high, vertical grooves. The ascent through this wild rock-labyrinth via the partly protected Oskar-Schuster Way offers a maximum of excitement and adventure. Alpine experience, freedom from dizziness, some skill on rock, good weather and ice-free conditions are indispensable preconditions for this expedition. On the other hand, the Plattkofel is the one summit in the Langkofel group which, via its south flank, is also accessible to the mountain walker.

Approach: From the Sella Joch it is advisable to use the cable-car to the Tony Demetz Hut in the narrow Langkofel Scharte (Forcella Sassolungo) 2681m. You avoid 500 weary metres of ascent. The path waymarked No.525 drops steeply on the far side of the pass through a maze of boulders (often filled with old snow) between very high rocks down into the Langkofel Kar (combe), as far as a stone-filled basin. On the left hand slope of this stands the Langkofel Hut (Rif. Vicenza) 2253m.

Ascent: The ascent, which is not altogether simple, but nevertheless waymarked, winds its way at first under the ragged walls of the Langkofelspitze and under the small Plattkofel glacier, passes the rock-strewn Plattkofel Kar (combe) and leads fairly steeply, often over a field of hard snow, to the beginning of the rock ascent. A craggy ledge between two deep ravines leads to the right up to a small rock shelf. Always following painted waymarks exactly, you climb, more or less exposed, via small clefts, crag, narrow ledges and scree steps; you come to a gap, often iced, with an exciting glimpse downwards, cross below a series of dark chimneys, lose some heights in crossing to the left, and stand in front of a smooth wall. This is surmounted surprisingly easily on wire ropes. Having reached the broad scree couloir the difficulties are at an end.

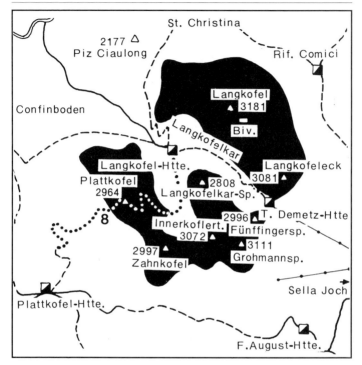

Brittle but easy crag leads up to the level of the exit-gap. From here along the ridge to the nearby middle summit with its large cross. The view all round over the Sieser Alm, Dolomite Groups and the northern glaciated summits is as over-powering as ever. Yet the principal fascination is provided by the view into the enchanted Dolomitic world of the Langkofel, with its thousand spires, indentations and precipices, which lies within shouting-distance opposite you.

Descent: The gigantic Plattkofel plateau, slanting obliquely towards the south, is a favourite high ski tour in late spring. On tracks, partly waymarked with small cairns and red paint, the route goes down the scree-covered plateau. Via meandering grooves, crag and grassy platforms you reach - without difficulty, but not very pleasantly - the Plattkofel

39

Route 8

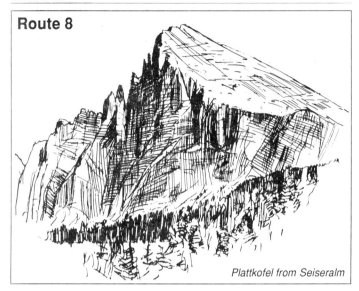

Plattkofel from Seiseralm

Hut (Rif. Sasso Piatto) on the Fassa Joch (Giogo di-Fassa). Now, the enjoyable ramble along the Friedrich-August Way (waymarks 617 and 4) to the Sellajoch is a worthy conclusion. Along by the rocky south walls of the Zahnkofel (il Dente). Innerkoflerturm and Grohmannspitze - all offering the hardest of climbing routes - the path winds its way with many views and without appreciable up-grade to the broad, grassy Rodella Scharte (Forcella Rodella) 2310m, which leads down via alm meadows to the Sellajoch.

Altitude Difference: Langkofel Hut 2253m - Plattkofel 2964m

Time Required: Descent, Langkofelscharte - Langkofel Hut ³/₄hr. Via the Oskar-Schuster Way to the summit 2¹/₂hrs. Descent to the Plattkofel Hut 1hr; high-level path to the Sellajoch 2hrs.

Difficulty: The Oskar-Schuster Way is not a route for the inexperienced; appropriate sure-footedness, freedom from dizziness and route-finding ability on rock are provisos. Danger of icing and stone-fall! Starting early from the huts instead of the valley is an advantage.

Base: Sellajoch House, 2180m, CAI. 62B, wardened throughout the year.

(Nearby Rif. Valentini, 2200m, private, wardened throughout the year); Demetz Hut, 2681m 18B, 32M, wardened throughout the year; Langkofel Hut 2251m, 13B, 37M, wardened from mid-June to the end of September; Plattkofel Hut on the Fassajoch, 2300m, 35B, 14M, running water, central heating, open from the end of June to September.

Note: In uncertain conditions - new snow, ice - get information in the Langkofel Hut. If mist prevails, care when descending over the plateau, too far left you come upon steep precipices.

9. Rosszähne (Denti di Terrarossa) 2653m, and Maximilian Way. Schlern (Sciliar) Area (Group b)

The curious forms which shut off the southern edge of the Seiser Alm (Alpe di Siusi) really call to mind a few completely rotten molars. These weathered peaks - the Rosszähne (Denti di Terrarossa) - neatly ranged alongside each other, look into every window of the Tierser Alp Hut. In 1968 the hut landlord, Max Aichner, decided to eliminate the difficulty of the ascent to the highest point of this impressive scene. He fixed four ropes with a combined length of 150m, enlarged a few rock-steps and holds - and his Mini-Ferrata and hut attraction was ready.

The continuation of this short route is the Maximilian Way: more demanding, somewhat brittle in parts and certainly extremely airy, it leads to the Roterdspitze (Cima Terra Rossa). The ground here is pregnant with history - on the slope before the summit, local history researchers found pottery fragments of the late Ice Age and a pre-historic brooch. The Schlern (Sciliar) too, a fine viewpoint and the climax of the round tour (recommended) is an ancient cultural and historical site. The nearby Burgstall (M. Castello) opposite the unforgettable mountain form of the Santnerspitze, where late Ice Age, Bronze Age and Roman objects have been found, was probably a site for prehistoric worship, still honoured in the time of the Roman emperors.

Approach: The Tieser Alp with its hut (2440m) is reached most quickly from the western edge of the Seiser Alm (Alpe di Siusi), Bellavista (Schönblick), 1854m (car park, bus station, information board). On a good path, No.7, to the Goldknopf Hotel (Hot. Punta d'Oro), 2070m. Here is the start of path No.2 which leads up steeply in serpentine bends to the Rosszähnscharte (pass) 2499m and ends on the south side at the Tierser Alp Hut with little loss of height.

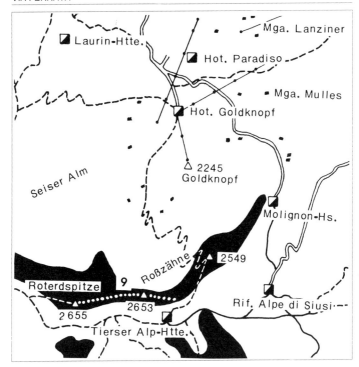

Ascent: Behind the hut the red waymarking leads through a short depression to the southern foot of the Rosszähne with the first rope protection. It goes round a rock corner and through a ravine into a clearly-cut gap which gives a free view over the Seiser Alm. Again on ropes up left over a small shelf and in a few steps to the highest point.

Descent: Exactly as for the ascent. 2nd possibility: From the summit over the steep, grassy south-west flank down to a small north wall, made easier with a 30m rope. In the notch begins the long ridge which the landlord of the hut has christened the Maximilian Way and waymarked well. Provided in part with enlarged natural footholds, the path, often narrow, leads over the Roterdscharte. Here on the left a new descent route begins via the Schotterkar, which was established in 1974 and provided with a 25m steel rope because of its initial steepness. It reaches the Schlern Way No.4 conveniently between the path-junction Bärenloch (Buco d'Orso) and the Tierser Alm. It is prettier to climb the nearby Roterdspitze (Cima Terra Rossa) 2658m by a short scramble up crag - always well waymarked and with the way out onto the ridge made easier with a fixed steel rope. The view over the Seiser Alm, Schlern and Rosengarten repays the slight effort.

Now westwards, descend gently in the direction of Schlern until one strikes Way No.4 which is followed over the broad grassy limestone pavement as far as the junction with the Schlern Tourist Route No.1, which brings one to the right, stonily and slabbily, northwards in zig-zags down slopes covered with dwarf conifers. At the first larch trees take No.5 to the right and further via a stream-cutting to the Saltner Dairy Farm on the Seiser Alm. At the curve in the next stream-ravine you hit the red waymark 'S', which rising first over grassy saddles, then level over alm meadows with a fine view to the Langkofel and Plattkofel (Sasso Lungo and Sasso Platto), reaches the top station of the Panorama chair-lift. Those who are tired go down on that. Perfectionists continue on foot following waymark 7 to Bellavista, where the round finishes.

Altitude Difference: Bellavista car park: 1834m; Rosszähnscharte, 2499m; Tierser Alp, 2440m; Rosszähne Summit, 2653m.

Time Required: Bellavista - Rosszähnscharte - Tierser Alm, 3hrs. Using the Panorama chair-lift, ½hr less. Climb to summit, ½hr. Maximilian Way to Roterdspitze, 1½hrs. Descent via the Tourist Route to Bellavista, 3hrs.

Difficulty: Because it is short the Mini-Ferrata up the Rosszähne is not exacting even for the inexperienced. Only footsure people should undertake traversing the ridge on the Maximilian Way: no novices. It is exposed in places and unsound. The remainder is an instructive walk with very beautiful views.

Base: Tierser Alp Hut, 2440m. Private (reduction for AAC Members) 26B, 36M. Wardened from mid-June to the beginning of October.

Tip: Walk from the Tierser Alp on a good path, No.4, to the Schlernhaus (Rifugio Bolzano), 2hrs. Stay the night there to see the sun-rise next morning from the summit of Petz (2563m) just NE of the hut.

10. Rotwand, Roda di Vael, 2800m, and Via Ferrata Masarè Rosengarten Group   (Group c)

You could describe the new climbing-path in the most southerly rock-ridge of the Rosengarten Group as being entertaining, even amusing, exciting and sporting, but not risky. Linked with an ascent of the Rotwand it can be rounded off into a delightful day's outing. If the convenient chair-lift to the Karer Pass is used, the approach is shortened to a refreshing stroll with a surprising wealth of good views. If bad weather blows up it is possible to make a rapid descent to the shelter of the hut from several sections of the route. The hut stands at the eastern edge of the arena of rocks and is both central and picturesque. Finally, if time is short the route can be limited to some sections and if necessary reduced to a half-day's undertaking. At any rate this new ferrata is a valuable addition to the climbing-paths on offer in the popular Rosengarten. Furthermore the possiblity of a traverse taking several days from the south of the Latemar Group via the Karer Pass to the northern Rosengarten - indeed even to the Seiser Alm - is not to be sneezed at. And this whole way on easy vie ferrate.

Approach: By the double chair-lift somewhat to the west below the Karer Pass to the Rif. Paolina, 2125m. (First trip: 8.00am.)

Ascent: A wide path leads fairly steeply south-west from the top station to the Christomannos Memorial, a huge bronze eagle on the broad south crest - a magnificent viewpoint (barely half an hour). The path now runs on the east side and leads - almost on the level - to the Rif. Roda di Vael (Rotwand Hut) 2280m, in a quarter of an hour. Now *not* on the wide path (No.541) but on the track directly east *[NB. surely this should read 'west'? Translator.].* In a few minutes the signpost is reached which shows all three climbing-path variations.

Take the track to the left (Via Ferrata Masarè), soon cross a wild basin full of fallen rock and climb diagonally up the scree-slope ahead. You reach the actual south ridge in steep curves. A further signpost now points to the first fixed rope, which leads over on to the west side. The well-protected route crosses the flank on wide rock ledges until a short, exciting chimney in an airy section of rock wall leads out on the east flank. Soon in bold switch-backs between wild rock-towers on the ridge, and then once more along under the ridge via earthy rock-ledges. A long descent on the terraced east flank of the final tower on the crest leads to a steep, grassy ridge. You climb up the path and, at a splendid viewpoint, meet the

44

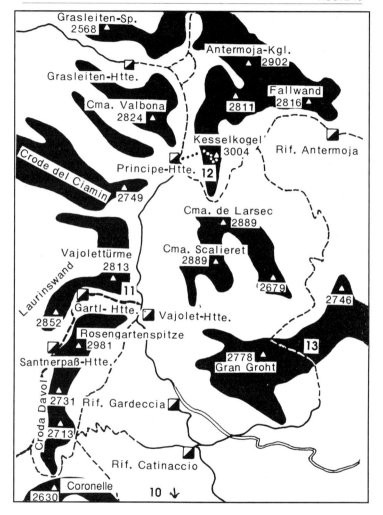

first direct approach from the Rotwand Hut, which joins your route here. (If necessary an emergency descent route, via an exciting via ferrata, including a chimney, in half an hour to the hut.) Soon you are standing in front of a marvel of nature - the Fensterlwand ["The Wall with a Little Window"]. Here a huge natural hole in the rock breaks through the thin wall. At the end of the steep grass ridge the most demanding section of via ferrata on the route follows now quite unexpectedly: a short section of wall, vertical in parts, is crossed very airily on a rope and with the help of some iron staples. Immediately after this section the second path up from the Rotwand Hut joins the climbing-path. (If necessary an emergency descent to the hut in 40 minutes.) After a short ladder and a few short ropes you climb up over the grassy east slope of the summit, gentle at the top, to the cross.

Descent: The descent of the wide, terraced north ridge with its faultless protection is enjoyable, entertaining and free of problems, with a splendid view of the wild Vajolon Towers and the rock panorama on the other side. The stop at the Vajolon Pass, 2650m, provides an unparalleled feast for the eyes: to the east you look over the Vajolon Basin to the Rotwand Hut; to the west the Latemar Towers gleam through the walls on each side of the gorge. Down to the west on steep serpentine bends over scree to the Panorama Path 549. To go straight down take path 539, which leads direct to the Rif. Paolina. If you want to enjoy the sight of the smooth, perpendicular Rotwand, you can wander further on the splendid Panorama Path until you get to the Christomannos Memorial again. From there in 10-15 minutes to the Rif. Paolina, where you can comfortably catch the last chair-lift at 6.30pm.

Altitude Difference: Karer Pass 1745m - Rif. Paolina 2125m - Rotwand Hut 2280m - Rotwand 2800m.

Time Required: Karer Pass - Rif. Paolina on foot by Path 552-542 about 1$\frac{1}{2}$hrs, Rif. Paolina - Rotwand Hut $\frac{3}{4}$hr, Rotwand Hut - Punta Masarè 1hr, Punta Masarè - Rotwand 3$\frac{1}{4}$-3$\frac{1}{2}$hrs, Descent of Rotwand - Vajolon Pass $\frac{1}{2}$-$\frac{3}{4}$hr, Vajolon Pass - Rif. Paolina 1$\frac{1}{4}$-1$\frac{1}{2}$hrs; complete round-tour from the Paolina Hut about 7hrs.

Difficulty: Via Ferrata Masarè moderately difficult; a short section of via ferrata above the Fensterlwand difficult. Protected descent from the Rotwand to the Vajolon Pass, without difficulties.

Bases: Rif. Paolina (top station of chair-lift) 2125m, wardened; Rotwand Hut (Rif. Roda di Vael) 2280 Wardened. Adequate overnight accommodation.

Tip: Path 541 leads *directly* from the Rotwand Hut to the Vajolet Hut, 2243m; from the last third of this route you can descend to the east to the Rif. Catinaccio, 1920m, and the Rif. Gardeccia, 1949m. This path is perhaps an ideal link between the most important bases for via ferrata outings in the Rosengarten.

11. Santner Pass 2741m, Rosengarten (Kölner) Hut (Rifugio A. Fronza alle Coronelle) - Vajolet Hut Rosengarten Group (Group c)

The name of the Rosengarten is very closely linked with the Saga of Laurin. As early as the thirteenth century a minstrel ballard from Bozen tells about Laurin, the good King of the Dwarfs: in a battle against Dietrich of Bern and his companions he lost his kingdom in the 'hollow mountain' of the Rosengarten and was taken as a prisoner to Bern (Verona), where he was baptised and concluded a pact of friendship with Dietrich.

Like the celebrated Santnerspitze, the Santner Pass is named after Bozen's daring pioneer of mountaineering, Johann Santner, who as early as 1878 found the approach route to this pass via the steep precipices of the western Laurinswand (Croda Re Laurino).

Whoever gets over the Santner Pass into the 'Gartl' (Little Garden) penetrates the very heart of the Rosengarten. During the two hour ascent you experience what is so inspiring in the Dolomites; the well-marked path often leads along close to the edge of the abyss, squeezes its way through wildly torn, shadowy defiles, surmounts narrow indentations and a steep snow-couloir. Overhead, sun and clouds pursue the play of colour upon the bright rocks, jagged combs and impending cliffs. And always more magnificent glimpses, both near and into the depths. A rapid scene-change and, as a startling finale, you are admitted into the broad, welcoming circle of the Gartle. Suddenly you are standing in front of the classically beautiful picture of the Three Vajolet Towers, one of the most singular and beautiful show-pieces of the Dolomites.

Approach: Saving your energies, you are swept up 500m to the Rosengarten Hut in the Laurin Cable-car from the Nigerstrasse (5km from the Karer Pass). Or using the chair-lift to the Paolina Hut from the Carazza (Kerersee) Hotel, you can also walk pleasantly almost on the level to the

47

Rosengarten Hut in 1¹/₂hrs via the Panorama - Hirzelweg, No.549 under the vertically sliced orange-coloured cliffs.

Ascent: Waymarking No.542 winds immediately behind the lift-station via the craggy shelf to a fork on a scree-terrace. The left-hand path, often somewhat steep, leads northwards for a while over broken stones to the rock massif of the Rosengarten. Then it becomes exciting. You climb up over iron rungs to a small saddle, and on the far side immediately down into a shallow defile (crux). An iron ladder and wire rope help you to reach a striking tower, that stands higher up, and via a steep shelf you climb down 30m into the 'Eisrinne' (Ice-groove). The most delicate section of the Santner Pass route is crossing the snow-couloir, which is often rock-hard, especially in early summer. If the wire ropes are damaged or buried under the snow it is an advantage to use a short rope to protect the traverse of the permanent snow, which is about 20m wide and breaks off steeply below, and thus avoid risk. New cable has recently been installed to avert this but care is always required. This is a dangerous place. Left via a small wall with good holds and protected with wire rope, up to a last little gap. Finally, vertical pegs and ropes again, then a helpful cleft provides the exit into the 'Gartl'. (Protection improved 1986-1987.) The small Santner Pass Hut nearby, in a situation with a wealth of views, might be made for a good rest in King Laurin's Rock Kingdom.

Descent: First you go down the broad basin in the direction of the Gartl Hut, to the foot of the Vajolet Towers. Always following the clear red waymarkings, you go on climbing fairly steeply down over slabby scree shelves to the Vajolet Hut. From there on a good path No.546 in half-an-hour to the Gardeccia Hut, 1950m.

To finish the circuit of the Rosengarten you traverse under the mighty east wall and further up towards the Tschagerjoch (Pso.Cornelle) 2630m, waymarks 541-550. On the far side you reach the Rosengarten Hut with a lift-station directly on a zig-zag scree path and short, easy rock ribs.

Altitude Difference: Rosengarten Hut 2339m. - Gartl 2621m; Vajolet Hut 2243m. - Tschagerjoch 2630m.

Time Required: Rosengarten Hut - Gartl, 2hrs, descent to Vajolet Hut 1+hrs; via the Tschagerjoch to the Laurin Lift - Rosengarten Hut 2¹/₂hrs. Descent from pass poor, otherwise delightful easy walk.

Difficulty: The partly protected Santner Pass is not difficult. Sure-footedness and mountain experience are of course prerequisites.

Bases: Rosengarten Hut, 2339m, CAI; Gartle Hut, 2621m, private, 23B, 30M; Vajolet Hut, 2243m, CAI, 51B, 44M. All wardened from mid-June to end of September.

Note: Special care demanded when there is icing and hard snow in the Santner Pass groove.

Tip: Experienced mountain walkers can climb Rosengartenspitze (Catinaccio) 2981m from the Gartl in 1½hrs. Normal route Grade II, exposed in places, but with good holds everywhere.

12. Kesselkogel (Catinaccio d'Antermoja) 3004m, Traverse Rosengarten Group (Group b)

The Kesselkogel (Catinaccio d'Antermoja) stands with its steep, terraced flanks at the middle point of the whole Rosengarten group. It is the only summit in this enchanted rock kingdom which exceeds 3000m, and for this reason alone attracts a goodly number of mountaineers every year.

As early as 1876 the Bozen 'father of mountaineers', Johann Santner reached the summit perhaps via the present west route. Even if much has altered since the mountain was first made accessible, the exciting view into Lake Antermoja far below, the panoramic view over the labyrinth of dolomitic peaks away to the Marmolada, and to the more distant glaciers of the Central Alps, have remained the same.

Since 1973 a most rewarding traverse of the Kesselkogel is available. The north-east flank, which is not difficult, has been marked and provided with some protection by the S.A.T. and the landlord of the Antermoja Hut. The upper part is - like the west side - crossed by a broad shelf which determines the ascent route.

Approach: Between Pera and Mazzin in the Fassa Tal (Val di Fassa) a recently asphalted mountain road forks off to the Gardeccia Hut (6½km.) Or with the funicular from Vigo di Fassa to Ciampedi and from there on route No.540, on the level, ¾-hour to Gardeccia and on route No.546 to the Vajolet Hut.

Ascent A): Past the Vajolet Hut on waymark No.584 gradually climbing to the Grasleiten Pass on whose edge stands the small private hut, Rifugio Passo Principe, and a sign indicates the way up to the via ferrata. After a short scree-combe, the first traverse with wire rope protection begins to the left. You slip through a ravine-like chimney, with good holds, which gives way to a somewhat exposed, steep passage. This is very exposed

49

Route 12

indeed, and quite cramped. Getting onto the ladder (or off it if the route is done the other way round) involves a long stride with limited headroom above. The bottom of the ladder is loose (1989) and there is a 5-metre stretch above a vertical drop of 50 metres with no cable. It hangs uselessly below. It is important to realise at an early stage, if travelling the other way, that this line is loose and not to be used for the final step to the ladder. You climb down for some metres on a fixed ladder to a narrow rib. Then up again, mostly with wire rope protection, via easy walls as far as the junction with the old route, which begins just under the Antermoja Pass and is now only rarely used. From now on you gain height on a broad ledge (crux - sometimes snow, no regular cable) that leads obliquely upwards across the whole west flank and ends in a narrow but distinctly defined gap.

You can look down the far side deep into the Grasleitin Kessel. But the ascent goes somewhat lower further to the right, fairly directly up over rock ribs and broken rock (look out for tracks and small cairns) to a rather steep arête together with the north summit. A little curve to the south and in a
50

few minutes you are enjoying the view and the summit by the great metal cross.

B) Almost in the middle of the great boulder-filled level tract of the Antermoja Kessel, ¹/₄-hour west of the lake and the hut, 2496m, stands a large boulder with a sign to the 'Ferrata' and red waymarks, which continue on tracks westwards over the combe. Where the rock and scree area begins, a distinct path can be seen with waymarks that begin well and then become faint. In easy curves for about ¹/₂hr over scree and easy rock steps up to a saddle-like rock ridge which leads over to the true cliff-face. The route sometimes holds late snow - beware!

Now from here you follow the wire ropes, surmount rocks lacking holds by means of two ladders and reach the big scree shelf which crosses the east flank from right to left. After some narrow places and over easy broken rock you advance to the south arête, and from this, turning north, easily to the summit.

Descent: As ascent A) or B)

Altitude Difference: Gardeccia 1950m - Grasleiten Pass 2599m; Start of the climbing path - Kesselkogel 400m. Antermoja Kessel - start of climbing path 200m, - Kesselkogel 300m.

Time Required: Gardeccia - Grasleiten Pass 2hrs; climbing path 1¹/₂+hrs; Antermoja Hut - Summit 2¹/₂hrs. Allow 6hrs, Grasleiten - Antermoja or vice versa.

Difficulty: Ascent A) without problems for those who are sure-footed and free of dizziness. Ascent B) somewhat more demanding, above all when there is new snow and icing because of its shaded situation.

Bases: Gardeccia Hut, 1950m. Private 36B. Wardened from the middle of June to the beginning of October (nearby also two further private huts; Catinaccio and Stella Alpina). Vajolet Hut. 2243m. CAI, 51B, 44M. Wardened from the middle of June to the end of September. - Grasleiten Pass Hut. 2599m. Private 12B. Wardened from the end of June to end of September. - Antermoja Hut. 2496m. CAI-SAT. Trient. 10B, 10M. open from June to the middle of September. (Hut recently considerably enlarged.)

Note: If you undertake the traverse - Grasleiten Pass - Kesselkogel - Antermoja Kessel - which offers a wealth of landscape experience - and want then to get back again to the Grasleiten Pass, you must take into account the 1-hour ascent (waymark 584) from the Antermoja combe to the Antermoja Pass, 2769m. On the far side via a scree path down for ¹/₂hr to the Grasleiten Pass, 2599m. Naturally you can also do the whole thing in reverse.

Note: Danger of slipping on scree and slabs, especially in the last section, in the event of new snow in summer.

Tip: From the Grasleiten Pass in 2hrs via the Molignon Pass, 2598m, to the Tierser-Alp Hut and the Seiser Alm (Alp di Suisi).

13. Passo di Lausa 2700m, Scalette Path
Rosengarten Group   (Group b)

Do not expect exciting sections of climbing on the Scalette Path. What you do find, however, are superbly extensive landscapes together with peaceful solitude such as is found in only a few places on the popular route from the Gardeccia Hut to the Kesselkogel. For connoisseurs this is a beautifully quiet day remote from the main routes; but it can also be a welcome bonus for summit-baggers with plenty of stamina: to round off the popular traverse of the Kesselkogel [see previous route] with a long additional route through the Larsec Group. Anyway, the frequent and surprising changes in the scenic moods make the great horseshoe worth while.

Approach: Rif. Gardeccia, 1949m, or Rif. Catinaccio, 1920m: access as for the Kesselkogel Traverse.

Ascent: Immediately before the last wooden bridge, before the big, gravel-covered parking area below the Rif. Gardeccia, is the sign for Path 538 ("Rif. Antermoja"). The path leads at once into a dense belt of latschen. After a few minutes, turn right at the first fork. First, low down below the steep walls of the Torre Gardeccia, in part almost on the level, but in places actually dropping easily to the east and crossing under the first, vertical outliers. Through open woodland to a broad, grassy slope where the first glimpse of the Scalette Pass ravine opens up. You easily cross the gentle, almost completely grassless lines of scree. Now the route goes north, steeply, but without any problems at all, up the ravine, which is still in shade in the early morning. Some staples make the already simple ascent over scree-paths and rock-steps even easier. In the top third there are actually some fixed ropes for protection. Then the ravine becomes wider and less steep, like a funnel. At the top end a broad plateau, rising to the north in terraces, takes one by surprise. The tower-like Cogolo di Larsec can be seen, to its left the distant Kesselkogel, and below one's feet the flat Larsec Basin, whose lake is always dry in summer. After a short stroll across a completely flat boggy meadow the terrain becomes steeper again. The path goes up through a landscape of barren scree and over short flat fields of old snow. The broad Passo Lausa, which opens up the view of the bold rock formations north of Lake Antermoja, is marked by a sign pointing right (south-east: "Sentiero Paola"). Now you stroll enjoyably down into the arena of rock with its wealth of views. After a short re-ascent over a gently rounded top, the magical Lake Antermoja soon comes into sight, and a little later you are at the Rif. Antermoja, 2497m. *Return:* From the Rif. Antermoja into the valley on a splendidly scenic path, past the lake, and continuing in a dry river-bed to a big boulder (sign: "Via Ferrata"). Here you have a choice: the "normal", comparatively easy return route via the Antermoja Pass, or a traverse of the Kesselkogel from east to west, with a choice of two possible ascent-routes.

The easy way goes straight through the ravine between the Kesselkogel and the Cima Scalieret and reaches the Antermoja Pass, 2769m, after a short, laborious ascent. From there the Cima Scalieret, 2887m, offers an additional summit stroll taking an hour. (Total time from Pass to Summit and back: 1$\frac{1}{2}$-1$\frac{3}{4}$hrs.)

From the Antermoja Pass a path leads across through the cwms and snow-fields under the west wall of the Kesselkogel down to the Grasleiten Pass. Here, if not sooner, at the tiny Rif. Passo di Principe, 2601m, your peace and quiet are at an end. On many weekends you must share the afternoon descent to your starting-point at the Gardeccia Hut with huge hordes of mountaineers and walkers.

In good weather no one fit enough should on any account miss the traverse of the Kesselkogel. [See Ascent Route B of that route.]

Altitude Difference: Rif. Gardeccia 1949m - Passo di Lausa 2700m - Rif. Antermoja 2497m - Antermoja Pass 2769m.

Time Required: Rif. Gardeccia - Passo di Lausa - Rif. Antermoja - Antermoja Pass - Rif. Gardeccia (circular route) 6hrs; with the traverse of the Kesselkogel 8-9hrs.

Difficulty: No problems at all if you are sure-footed. Route-finding difficult in mist.

Bases: As for the Traverse of the Kesselkogel, plus the Rif. Antermoja, 2497, if necessary.

53

14. Grosser Latemarturm 2842m, Sentiero attrezzato Campanili del Latemar Latemar Group (Group b)

The Latemar Group south of the Karer Pass always used to be a bit overshadowed by the splendid Rosengarten, which was also better developed with paths and huts. Since 1982, because the via ferrata and the new Rif. Torre di Pisa have been established, a very attractive traverse of this romantic Dolomite group has become possible, on which the two highest peaks can easily be climbed. The route passes through the southern flanks of the Latemar Towers, 2800m, at an average altitude of 2700m. These flanks are only moderately steep and break off into the steep walls on the northern side. The route runs predominantly on natural ledges and walking terrain; the protection is limited to one part. But there are really exciting sections on the two ascents and at the five wind-gaps, where there are breath-taking views straight down. Though the high route is exposed it is largely free of problems and numerous surprises add to its flavour.

Approach: The shortest approach is from the Meier Alm, 2037m, which is reached in 3.7km on a good minor road from Obereggen, 1561m, situated on the western slope of the Latemar Group. (Signs at the highest point of the road above Obereggen.) This cosy alpine inn offers simple food and adequate parking-space. You should not rely completely upon the chairlifts running in summer, but there is a lift from Obereggen to Path No.22, which runs near the Meier Alm.

Ascent: From the Meier Alm climb directly up in a few minutes to the top station of a chair-lift which is visible from the alm. (You can also reach this point if you have come by lift from Obereggen.) You meet Path 22, which soon leads very steeply up a scree-covered ridge. Here you meet the path leading up from Predazzo and, after a steep ascent, you reach the hospitable Rifugio Torre di Pisa, 2675m, situated in the south-west part of the Latemar Group, near the bizarre "rock-circus". Here you first follow Path 516 to the ridge and then climb down a short distance into a snow-filled rock-basin surrounded by pinnacles, towers and ridges. A scree-covered path continues northwards on the east side of a towering rock ridge and crosses a gigantic wilderness of stone, called the Valsordakessel, with its mysterious, deep rock-crevasses.

Shortly after a waymarked path to the Bivacco Latemar, above a helicopter-pad, you reach a broad, grassy saddle on the rock-ridge, the Forcella dei Campanili. Here a steep path leads up in a few minutes to the
54

start of the via ferrata - Path 511 (big signs at exactly 2600m). Up a steep track over the scree-covered flank to reach the first rope in a few minutes. The route leads without difficulty diagonally along by a wall and soon leads via a flat ledge to a grassy spot. A further rope leads via a nick and up the next rock ridge. Obliquely up over a scree-covered flank interspersed with grass, and easily on an almost level scree-path to the next nick, with wire-rope protection. Soon you cross two small hollows, one immediately after the other, from which the view to the north is blocked by a striking twin-tower. On the long way across a moderately steep scree-slope you are on the south flank of the main summit. Near the middle of the flank you will notice the marks of descending footsteps in the scree above and below the path. The main summit, which is not distinctly visible from here, is immediately above this spot. It can be reached without difficulty in about twenty minutes: no path, but footmarks, and cairns in places.

This main summit, the Diamantidi-Tower (Grosser Latemarturm; Cimon del Latemar) 2842m, offers incomparable views down and around in all directions!

The path itself leads, after a small nick, into more rocky scenery again. You reach a vertical drop via several scree-covered ribs. An iron ladder with staggered rungs leads down into the next nick and a little way up on the other side. The last bit of the via ferrata goes down steeply into the broad, grassy Forcella Grande del Latemar, 2620m; here is the Bivacco M.O.Mario Rigatti. Even if you have decided to return from here (and not to continue the crossing in the direction of the Karer Pass) you are recommended, if fit enough, to climb the next summit, the Eastern Latemarspitze, 2791m, with its big cross. The steep, waymarked path can be surmounted in $^{1}/_{2}$-$^{3}/_{4}$hr.

Descent: A) The 'Normal Route' (No.18) leads from the Forcella Grande del Latemar back across the south flank of the Latemar Towers - several hundred metres lower than the via ferrata - to near the start of the via ferrata below the Forcella dei Campanili. The path is easier and shorter than the via ferrata. You come to the fork to the Bivacco Latemar and can get to know the harsh appeal of the Valsordakessel better by the detour via this bivouac. Soon you come to the main path, 516, again, leading back to the Rifugio and the Meier Alm.

B) If you have solved the problem of getting back from the Karer Pass to the Meier Alm with the help of a friend with a car, you can climb to the Eastern Latemar Summit in $^{1}/_{2}$-$^{3}/_{4}$hr on the steep path, 18. From there Path 18 leads without problems and well waymarked along the ridge and down to the Karer Pass, 1745m. (It is not possible to make the return journey by public transport!)

Altitude Difference: Meier Alm 2037m - Rif. Torre di Pisa 2675 - Cimon del Latemar 2842m. Altitude differences within the via ferrata about 200m.

Time Required: Meier Alm - Rif. Torre di Pisa 1½hrs; Rifugio Torre di Pisa - Forcella dei Campanili 1hr; Forcella dei Campanili - Forcella Grande del Latemar 1½hrs; return on Path 18 to the Rifugio Torre di Pisa 2hrs; descent to the Meier Alm 1hr; total time 7hrs; total time with additional ascents of the Grosser Latemarturm and the Eastern Latemarspitze, about 9hrs.

Difficulty: Almost horizontal paths on the rock and scree terrain on the south side. Very good protection and problem-free going in both directions make this a day's outing without difficulties, though long.

Bases: Rif.Torre di Pisa, 2675m, privately owned, 16 beds and sleeping-places, open from beginning of June to mid-October; Bivacco M.O.Mario Rigatti, 2620m, emergency accommodation, sleeps 9; if necessary there is also the Bivacco Latemar, 2355m, a little off the main route.

15. Punta Polse 1450m, Sentiero attrezzato Attilio Sieff Latemar Group (Group c)

North of Ziano di Fiemme vertical rock-walls of varying height rise above a steep belt of forest. Above the centre of the village a broad, clearly isolated rock-tower with a large white cross stands in front of a compactly formed cliff. The via ferrata up it is surprisingly exciting and novel and is certainly worth the rather monotonous climb through the belt of forest.

For those interested in folklore there is a very unusual record of the life of herdsmen in bygone times before the start of the climb. There are some 500 inscriptions in red chalk scattered along a stretch of several hundred metres on the rocks at the foot of the cliff. These consist of initials and dates as well as a series of additional drawings. Most of the dates come from the period between 1750 and 1800, but many are also to be found from 1800 to 1925, and occasionally even primitive representations of animals. For almost 200 years the herdsmen have immortalised themselves here on the rock-walls - an entry for every summer's grazing.

The belt of forest between the valley and the rock could originally be used for grazing by every farmer in the village. Throughout the grazing season the cattle were placed in the care of professional herdsmen, who presumably had to remain up here by night as well, to prevent the cattle getting into difficulties.

Approach: Ziano di Fiemme, 954m, lies 3.5km southwest and downstream of Predazzo. The village burial-ground is directly opposite the church, on the other side of the road. A narrow hard-top road passes behind it. A sign to the access into the forest is only a few steps higher up.

Ascent: The fine, shady path soon crosses a forestry road. Here you go to the left across the sharp bend and only 10m beyond you come to the sign to the via ferrata. The route now goes, with many sharp bends, via a very steep but shady path somewhat monotonously to the foot of the rock-wall with its fascinating inscriptions by the former herdsmen. Along this wall, left, to the first rope by the commemorative plaque. Up on a firm new rope at the edge of the vertical rock-wall, partly over steep steps, partly via more level grassy ledges. Across a scree-covered ledge to the vertical wall of the Punta Polse, at the edge of which you climb up on a rope: a few steps in clayey ground. A novel pitch follows through a "squeeze-chimney". You work your way up on the rope under huge jammed boulders. Through a very steep, earthy groove with the help of a further rope and to a stance on the little saddle between the rock-wall and the Punta Polse. The last steep step up the rock-tower is very well protected.

Descent: Only as ascent.

Altitude Difference: Ziano di Fiemme - Punta Polse 490m.

Height of via ferrata: About 130m.

Time required: Ziano di Fiemme - Punta Polse 1³⁄₄hrs, descent 1hr.

Difficulty: Short but exciting and technically demanding via ferrata. Not for children or beginners.

Bases: None.

16. Pössnecker Path (Piz Selva 2941m)
   Sella Group   (Group f)

The Pössnecker path is the oldest protected rock path in the Dolomites. As early as August 1907 Paul Mayr and Georg Haupt from Bozen reached the western edge of the Sella and Piz Selva by roughly the present-day

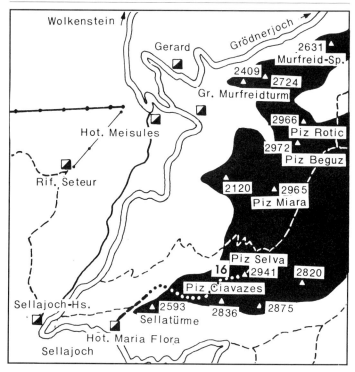

ascent-route. These alpine pioneers found the ideal route through the forbidding rock wall at the first attempt: it is about Grade IV. A few years later the route was made easier by means of pegs, iron ladders, wire ropes and enlarged holds, by the Pössneck Section of the DAV under the name Pössnecker Weg.

To climb it demands, in spite of all the climbing aids, alpine experience, security on rock and absolute immunity to exposure. On this route the inexperienced feel decidedly better on a safe partner's rope.

Approach: From the Sellajoch (Passo Sella) you cross eastwards on a good path (No.649) over grass and scree to the characteristic Sella Towers and go along, half-way up the combe, by the series of walls to about 500m north of the third tower. The start of the climb is by the grey-black, water-streaked wall, opposite a small rock pinnacle, exactly under the deepest indentation in the west bastion that rises above.

Ascent: A wire rope leads via the vertical rock-foot into a steep part of the wall by a watercourse. From here into a gloomy cleft which leads to a completely vertical section of the cliff. Here the smooth rock wall and detached pillar form a narrow chimney which is climbed with the help of protection. The climb out of this chimney on to the tiny summit of the pillar is very airy. Via a short iron ladder about 150m above the floor of the combe extremely airily from the top of the pillar over on to the now extraordinarily exposed, vertical, open wall. The route now goes the remaining 100m of height over changing clefts and chimneys, almost vertically and always very exposed up to a basin-like scree-step. Here you can breathe a sigh of relief, for moral and technical demands of this sort are no longer to be expected.

The route now crosses the craggy flank to the left and leads into a well-protected ravine comparatively comfortably over the last steep rock on to the scree-covered plateaux of the Sella massif. It now goes on easy walking terrain to the weathered rock summit of Piz Selva 2941m. The summit, is a dominating point in the silhouette of the ragged, rocky and bare plateau, with an exciting view toward the Langkofel opposite and the glittering Marmolata beyond the southern edge of the plateau.

The continuation of the route over the Altopiano di Meisules will fully satisfy peak-baggers and connoisseurs of views. Waymarking No.649 leads northwards in wide arcs to the Gamsscharte, 2919m. On this splendid, almost horizontal, high-level walk you can take in, with minor diversions from the path, altogether eight flat-topped summits between Piz Gralba and the western Meisules.

At the pass you strike the fork with the much-frequented path No.666, which connects with the Hut (Pisciadù Hut).

Descent: As most people want to avoid descending the vertical ascent route, the choice of descents, especially in regard to base, is particularly significant.

A) Anyone who want to spice the expedition with a particularly airy descent chooses the Pisciadù Climbing Path, on which you reach the Grödner Joch without much detour. On path No.666 down left to the Pisciadù Hut. From here, see Route 17 (in reverse).

B) From the Pisciadù Hut through the Val Setus (see descent from Route 17) - the shortest way to the Grödner Joch.

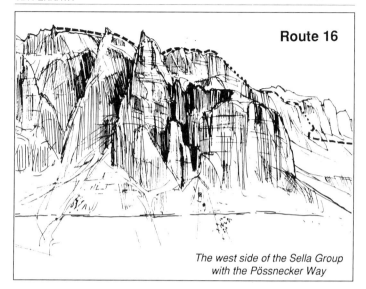

Route 16

*The west side of the Sella Group
with the Pössnecker Way*

C) From the pass southwards to the right, and half way to the Cavazza Hut to the right of path No.647 and through the magnificent Val Lasties and up the road on the south side of the Sella Joch.

D) From the Gamsscharte on path No.666 to the Cavazza Hut, from here on path No.651 through the famous Val de Mesdi (Mittagstal) to near Colfuschg.

E) From the Cavazza Hut in wide arcs over to the Pordoispitze (Sass Pordoi), from here either on foot, or more easily with the cable-car to the Pordoi Joch (Passo Pordoi).

Altitude Difference of the Climbing Path: about 800m.

Difficulty: Very exposed in places. Only for very sure-footed mountaineers, free from vertigo. Rock-climbing skill essential.

Time Required: As far as Piz Selva 3-3¹/₂hrs. (Larger groups will take longer because one-at-a-time movement is necessary in places). Descent, according to route, 2¹/₂-4hrs.

Base: Sellajoch House, 2180m, CAI, 62B, wardened throughout the year; (Nearby Rif. Valentini, 2200m, private, wardened throughout the year);
60

Boè hut, 2871m, CAI, 28B, 20M, wardened from the beginning of July to the end of September; Pisciadù hut, 2583m, CAI 18B, wardened from the beginning of July to the end of September.

Notes: Do not start too early on the cliff, which is shaded in the morning, often iced. Mist on the plateau makes route-finding problematic - keep precisely to the waymarks. Because you may perhaps have to get back to the Sellajoch if occasion arises, make sure of the bus connections! It is ideal if before you start you can put a second car where you intend to come down.

17. Pisciadù Climbing Path (Via Ferrata Brigata Tridentina) Sella Group (Group d)

The second protected rock path in the Sella group exists thanks to an initiative of the CAI Bologna and an anonymous donor. The route forces its way through one of the wildest and most romantic folds in the north flank, to the right by the waterfall, up to the scree balcony which goes round the whole Sella massif. Up there, there is space enough for Lake Pisciadù and the friendly refuge. When this first-rate and skilfully planned climbing-path was first set up, the hut warden and mountain guide, Germano Kostner, was decisively involved, together with soldiers from the Trentino region. For this reason, too, the official name, 'Via Ferrata Brigata Tridentina - Versicherter Pisciadù-Klettersteig'. So it reads on a sign at Kilometre 8 on the Grödner Joch-Colfuschg road, which points to the start of the 'iron way'. The route stretches to the top of the waterfall, is fitted with 440m of fixed rope and 130 iron brackets, is in parts really exposed but always well protected, with good holds and excitingly beautiful.

The second section was not finished until the summer of 1968, again with the leadership and assistance of Germano. This upper section leads up, even more airly and a trace harder, on wire ropes, ladders and a suspension bridge, to the height of the Exner Tower and into the midst of classic rock scenery that rises around the jade-green lake. The elegant wall of the Cima Pisciadù, edges, ridges, walls and the bold form of the Dent de Mesdi, rise steeply out of the snow-flecked scree corrie into the southern blue sky. A Dolomitic picture, with a changing play of colours that imprints unforgettably on the mind when seen from the sunny hut site.

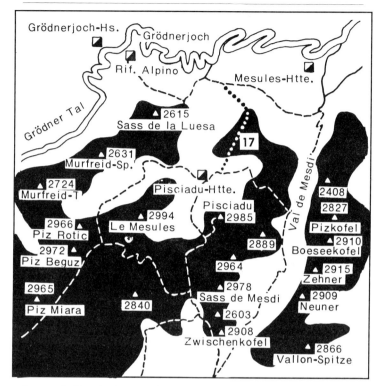

Approach: If parked at the Grödner Joch use first path No.666, which leads along about horizontally under the broad range of cliffs, crosses the lower scree-shoots of Val Setus, and then - no number - reaches the Pisciadù waterfall (or reach the waterfall by the lower pitches mentioned below). The more interesting possibility: with your own car (or taking a short cut on foot over the meadows) about 2½km down the road in the direction of Colfuschg. By a scree scar, the goods ropeway for the hut and good parking (1950m).

Ascent: Left up the distinct path through the last trees to the rock. The first protection, massive iron brackets, surmount the lowest rock step - usually wet. Above that the path continues to the waterfall. Shortly before it, the

Sella, north side, -
Pisciadu Climbing-path

Route 17

junction of the Grödner Joch variation. In the right-hand wall (climber's viewpoint) of the waterfall course with interesting gymnastics up wire ropes and iron pegs - at one point a section leads up really near the cascade - the going is now somewhat less steep, along a wall to a crag-basin. Anyone who has had enough of rungs and metal ropes can easily cut out here to the left (old anchorages and washed-out markings) and climb up by the stream to the hut over traces of a path interspersed with

63

scree and grass. Those who enjoy scrambling, climb with the aid of a wire rope up to the right to a very steep piece of wall. An exposed traverse to the left (good place for photos) introduces the very exposed final ascent. Up through a steep, chimney-like groove, then right to an almost vertical ladder, up this and airily further until just under the conspicious Exner Tower, 2470m. The final surprise is a boldly constructed suspension bridge which spans a deep rock cleft and leads over to the red-waymarked path, on which the terrace-ledge with the hut is soon seen.

Descent: From the hut east into the Mittagstal on a marked path, protected in places. Down through this and just before the last steep drop go left (west) over grassy slopes below the Masores Walls to the Pisciadù via ferrata again, which you reach above the first step in the cliff, protected by iron staples.

[Note: The first edition gave the following descent:] A little way north-west from the hut No.666 leads steeply down through the Val Setus via coarse scree and partly protected sections (hard tongues of snow in early summer). At its end a clear red direction arrow on a boulder pointing left to Passo Gardena (Grödner Joch), or on the usual path directly down to the scree scar and parking place.

Altitude Difference: From lower starting place (1950m) to the suspension bridge, about 550m.

Time Required: Ascent 2¹/₂-3hrs. Descent 2hrs.

Difficulty: First part fairly difficult, second part technically more demanding and extraordinarily airy; perfectly protected throughout.

Base: Grödner Joch, 2130m (several guest-houses); Pisciadù Hut, 2583m, CAI, 18B, wardened from the beginning of July to the end of September. (Recently enlarged).

Note: Only for mountaineers really free of vertigo and accustomed to rock, in good weather from mid-July. Val Gardena can have lengthy thunderstorms - dangerous.

The Pisciadù is also one of the most popular vie ferrate. You may perhaps avoid the worst crush by starting very early.

Tip: If there is time there is an opportunity to climb the Pisciadù Summit 2985m - good views, not difficult. From hut about 1¹/₂hrs.

A high traversing ledge on the Senterio delle Bochette Centrale. Photo: G.Sellers

18.   Boèseekofel, Piz da Lec 2908m, Via Ferrata Piz da Lec Sella Group   (Group d)

Little notice used to be taken of this summit on the east side of the Val oe Mesdi: it is rather monotonous to climb by the normal route. But since 1984 it is part of the Sella Group's via ferrata scene. The ferrata is short but exciting; the approach using the lift extremely easy. It is suitable for your day of arrival or departure, as it takes only half a day. If you are really fit you can still climb Piz Boè on the same day. This mountain has a steep west wall, so from the summit there is an unusual and comprehensive view down into the Val de Mesdi. The Boèseekofel is ideal for a family gathering on the summit: while the via ferrata satisfies the demands of connoisseurs, the normal route suits all mountain walkers reasonably free of vertigo.

Approach: A) From Corvara by the large-cabin cableway, the "Funivia Boè" to the top station, 'Crep de Mont', 2198m, and then by double-chair-lift to its top station 'Vallon', 2553m.

B) From the Passo di Campolongo, 1876m, 400m north down to the Hotel Boè 1867m. Immediately north of the hotel a wide gravelled track leads steeply in big curves, past an alm, to the top-station Crep de Mont (1hr). By chair-lift to its top station Vallon or on foot to the same spot on path 638, past the idyllic Boèsee and chiefly under the line of the lift.

Ascent: You walk a short distance west over a rocky hillock and pass a tiny open hut. (A very steep unmarked approach to the normal route branches off here to the right.) Keep on to the left, quickly reaching the cliffs, on a scree-covered ledge. The start is immediately behind an overhanging rock. Via a short ledge round the first boulder. Steep rock steps then follow. The rope now goes up to the right into the big ravine and via steps - good going, very steep in places, but hardly at all exposed. You cross a small wall, climb up into a short cutting and surmount some vertical sections of wall - the very first exposed section. A scree-covered ledge is good for a breather. Then follows the final test of your courage: two almost vertical, very exposed long ladders. The exit tends to push you gently off. When you have finally overcome this with the help of several iron staples you can breathe more freely. The rock steps that follow - sheltered under a small overhang - are easy. Ropes still lead you for a short distance over some wide, gentle ledges to the exit crags. An easy, wide scree-ledge

The crux of the via Giovanni Lipella. Photo: A.H.Pilkington

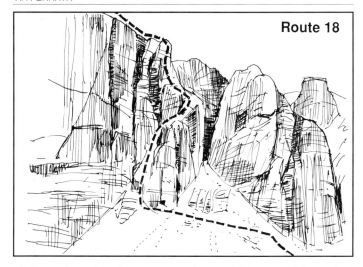

Route 18

winds gently up broad, scree-covered ground. The summit is reached from the south via a broad ridge.

Descent: The way-marks of the normal route (646) lead down east via gentle rock-steps and areas of scree. At one point you notice a gorge-like basin on the right. After rather monotonous scree-fields steeper crags follow. At the end a series of iron staples leads down over the almost vertical rock-plinth. Once again you stroll easily over an almost level scree-field, with fine views, until an iron ladder leads down over the next rock step. In serpentine bends down to a little nick, from which you can enjoy a surprising view down to the Boèsee. Down via low rock steps and in a gentle curve round the rock-flank, to the right to the Crep de Mont top-station.

Altitude Difference: Corvara 1568m - Passo Campolongo 1876m - Crep de Mont top-station 2198m - Vallon top-station 2553m - Piz da Lec 2908m; height of via ferrata: about 240m.

Time Required: Vallon top-station - Piz da Lec 2¹/₂hrs; descent 1¹/₂hrs; Passo Campolongo - Crep de Mont top-station 1hr.

Difficulty: 240m of height moderately difficult and in places really exposed. Descent (Normal Route) - no problems; two short vertical steps in the wall are perfectly protected.

Bases: None.

Hint: If timing is appropriately planned Piz Boè can also be climbed either by the Lichtenfelser Steig (next route in this book) or by the normal route Roa di Pigolerz (No.638): either route 2¹/₂hrs from Vallon top-station.

19. Piz Boè 3152m, Lichtenfelser Steig
Sella Group   (Group a)

The Lichtenfelser Steig is perhaps the most quiet and peaceful of the dozen or so marked routes to the summit of Piz Boè; admittedly it is not a via ferrata in the narrower sense but rather an alternative route if you have to avoid an exciting via ferrata in the Piz Boè area because of doubtful weather. Neverthless, to do this route - protected in some places - is really stimulating for beginners, the less experienced, and also for children. Using the lifts it is not too taxing, but there again, not as easy as using the lift from the Pordoi Pass.

Approach: By cable-car and chair-lift, or on foot as by the previous route to the Vallon top-station, 2553m.

Ascent: You follow the "Boè" signs from the top-station and walk over the hillocky scree-plateau, perhaps with a little detour via the ruin of the old Vallon Hut, visible from a considerable distance. Then the path becomes steeper and a final fork on the slope opposite the ruin is sign-posted to the right "637 - Lichtenfels". Eventually you reach a rock basin. Easy, broad ledges with steps cut out of the rock in parts and with fixed wire-ropes in places, wind along the eastern flank of the basin into a shallow funnel. Then, describing a wide curve, the path leads above the whole basin on flat ledges to the south side of the scree-covered secondary summit of the Vallonspitze. A surprisingly beautiful and rewarding part of the route! You now enter upon a broad saddle with scree-covered hillocks and hollows. After this follow scree-covered steps marked with big cairns. After a last flat terrace the way goes up on the steep north flank on to a broad ridge which leads up to the actual north-east flank of the summit with a gentle gradient. You wind steeply up to reach the broad ridge, with its great rocky blocks, which leads very excitingly to the summit. Shortly before this, your path is joined by the popular ascent-route from the Bamberger Hut (Rif. Boè).

Descent: A) As ascent

B) Via the normal route, "Roa da Pigolerz", path No.638, - well waymarked - back to your starting point, the Vallon top-station. This route at first leads due south from the summit. (Do *NOT* follow the much used descent to the Pordoi Scharte.) It soon turns off to the east, however, and follows roughly the ledges of the summit massif until it joins the Lichtenfelser Steig.

Warning: Beware of straying on to the difficult Via Ferrata Cesare Piazzetta during the descent!

Altitude Difference: Vallon top-station 2553m - Piz Boè 3152m.

Time Required: Vallon top-station - Piz Boè 2¹/₂hrs. Descent A) or B) 1¹/₂hrs.

Difficulty: No difficulty the whole way; nowhere exposed.

Bases: Capanna Piz Fassa am Piz Boè, 3152m. Simply run.

20. Piz Boè 3152m, Via Ferrata Cesare Piazzetta Sella Group   (Group g)

The "easiest three-thousander" in the Dolomites can now offer a diametrically opposed superlative: the most difficult of all vie ferrate yet constructed! Of course this rating only applies to about 150m of its height, which are deliberately made extremely strenuous and demanding. In its original state the route, which was 'protected' in 1982, would have been rated Grade V in places. The large vertical part of the rock wall lies predominantly on the south side, so that there is hardly any fear of icing or wetness.

The via ferrata was named in honour of the mountaineering author Cesare Piazzetta from nearby Arraba, who met with a fatal accident some years ago in South Africa. His friends and some specialists from the Arraba Police School completed the "alpine masterpiece": two hours of extremely hard hammer-and-chisel work for every anchor, without any mechanical aids. It was ten days before the cement was sufficiently hard. Only then could the ropes, which have a good grip, be tightly fitted in.

Signs at the start, brochures and other publications warn of the difficulties of this via ferrata. But you can make the following assumptions: anyone who has mastered the "Possnecker", the "Tomaselli", the "Constantini" in the Moiazza, the "Stella Alpina" on Monte Agnèr and the "Rino Pisetta" north of Lake Garda, can confidently tackle the "Cesare Piazzetti" - solo, of course. Nevertheless it is imperative that you wait for

Route 20

good conditions.

Approach: By car from the Pordoi Pass, 2242m, on a narrow hard-top road to the east in a few minutes to the small car park in front of the widely visible memorial to German soldiers. From the attendant's kiosk on foot on a good path to the mausoleum, 2229m, (open 8.00-1900).

Ascent: The path to the start of the climb begins immediately on the north side of the mausoleum. It is waymarked throughout, but only sparingly. In places there is only a beaten track through the sheep-pastures south of the whole rock precipice (Edelweiss grows hereabouts). The path leads north-east above a well-detached rock spur. After going up steeply for 1¹/₂ hrs you finally reach the vertical rock along which the waymarked track No.7 also leads. You are soon at the start of the climb about 2600m up. The famous 'suspension bridge' is already clearly visible from here. Tightly stretched ropes, faultlessly anchored, thick enough, and with a very good grip, lead first for about 10m up vertical rock with very few footholds. Now the first 80m really are a genuine test of strength in places. The line of the ropes varies between vertical and slanting sections, and short traverses with few footholds. You get to a crucial step with the help of two iron staples. You can pull yourself out of this over a bulge. Conventional foothold aids are put in at several awkward spots, too. The

69

route leads up far to the right and is always very exposed. Finally a gravelly ledge leads out to the left. Here you can take a rest and heave a sigh of relief: the tests of your strength and courage have been passed!

A short chimney, which you must squeeze through, leads to the suspension bridge (safety rope on the left) stretched over a deep cleft. Then continue without problems over well-stepped rock. The rope leads up along short ledges over low but vertical sections of wall and so some distance east to a big, scree-covered terrace with a view. Here the vertical steps begin to break up into several ribs no more than moderately steep. Another short pull-up on the rope, then left on a broad ledge, on rock nowhere harder than Grade II, *and* no longer protected, though well waymarked. The way-marking leads skilfully among steps barely a man's height and up over ledges to the right on to the south-east side, which is bathed in sunlight even in the morning. After climbing a shallow groove, a steep but very short pull-up in a kind of chimney follows. It is not as severe as one fears, on account of an iron peg at the bottom right and a real jug at the top left. Easy rock leads to a ledge. Follow it left to a sign and scramble up a well-stepped gentle rib. Up a steep track to the left to an earthy terrace from which, going half-left, you get into a maze of boulders. A shallow little chimney leads to the junction with the normal route 638 from Corvara, by which you reach the summit without problems.

Descent: A) If you want to get back to your car it is best to follow the normal route (No.627/638) to the Pordoi Scharte, 2849m, with a little restaurant (Rif. Forcella Pordoi). Climb easily up to Sass Pordoi, 2950m, and take the cable-car down to the valley. Another really easy way down is through the famous 'gorge' (ski-route). Good rope-protection on the west side makes the descent easier. The middle section gives an opportunity for scree-running. If you keep steadily half-left at the exit to the gorge you can reach the mausoleum direct through very beautiful terrain - pasture and boulders, - with no path.

B) Descend by the Lichtenfelser Steig (previous route) or the normal route 638.

C) Go through the Val de Mesdi (see Pössnecker Path, Piz Selva).

Altitude Difference: Pordoi Pass 2242m, Piz Boè 3152m, Height of via ferrata 300m (2600-2900m).

Time Required: Memorial to German Soldiers - Start of via ferrata 1¹/₂hrs. Start of via ferrata - Piz Boè 2-3hrs. Descent on foot 1¹/₂-2hrs.

Difficulty: About 150m unusually demanding, exhausting and exposed.

The remainder of the route is at most moderately difficult, but nevertheless demands free climbing to Grades I & II - not exposed. Descents A) & B) are totally free of problems. Descent C) may require an ice-axe in some conditions.

Bases: Capanna Piz Fassa on Piz Boè, 3152m, simply run; Rifugio Forcella Pordoi 2849m; Restaurant at the Sass Pordoi top-station. 2950m; Rif. Boè (Bamberger Hut) 2871m - if you use the way down Val de Mesdi.

Tip: To be climbed in good, dry weather! Under no circumstances carry a heavy rucksack! Be sure there is no mud on the soles of your boots!

21. Cima Dodici - Sass Aut (Sasso Alto) - Punta della Vallacia, Sentiero attrezzato di Sass Aut dedicato a Franco Gadotti (dedicated to Franco Gadotti) Marmolata Area   (Group c)

South-east of the popular and busy Rosengarten the Vallacia massif towers up from the Fassa Valley. The narrow, high-lying, consistently steep Vallacia Valley is framed by a U-shaped mountain massif open to the north. The summits of this "U" are: in the north-east Torre di Vallacia, 2143m; in the south-east Sasso delle Undici, 2563m; in the south Punta della Vallacia; in the south-west Sass Aut (Sasso Alto) 2376m; and in the north-west Cima Dodici, 2443m. The via ferrata which was constructed on the rocks in 1978 opens up the western (*NB: The German guidebook says 'eastern', but this is clearly an error. Translator*) chain of summits. It offers a more peaceful experience of via ferrata climbing away from the huge streams of tourists, with a magnificent view of the neighbouring rock-massifs - and with some surprises.

Approach: By car from Pozza di Fassa, 1320m, into the San Nicolo valley as far as the Soldanella inn.

Ascent: Downstream of the bridge there is a sign to the Donato Zeni bivouac, path No.615. Up a path through tall forest, easily at first but later laboriously and consistently steeply into the steep, lonely, high-lying valley. A wire rope leads over a ramp of a block that is to be crossed. Soon after, you arrive at the Zeni bivouac at about 2100m on a small plateau at the narrow valley-head. A sign points to the start of the via ferrata, which is reached in five minutes.

The route over the first ledge of rock is startlingly bold and has one very exposed spot. Further protected rock ledges below rugged overhangs follow after walking steeply on a short path. Soon an easy protected rock step follows on to a steep grassy path.

A further, very steep grass-path leads into a wide, steep scree-groove which leads to the first wind-gap, the Forcella Vallacia. Down over a rock slab and in wide curves through a corrie on to a broad, grassy crest. A ten-minute detour to the right leads to the Cima Dodici, 2443m, a broad, grassy hummock with a new summit cross and a superb panoramic view of the Latemar, Rosengarten and Marmolata groups. Now a very simple via ferrata section leads over broad rock ledges to the summit of Sass Aut, 2376m, a grassy hummock. Very scanty way-marking leads south through the grassy terrain to a steep and gloomy rock ravine. You climb down about 100m on good wire ropes until a red circle on the rock wall to the right marks the surprising crux. Here, where the route apparently goes no further, you turn left for a few steps and find a wire rope that leads down into a grotto formed by huge jammed boulders. You creep down through the rocky vault and must then climb down about 100m once more, well protected. The via ferrata adventure ends at the foot of this ravine; a long rising traverse along by steep walls leads into a corrie or basin, then up to a grassy wind-gap from which you reach the third summit, Punta della Vallacia, 2637m, - again a grassy flank - in a few minutes. Once again the long-distance view is magnificent and includes the Pala Group as well.

Descent: Path No.624 leads from the grassy ridge below the summit to the crossing with the connecting-path to the Rif. Taramelli. The detour to the hut - about $1/2$hr - is worthwhile for its great hospitality. The further descent now leads into the Valle dei Manzoni, where a road for vehicles leads on downhill back to the Val San Nicolo. Here you pass the big new Manzoni Alm, 1829m, and the "Rifugio Manzoni", 1782m, a former, and older, alm, now an inn. About $1^1/2$km before Soldanella you can take a look into the Capella di Crocefesso, 1522m - a moving experience. Nearby there is a simple inn. And so, back to the car.

Altitude Difference: Soldanella 1450m - Cima Dodici 2443m - Sass Aut, 2376m - Punta della Vallacia 2637m.

Time Required: Punta della Vallacia 4-5hrs. Descent about 3hrs.

Difficulty: Some rather exposed sections at the start of the via ferrata, otherwise free of technical problems. Navigational difficulties in mist on the high grassy summit areas.

Bases: Bivacco Zeni, 2100m, sleeps 9, no water. In descent, if necessary, Rif. Taramelli, 2046m ($^1/_2$-$^3/_4$hr detour); Rif. Manzoni, 1792m, wardened.

22.   Collàc 2715m, Via Ferrata dei Finanzieri
Marmolata Area   (Group e)

Since the ferrata and the cable-car have been set up, the massive Collàc, which formerly was barely noticed 'on the wayside' *en route* for the Marmolata, has become a via ferrata classic. The great cleft half-way up, which leads up through the western half of the north wall, attracts the eyes of all via ferrata connoisseurs driving on the road between Canazei and the Sella Pass. This cleft, which forms half of the ascent, is the key to this exciting route on steel rope, which can be started without a tiring approach. If you want to round off the comparatively short route quietly, there are several possibilities: a long descent through the Val di Contrin or, as an addition, the magnificent, protected Lino Pederiva high-level route. (See next route.)

Approach: From Canazei to Alba (3km), to the valley-station of the Ciampac cable-car (first trip 8.30am).

Ascent: Go down to the east from the top-station for a few steps on the marked piste-route; turn sharp right at the first junction in the path and down to the big gravelly hollow, 2090m, already visible from above. Red arrows mark the winding path which leads over a big scree-cone - grassy in parts - to the start of the climb (2175m. Memorial plaque). For a short distance up on a rope through a shallow groove to a further scree-path; then on a rope over an easy step in the wall, left, to the great cleft. The route now goes up very strenuously over slabs, smooth in parts, which are especially damp in the morning. A very smooth, mostly wet section of slab has recently been by-passed on terraced, but nevertheless very steep, rock. Before the end of the cleft, iron pegs lead up very airily over a completely vertical section of wall on to moderately steep rock interspersed with scree. The biggest efforts are now over. Rocks with jointed structure follow. The rope follows the fall-line via small terraces and through groves up to a short band of scree, where you turn left. Steep ribs and sections of wall, grooves and small chimneys, follow some easier rock steps. A last steep groove finally leads out on to the north ridge, with an unexpected view of the Marmolata. Up the ridge and through an easy groove to the summit.

Descent: A) The inscription "Ciampec" in the saddle between the main and subsidiary summits indicates a short, wide scree-groove. Before it breaks off, a rope leads right through a narrow rock fissure into a short cleft. Go right on an easy ledge into a scree-covered ravine, through which you climb down on ropes without problems. Go through a small rock-gate to get into the next ravine, where you climb down on the right side on sloping paths. A short rope leads over ledges to the right on to grassy ledges, then via further ledges, sloping but protected, to the bottom end of the ravine, on the right. An easy ledge of grass finally leads west round the walls and to the wide grassy gap between Collàc and Sasso Nero. A boulder with the inscription 'Ciampac' indicates the descent via alpine meadows down to the top station (Path No.644).

B) Eastwards on the gap between Collàc and Sasso Nero, and then continue in a south-easterly direction on Path No.613 to the Passo di San Nicolo, 2338m. You can finish this scenically very beautiful high-level walk by going down to the Rif. Contrin, from which, perhaps, you can climb to the Marmolata the next day. (See Westgrat zur Punta Penia and cf 'Cima Ombretta'.)

C) At first as for descent B), but immediately behind the Passo di San Nicolo down to the left into the Pra Contrin. This shortens the way back to the valley station considerably.

D) At first as for descent B) but when east of Sass di Roca take a path north into the high valley Ciamp de Mèz (Campo di Mezza), a branch valley of the Val di Contrin. You join the well-known approach path to the Rif. Contrin (Path 602) half-way along it and soon reach the valley station of the cable-car.

Altitude Difference: Start of ferrata 2090m - Collàc 2715m.

Time Required: Ciampac top station - Collàc 2hrs (in descent 1$^{1}/_{2}$hrs); descent B) 4hrs; descent C) 3hrs; descent D) 2$^{1}/_{2}$hrs. Ascent from Alba to Cimapac top station on foot 2hrs (in descent 1$^{1}/_{4}$-1$^{1}/_{2}$hrs).

Difficulty: The Ferrata di Finanzieri is difficult and strenuous in its lower and middle sections. The route is exposed in parts and endangered by stone-fall. The normal way is comparatively simple and considerably less demanding in descent as well.

Bases: Restaurant at the Ciampac top station. Four other restaurants in the immediate vicinity (sometimes closed in summer).

Tip: After climbing Collàc, a detour to Sasso Bianco (see next route) is recommended if you have adequate stamina.

23.   Sasso Bianco 2431m, Sentiero attrezzato dedicato a Lino Pederiva Marmolata Area   (Group a)

This high-level path, with many good views and protected in places, offers a welcome way of rounding off a day on the Collàc Via Ferrata, but in less good weather it is also an alternative goal which can be extended to a full day's outing. The well laid-out path leads from Buffaure over the gentle ridge to Brunec and then across the northern slopes of Sass de Roca as far as the Passo San Nicolo. *En route* you walk past the little Sass de Bianco, which was a part of the strongly fortified Austrian defence system. Tyrolean outposts stood here summer and winter, as too on the Contrin Pass, the Punta di Nicolo, the Col Ombert, the Passo di Uomo and around the Costabella. The whole line of defence in the Fassa Dolomites withstood all attacks until the front was disbanded in November 1917.

Approach: A) Best as for Collàc (previous route) by cable-car to the Ciampac top station.
B) After climbing Collàc the Forcia Neigra, 2530m, is an ideal starting-point.
C) For a day's outing you can decide to start from the valley village of Pozza di Fassa (in the part of the village called Meida) and ride up to the Rif. Buffaure, 2020m, on the gondola. From there the waymarked path 613 leads over Sass de Dama, 2430m, to Sella Brunec, 2428m (top station of a ski-lift from Ciampac).

Ascent: A) From Ciampac top station the route goes in 40mins, partly through flowery alpine meadows, partly over ski-routes (piste), to Sella Brunec, 2428m, top station of the big western ski-lift about 40m lower than the ridge. The waymarking 613 starts here. First you cross on the south side a fairly steep grassy flank of a high rounded hilltop. Then the path runs directly on the ridge in easy switchbacks. It is occasionally a bit narrow and airy but offers a magnificent view on each side. Soon you reach the grassy saddle in front of the massif of dark volcanic rock which now suddenly towers up. With a few curves the path leads down on to the south flank and goes round the whole rocky eminence on grassy banks, sometimes leading downwards. An exciting section with good views follows: it is well protected in the few rather exposed places. At the foot of light-coloured limestone rocks you reach a saddle from which Sass de Bianco comes fully into the field of view: a ruggedly chopped-up, low rock ridge which reveals wide yawning caverns even at a distance. Once more you go a

75

short distance down over meadow-land and after a few minutes' easy re-ascent are standing in the midst of the former battle-positions of the First World War. A small detour to the left leads through the ridge, which is hollowed out with caverns. You step on to the west side directly over a concreted parapet. A few paces from there a concreted arch with the date 1917 is still standing. The summit of the highest jagged peak on the north side is likewise reached with a few steps. Much needed refreshment is available at the Rifugio Passo San Nicolo, 2340m.

B) Anyone who has climbed Collàc is probably best advised to approach from the Forcia Neigra. From there on the waymarked path 613 east of Sasso Nero in the direction of Passo San Nicolo. You reach the Lino Pederiva path near Sasso Bianco and can use it as the return-route to Ciampac.

Descent: As ascent A) or B) or the continuation of the path to the Rif. Contrin. (See previous route, descents B), C), D).)

Altitude Difference: Ciampac 2147m - Sella Brunec 2428m - Forcia Neigra 2530m - Sasso Bianco 2431m.

Time Required: Ciampac - Sella Brunec 40mins, Ciampac - Forica Neigra 1hr, Rif. Buffaure - Sella Brunec 2hrs. From Sella Brunec or from Forcia Neigra to Sasso Bianco about 1-1$^{1}/_{2}$hrs.

Difficulty: Easy throughout.

Bases: As for Collàc; Rifugio Passo San Nicolo, 2338m, wardened.

24. Bec de Mesdi (La Mèsola. Mittagsspitze) 2733m, 'Via della Trincee' Padon Ridge
Marmolata Area   (Group f)

One of the climbing-paths based on old wartime fixtures, traverses the jagged, dark, Padon Ridge and reaches its culmination in the Bec de Mesdi (marked also on the Kompass Map as 'Mèsola' or 'Mittagsspitze'). Although this path is not among the longest Dolomite ferrate it can be counted among the most interesting. Apart from the keen excitement as to whatever is coming next, the special fascination of this (not entirely easy!) climbing-path is provided by the wealth of variety and the splendour of its viewpoints. It is extremely popular.

You could perhaps describe it as the sporting counterpart of the

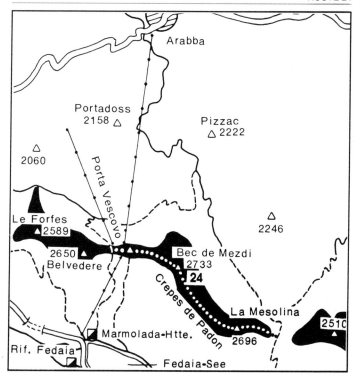

neighbouring, comfortable Bindel way, which is likewise eclipsed by the glacier-covered Marmolata opposite.

A guide from Arabba, Gilberto Salvatore, constructed the path and christened it 'Via della Trincèe', which means much the same as 'Trenches Way'. In fact this route leads through the narrowest battle-ground of the First World War, with numerous strong-points firmly clamped into the black volcanic rock.

Approach: To avoid three tiring hours of ascent, take the cable-car from Arabba up to Porta Vescovo, 2516m; from Fedaia (Marmolada Hut) on a steep path 1¼hrs.

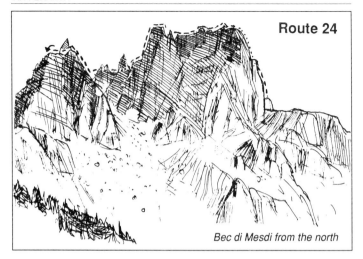

Route 24

Bec di Mesdi from the north

Ascent: At the Porta Vescovo in summer there are reminders of the winter ski-circus which takes place up there from November to April. Only a few enthusiasts for views value the grand sight towards the majestically spread out Queen of the Dolomites opposite - the Marmolata in her silvery mantle of snow. From the top station you first turn east over steep grassy slopes ornamented with fragments of rock. The red waymarks bring you in about 20mins to the start of the rock climb with a sign, 'Ferrata della Trincèe'.

The whole Padon Ridge consists of dark, compact volcanic rock. Even the start is harder than it looks: a rock about 35m high with small holds must be outwitted (very exposed). Only a loosely fixed guide-rope offers some help towards protection. Over grassy crags, stone slabs (iron holds) - but always really airily, often with mini-footholds, but with exciting glimpses into the depths - you reach a narrow ridge. Wire ropes indicate the continuation, which leads elegantly and smoothly, always up and down along the jagged knife-edge ridge to a swinging suspension bridge. This spans a deep indentation. The route-book is kept there in a metal box. A breather is rewarding. In the north the enormous Sella Group, to the right Sass Songher, Lavarella, Fanis and the other colossi of the Cortina Dolomites.

Climbing down along a fairly smooth slab (not altogether simple) and again up to the next rise in the ridge, you arrive at the highest point on the protected path, the Bec de Mesdi. After the next indentation there is an old wartime path and strong-points alongside, a cave and a broken field-kitchen. Just above is the East Summit, on which a small flat platform has been fixed on which searchlights were sited during the war, to be directed on the Austrian-occupied Col di Lana.

Finally another exposed ledge across a steep wall, bulging rock sections, which are provided with brackets and ropes. After the final protection you turn right to a steep grass ledge that leads to a gap, which turns out to be a wartime eyrie hewn out of the rock. Red waymarks show the return route to the cable-car station.

The Ferrata della Trincèe is not an undertaking for mountaineering greenhorns. Anyone who is advanced enough for this expedition can take home a memorable Dolomite experience of wartime history, as well as the personal alpine satisfaction given by this by no means commonplace route.

Descent: By cable-car to Arabba, or from Porta Vescovo by the old wartime path down the southern grass slope to Fedaia, ³/₄hr.

Altitude Difference: Arabba 1605m - Porta Vescovo 2516m - Bec de Mesdi 2733m - Fedaia 2044m.

Time Required: For the complete crossing from the Porta Vescovo back to the cable-car station allow 3-3¹/₂hrs.

Difficulty: In spite of the relative shortness of this protected eastern traverse of the Padon Ridge, the route is to be reckoned as technically difficult. Only for those really experienced on rock, surefooted and free of vertigo. Special care in bad weather or if there is icing. Danger of stonefall at the start.

Bases: Hotels and guesthouses in Arabba, 1605m (Rhaeto-Romanic, Reba); Mountain restaurant (self-service) at Porta Vescovo 2516m; Rifugio Marmolata - Fedaia 2044m, CAI, 72B & M, wardened all the year round.

Tip: Descent towards Fedaia. Shortly before Fedaia you meet the well-known Bindelweg (Rhaeto-Romanic, 'Viel del Pan') No.601, that leads further to the west to the Belvedere chair-lift station and to the Pordoijoch. A panorama of the first rank, also very interesting botanically and geologically.

Note: The "Delle Creste" high-level route begins in the gap where the Via delle Trincèe ends. This leads in an easterly direction falling gently to the Ernesto **Bontadini** Bivouac, 2696m, and steeply down to the Rifugio Padon. This high-level route is protected by wire ropes in airy places and sometimes runs through old wartime tunnels (torch needed). Although the route is not difficult in comparison with the Via della Trincèe it forms a rewarding continuation of this climbing-path. Descent to the Caprile/Fedaia road from the Rif. Padon on Path No.699. Total time from the start of the high-level route 3hrs.

25. Marmolata, West Ridge to the Punta Penia 3344m
Marmolata Area   (Group e)

The Marmolata mountain massif has not only the highest summit in the Dolomites but also the largest glacier. To the south the summit mass falls abruptly with vertical cliffs into the combe; to the north the slope is less steep; here, instead of naked walls, are ice-streams and areas of permanent snow, into which two ridge-like, isolated rock pillars, the Sasso delle Undici and the Sasso delle Dodici penetrate from the north side; small rock spurs can also be seen further west. The ridge-line swinging round above the glacier carries three elevations: the Punta Penia 3344m,

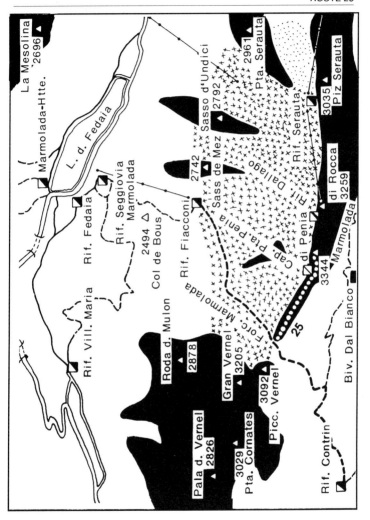

the dream-goal of mountaineers of all styles and standards, the Punta di Rocca, 3259m, Mecca of summer skiers; and the more isolated Mount Serauta, 3218m. In the north-west of this massive rock ridge is the notch of the narrow Marmolatascharte (Forcella Marmolada) from which rises to the west the rock mass of the Grosser Vernel (Gran Vernel) and its subsidiary peaks. In 1898 two Nuremberg men climbed the summit for the first time from this pass up the very exposed west ridge, after the first ascent via the normal route from the north had been achieved after several unsuccessful attempts by that Dolomite pioneer, Paul Grohmann as early as 1864. The climbing-path, protected by numerous brackets, iron pegs and wire ropes, which was set up even before the First World War, leads up this west ridge.

This climbing-path, joining rock and snow, offers a magnificent and varied Dolomite experience. Even when the route does not exhibit any really difficult sections, and protection and artificial footholds make a rapid ascent possible, a sudden change in the weather, new snow or indeed, icing, can bring with it very serious problems, especially when individual items of protection are damaged or buried. This is frequently the case - the ferruginous west ridge is endangered by lightning, and the knife-edge of the highest Dolomite mountain is moreover renowned for sudden changes in weather. Anyone who climbs the snow-covered summit of the Queen of the Dolomites, shimmering with permanent snow, must therefore have sufficient reserves of strength, adequate experience of high mountains and equipment appropriate to the conditions, to abandon the lightning-endangered ridge by the quickest route if a thunderstorm comes up - and this is not easy to manage.

Approach: From Canazei, the principal place in the Fassa Tal, east to Alba (2km). Here the cart-track No.602 branches right to Contrin. After a steep, wooded rise, you wander almost on the level in the scenically extremely attractive Contrintal (Val de Contrin) up to the Contrinhaus (Rif. Contrin) 2016m, where you spend the night.

Ascent: From the hut on the distinct path No.606 in the direction of the Ombretta Pass as far as the fork with signpost. Left up a steep, zig-zag scree path towards the deeply indented Marmolatascharte (Forcella Marmolada) between Vernel and Marmolata. Finally laboriously through a stepped groove and up an iron ladder into the gap, 2896m. The route to the west ridge begins by old wartime dugouts.

Even the prelude begins really airily. Up immediately by the rock-

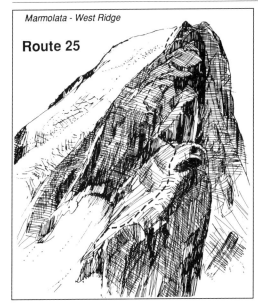

Marmolata - West Ridge

Route 25

caves, following the protection up the first smooth rock step to the left. After a shallow cutting, the pegs and metal ropes indicate the route over exposed, steep slabs fairly far into the north flank. Once more, a long exposed series of slabs, climbed up to on massive ladders, to a prominent tower. Wire ropes go round it and lead up the highest permanent snow (from the gap, 1hr). Over snow-fields and tops without difficulty to the Punta Penia summit with a hut offering limited refreshments.

From the triangulation sign the view seems almost boundless; from the Julian Alps to Graubünden, from the Tauern to the Adamello and Ortler, over all the Dolomitic groups away as far as the Venetian plain and Adriatic - everything is to be seen, provided the weather co-operates. In the great depths below, the clefts of the Contrin and Ombretta valleys and on the north side the emerald-green Lake Fedaia snuggling against the curved wall of its dam.

Descent: By the normal route. A sharp snow-ridge drops steeply and exposed to a craggy, unprotected rock wall. You scramble down 200m on good holds via shallow grooves and chimneys to the big bergschrund, which is not always easy to cross. The continuation over the Marmolata glacier winds skilfully over some crevasses and by fine ice-falls. It is generally well marked in advance by old tracks. Finally via snow-free rock slabs to the mountain chalet and the lift-station Pian dei Fiacconi, 2626m. By the cable-car or on foot over steep moraine terrain to the lake with its dam and the Fedaia saddle with several private huts and the well-equipped Marmolata mountain hut (Rif. Ettore Castiglioni, CAI). This fine refugio lies on the road which comes up from Pian Trevisan, with bus connection from Canazei. A motor-road which continues to Fedaia and the Rifugio Marmolata, comes from the east, from Caprile and Sottoguda to Malga Ciapèla (bottom station of the glacier cable-way).

Altitude Difference: Alba about 1500m - Contrinhaus 2016m - Punta Penia 3344m.

Time Required: Ascent to hut 2hrs; Contrinhaus - Marmolatascharte 2¹/₂hrs; West Ridge 2hrs; Descent to Pian Fiacconi 2hrs. From there to Lake Fedaia, 1hr.

Difficulty: For an experienced mountaineer in good conditions the west ridge of the Marmolata is without any problems worth mentioning, if all the conditions set out in the introduction are fulfilled. In mist the crevasses can be dangerous, and when there is icing or a thunderstorm the metal protection can also be dangerous.

Bases: Contrinhaus, 2016m (private) wardened from mid-June to mid-October, 90B.&M; Summit hut, 3340m, open, emergency sleeping with minimal emergency provisions (payment on basis of trust); Rif. Pian dei Fiacconi (Lift) 2626m; Rif. Marmolada-Fedaia, 2044m, CAI, wardened all the year round, 72B.&M; Gasthof Pian Trevisan (Bus), 1717m.

Note: Glacier experience, endurance at altitudes of over 3000m, as well as warm clothing, are indispensable; as are ice-axe, rope and crampons.

26. Cima Ombretta 3011m, Sentiero attrezzato Cima Ombretta Marmolata Group (Group c)

This little-visited rock crest with three summits stands immediately facing the south wall of the Marmolata. There is no place which commands such a complete view of the Marmolata's sheer size, nor from which one can experience it so impressively or at such close quarters as from this easy crest of jagged peaks, whose proud height, of course, pales into insignificance before that of the Queen of the Dolomites. Thanks to a good connecting path, those with adequate stamina can take in the Ombretta on the same afternoon after climbing the Marmolata, look once more from below at the goal of their dreams already reached, and by going down to the Rif. Contrin make the trip into an exceptional scenic experience. During the First World War the Italian front line here ran over the main summit, turned east to Passo Ombretta and reached its most dangerous position on the Piz Serauta ridge. When on the Cima Ombretta one can form a frightening picture of the dramatic struggle on this line, from the Italian point of view: in an ice-cave on the Punta di Rocca, 3259m, the highest placed mountain-cannon of the whole Austrian Dolomite Front was stationed. From there the Austrians were able to bombard the Italian supply-lines in the Val Ombretta down from the 1000-metre-high vertical south wall.

Approach: To the Rif. Contrin, as for Punta Penia. (See route sketch p80)

Ascent: A) From the Rif. Contrin, at first as for Punta Penia on Path 606 in the direction of the Marmolata Scharte (Forcia Marmolada), but about half way up the ascent turn right and on Path No.610 to a prominent rock-gate. Past a tiny lake, more often than not dried up, and up to the Passo Ombretta, 2704m, where the Bianco bivouac stands. Now you follow an old disused military path south and climb up over rocky terrain with old worn-out rope-protection. A steep scree-path leads tiringly over the north-east flank to the ridge, where a magnificent view on both sides rewards you for the effort of getting up there. At first on a level, rocky ridge, then east in bends to the principal summit of the three-peaked ridge (Summit Cross, 3011m). The Middle Summit, 2983m, and the West Summit, 2998m, can only be reached with difficulty.

B) An unwaymarked but distinctly trodden-out path leads from the Marmolata Scharte, below the south walls of the Marmolata to the Passo Ombretta. This makes it possible to cross over quickly after climbing the Marmolata, but it is also useful if you have to give up an ascent of the Marmolata because of unfavourable conditions and switch to the problem-free Ombretta as a substitute.

Descent: From the summit down to the lowest point of the ridge again. A very scantily waymarked track now leads diagonally down south-west into the huge, desolate wilderness of scree between the eastern summit ridge of Cima Ombretta and Sasso Vernale with its diminishing hanging-glacier. The path turns left in broad, gentle curves and follows in places a lateral moraine between two former glaciers, whose wide, deeply-trenched, dead channels characterize the unvegetated but very impressive scene. At last you reach a steep drop of about 55m down whose weakest point leads wire-rope protection, - unfortunately in disrepair. In 1985 the rope was lacking for 3m on a short traverse in the upper part (Grade II), and lower down in a shallow chimney about 6 or 8 metres of wire-rope are missing (Grade II). Afterwards, keep right near the vertical rock walls and go down in a steep scree-slope, until soon you meet the much-frequented Path 607, which leads down the Rif. Contrin - which is already visible from a distance.

Altitude Difference: Rif. Contrin 2016m - Passo Ombretta 2704m - Cima Ombretta 3011m (East Summit).

Time Required: Rif. Contrin - Cima Ombretta about 3½hrs; from the Marmolata Scharte to Passo Ombretta about ¾hr; from there to the summit about 1¼hrs.

Difficulty. Path 610 to the summit presents no problems, nor does the crossing from the Marmolata Scharte. The 55m drop on the descent described demands free climbing (Grade II) or abseilling, on account of damaged sections of rope. Under some circumstances there are great problems of navigation in mist above this drop.

Bases: Rif. Contrin, 2016m, fully wardened; Bivacco Marco del Bianco on the Passo Ombretta, 2704m, emergency accommodation, sleeps 9. No water.

27. Cima di Costabella 2762m, Via alta attrezzata Bepi Zac Marmolata Group (Group c)

An impressive rock ridge towers up above the broad, green alpine meadows north of the Passo Pellegrino. Its highest point is the Cima del Uomo, 3010m, at its eastern end. On this peaceful high pass - a ski-centre typically sleepy in summer-time - hardly anyone would suspect at first that this was a focal point of the First World War. The whole ridge was part of the Austrian front line. Here the Italian mountain troops, the "Alpini", tried to force their way into the Val di Fassa. For months on end the opposing forces faced each other, often only a few yards apart; but the Austrian Imperial Mountain Troops and above all the Bavarians of the German Alpine Corps held the hotly contested Costabella with great losses. Some 2,000 men also lost their lives here, through stone-fall and avalanche. Even today the ridge is peppered with gun-emplacements and cut through with trenches, several rock-towers and undermined with tunnels and caverns. For decades barbed wire and planks have been sliding yard by yard down the north corrie.

A well protected high-level path which only in places has the character of a via ferrata, leads through this open-air museum of two years of positional warfare. It is difficult to say what is most fascinating about this four-hour trip on the rocks: the shattering evidence of the events of the war, the indescribably varied panorama in all directions, or the switchback path through various kinds of rock formation, chilly corries and lush zones of vegetation. This route remains unforgettable.

Approach: A little lower than the highest point of the Passo Pellegrino, 1919m, and to its west is the bottom station of a chair-lift (1890m) by which you can ride up to 2160m (In operation 8.30am-5.00pm). The path, a very easy vehicle track, begins just 200m further west at the bottom station of the Campignol ski-tow (Sign, and marble memorial: 5.10.1916 BTG ALPINI "EXILLES") and leads north at first; after half-an-hour, at the fork, go left to the Passo de Selles (Sign). You soon reach the top station of the chair-lift and go leisurely on up until you reach the Passo de Selles after a short, steep section. Here on the airy crest at 2600m you will be surprised by the new and novel "Mountain Vagabonds" Hut - an ideal spot for a substantial second breakfast.

Ascent: On the ridge rising to the west, just after the disturbing "Barbedwire Cross", you reach the sign to the via ferrata with a photograph of Bebi Zac, honoured here as a hut and via ferrata builder. Now you traverse summit after summit: Lastei Piccolo, 2697m, Lastei Grande, 2716m, Cima della Campagnaccia, 2737m, and, free from problems all the way, walk on the traces of the former chief line of battle. On Cima di Costabella it becomes even more exciting and the views improve; the path leads through a long, low military tunnel and traverses more summit-points (2705m, 2726m, 2730m and 2697m) sometimes on the north flank, with some 'sporting' sections. At the Forcella di Ciadin, 2664m, there is a safe way down to the valley in case of emergency. After a rather more difficult part, where you have to squeeze through a very narrow fissure, you enter a steep corrie, very tiring to climb up through. Via an easy path on the north side you reach first a basin, then the summit of Punta di Cadino 2837m. At the Cima del Colbel, 2805m, you meet a protected path which leads up here from the top station of the highest ski-tow (Sentiero attrezzato Cima del Colbel). It provides an emergency descent.

The last section of the via alta, which at first climbs easily again, always follows natural ledges on the south side of the next rock massif.

The bold "Torre California" (inscription) rises clearly from a series of free-standing rock towers. Extreme rock gymansts climb it occasionally. Now the path becomes more rocky. A short, protected little chimney leads to a higher ledge. In a continuous switchback, with the rugged west flank of the Cima del Uomo in sight all the time, you finally reach the last bulge, on a rope leading diagonally across a wall. From there you reach the last gap before Cima del Uomo (Shelter: a small, open hut).

Descent: Go down steep scree into the bottom of the corrie and on a clear track to the bottom station of the highest ski-tow. From there a drivable road leads west of the lift to the road over the pass.

Altitude Difference: Passo del Pellegrino 1919m - Passo de Selles 2600m - Cima di Costabella 2762m (many re-ascents, often long).

Time Required: Passo del Pellegrino - Passo de Selles 2¹/₂hrs; Via Ferrata attrezzato Bepi Zac to the gap between Cima del Uomo 4-5hrs (according to how much time your curiosity delays you!); descent 2hrs.

Difficulty: Apart from some airy sections, not difficult and free of problems - but long. Escape routes down are possible.

Bases: Rifugio Passo de Selles (Mountain Vagabonds Hut), in summer simply run. Overnight accommodation in emergency only.

WARNING!

Cima del Uomo, 3010m, Via Ferrata Bepi Zac.
This via ferrata, formerly recommended to experienced climbers as an exciting continuation of the Via alta attrezzata Bepi Zac from the Forcella Uomo to the summit of Cima del Uomo, has been dismantled following a fatal accident caused when the anchoring of a fixed rope gave way. It will presumably never be reconstructed. The summit can now only be reached by the normal route on the south side, endangered by stone-fall.

28.　Cima dell'Auta Orientale 2624m, Via Ferrata Paolin-Piccolin　Marmolata Area　(Group c)

The Cima dell'Auta area, which lies somewhat apart from the great via ferrata centres of the Pala, Civetta and Marmolata, is seldom visited by mountaineers from countries north of the Alps. Anyone who decides to climb the Cima dell'Auta Orientale will have the experience of a satisfying and really solitary rock route. Resting afterwards on the summit you see an unfamiliar view, especially of the Marmolata Group. For descent you can choose between a short, barren, solitary route and a longer one which is scenically extraordinarily delightful: between the high-lying, deep blue Lago di Franzei and the Via alta dei Pastori, overgrown with splendid Mediterranean flowers, the alpine plants on the sunny south flanks "pull out all the stops".

Approach: In Caviola, on the road between Cencenighe and the Passo San Pellegrino, turn off to the hamlets of Colmèan and Feder. At the last big right-hand bend on the road to Feder the short branch-road to Colmèan branches left immediately after the bridge. Now go another 450m to the last house, Al Bar Colmèan. To the left, above, there is an adequate car park.

Ascent: A sign and detailed waymarking lead the way through a number of parallel paths, confusing at first. The correct way is narrow, like a defile, and crosses a new vehicular road; then it leads really clearly through the tall, shady forest to the foaming Caiado stream, which is crossed. There is a good view from there of the summit that you are aiming for. Soon after this, going west, you reach the extraordinarily romantic Rif. Cacciatori, 1751m. After a short ascent a sign points to the new Baita Giovanni Paolo I, a log-hut, no less romantic than the Rifugio, but private.

[This point can also be reached by taking the Alta Via dei Pastori (waymarked blue) from the Rif. Cacciatori and climbing up left at the sign shortly after the little chapel at the hut.] A little below the hut sign, go right to a little well. Immediately in front of this the route goes up to the left [NOT straight on, although that is also waymarked]. The path now goes up very steeply to the wind-gap, following the fall-line - in one place going round an overgrown mass of rock in an easy curve to the right - and leads diagonally left under the first rock walls, laboriously on scree, up to the start of the climb. Ladders, staples and faultless fixed ropes lead up the first really exciting steep step west of a ravine-like groove. After climbing up 50m, go right into the broad groove and laboriously up on scree on its western side. A short rope can soon be seen on its left edge. The top quarter of the ravine is a nasty scree-slope, and you are really thankful to find thin guide-ropes again on the left edge of the rocks. These lead without problems over easily stepped rock to the gap. You find the first red spot just at the foot of the eastern summit massif. Via short ledges and through little scree-covered grooves, somewhat left of the north ridge - not very distinct now - to the first rope; then in bends over ledges to where the rock first sweeps up steeply: a short ladder overcomes this. At first the route goes on ropes over some short ledges, then, following the fall-line over not very steep rock to a little stance with a view. Now a broad ledge leads past a small cave left to a little gap from which a rope and a short path lead quickly to the summit.

Descent: A) Down again to the little wind-gap and up on a rope to the small northern subsidiary summit. Down on a narrow path on its grassy east crest into a broad green hollow above the helicopter pad, now visible from above. After a short re-ascent the path leads evenly through the sunny steep south flank of a weathered group of small, dark, basalt towers and drops down once again to a wide grassy saddle. Shortly before this the quickest way down (via normale), branches sharp right, traverses under the vertical south walls over steep grass-slopes and joins the approach route above the Baita Giovanni Paolo I.

B) The descent to the east to the Forcella Negher is scenically more attractive but about ³/₄hr longer. The almost circular and surprisingly beautiful Lago di Franzei lies to the north below the path, which leads in wide curves over the edge of the huge green basin. From the Forcella Negher, 2266m, a path, frequently branching, now leads fairly steeply through lush alpine meadows down to the Baita Colmont, 1954m, a little hut, usually open, but uninhabited. Above this to the west a big boulder marks the blue waymarked Alta Via dei Pastori, which begins with an unwelcome, but short, re-ascent. This path through very rich alpine flora becomes ever more beautiful and strange. It crosses seven ravine-like grooves, with running water, and finally leads directly back to the Rif. Cacciatori. From there go back to the starting-point the way you came up.

Altitude Difference: Colmèan (highest part of the hamlet) about 1280m - Cima dell'Auta 2624m.

Time Required: Colmèan - Cima dell'Auta 4¹/₂hrs. Descent A) 2¹/₂hrs, B) 3hrs.

Difficulty: Except for the first steep upswing of rock, which is more difficult, not difficult to moderately difficult. Descents easy.

Bases: Baita dei Cacciatori, 1751m, wardened; Baita Giovanni Paolo I, 1900m and Baita Colmont, 1954m, not wardened. (Bad weather shelter.)

29. Via Ferrata Bolver-Lugli (Cimone della Pala)
Pala Group (Group f)

A protected rock-path was given to the Cimone in the summer of 1970 to celebrate the centenary of its first conquest. The idea, which stemmed from the Guild of Guides at San Martino di Castrozza, was then made a reality in three weeks of unremitting work by the guide-priest Don Martino Delugan from Tèsero together with Saverio Scalet and Camillo de Paoli. The expenses were largely met by the mountaineering family Bolver-Lugli from Fiera di Primiero, and the 'Ferrata' therefore named after it.

It is one of the finest iron routes in the Dolomites and very dynamic in its route-line. It uses the old 'Higusi' route in the broad west wall. Improved with over 500m of wire rope as well as absolutely reliable pegs and chiselled-out foot - and hand-holds, the climb makes possible an airy and exciting gymnastic ascent to the south shoulder.

Approach: To Col Verde as on Route 30. Unfortunately the first chair-lift does not start until 7.30 in the morning.

Ascent: By the chair-lift station Path No.706 begins (sign). Walking due north leads in one hour via crag, grass and scree terrain to the start of the climb at about 2250m (Bolver-Lugli memorial sign) - a spectacular approach. At first without protection - as a 'trial by fire', so to speak, for the difficulties to come - via a steep rock spur marked with red spots, up to the first wire-rope. In a bad year this first part may be iced-up, as may the entire route.

Now through grooves and chimney pitches which have been worn smooth, up to a big platform. From there the guide-ropes lead up, at first fairly steeply and then ever more airily to a vertical wall about 50m high. This and a chimney which follows are the hardest and most impressive pitches. Some loose rock - helmet advised. The edge of the cliff at about 2950m is reached over less steep rock. Now in 10mins to the Fiamme Gialle bivvy-box. To climb further from here to the summit of the Cimone, 3185m, is no light undertaking but an unmistakably often extremely exposed rock-climb (Grades II & III). A narrow rock tunnel to crawl through, a frequently iced traverse, a steep tower-wall, an overhanging chimney, a sharp knife-edge ridge, are refinements which an ordinary ferrata-climber may hardly attempt without a guide.

On the other hand in good weather and with good visibility you should go further over the snow-field of the Ghiaccia di Travignolo, via rock terrain

91

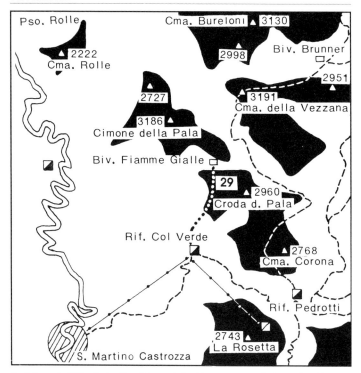

that is not difficult, to the Cima della Vezzana, at 3196m the highest summit of the Pala and a viewpoint of the first rank.

Descent: A) First from the bivvy-box north-east over easy broken rock towards the Travignolo Pass. But before you reach it go down to the right (often hard snow or ice) into the Val dei Cantoni. Down in this. A steep rock step is circumvented on the right on broken, rocky terrain; then continue on a scree-track and over broken rock out to the right towards the Passo Bettega, 2610m, which is reached by a short re-ascent. Easily down on the far side, then once more over broken rock to a fork in the path. Left (south) down to the Rif. Rosetta. From there either 10min to the top station of the cable-car or on foot to Col Verde and further to S.Martino di Castrozza: the upper part of the protected descent path from the Rosetta

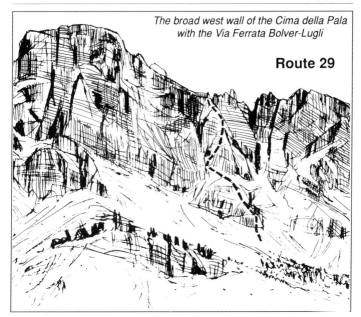

The broad west wall of the Cima della Pala
with the Via Ferrata Bolver-Lugli

Route 29

Hut to Col Verde is seldom used. The descent is free of problems in normal weather conditions and solitary in any case.

B) It is also possible to reach the Rosetta Hut/Col Verde path by a direct descent from the fork. (This saves at least one hour.) This route winds ingeniously through the weaknesses of the western cliffs of the Cima Corona. Finally, a steep wall (about 10m) protected by wire rope leads on to the aforementioned path, which you reach on its easy section. Absolute sure-footedness, freedom from vertigo and rock-climbing experience (some places are Grade I) are essential for this variant descent.

C) If the highest Pala summit, the Cima della Vezzana, is taken in as well from the Travignolo Pass, there is an interesting descent via the Via Ferrata Gabitta d'Ignotti to the Rif. Rosetta.

Down to the east over loose scree from the wide, scree-covered east ridge of Cima della Vezzana. Be prepared for icing, damaged ropes and the danger of stone-fall. Wire ropes assist you over the rock barrier about 120m high; then you are walking on the little Val Strut Glacier (few crevasses) and soon after that reach the Bruner Bivouac, 2665m. After the path branches (to the left it goes to the Passo di Val Strut) the Sentiero delle Faragnole (No.703) leads directly south to the Pian dei Cantoni in the highest part of the Valle delle Comelle. From here an easy re-ascent to the Rif. Rosetta.

Altitude Difference: Col Verde 1965m - exit at the bivouac shelter 3005m - Travignolo Pass 2983m - Rosetta Hut 2578m, altitude difference of the climbing-path 400m.

Time Required: Col Verde - Bolver Lugli sign 1hr - via ferrata to the shoulder 2¹/₂hrs. Descent via Travignolo and Bettega Passes to the Rosetta Hut 1¹/₂-2hrs. - Col Verde 1¹/₂-1³/₄hrs. Descent from Cima della Vezzana via the Via Ferrata Gabitta d'Ignotti to the Rif. Rosetta 4-5hrs.

Difficulty: The Via Ferrata Bolver-Lugli is to be recommended to experienced, vertigo-free and naturally footsure mountaineers as a very satisfying rock route. Not simple for the less experienced: they must be roped up. Missing items of protection increase the difficulty considerably.

Bases: Bivacco Fiamme Gialle 3005m, emergency accommodation for 9 persons, established primarily for those climbing the hard routes on the N.W. ridge and S.W. wall; Rosetta Hut 2560m CAI, 66B.& M., wardened end of June to end of September.

Note: The climbing route should not be used in threatening weather. Lightning danger on account of continuous wire ropes. Stone-fall danger when several parties are climbing it at once.

For the descent over the steep snow-slopes and perhaps steep snow-free ice-slopes in the Val dei Cantoni crampons are not a luxury!

30.   Via Ferrata del Velo (Cima della Madonna: Kl. Sass Maòr) Pala Group   (Group d)

Via Ferrata del Velo - The Iron Path of the Veil - an unusual name for a protected rock path. It was set up as an approach to a summit of a certain prominence: the Cima della Madonna in the Pala Group. Not less prominent is the Edge of the Veil - Spigolo del Velo - which shoots like an arrow into the sky and was first climbed in 1920 by Gunther Langes and Erwin Merlet. The 'Madonna's Veil' of light, compact rock falls with a wonderful leap down to the green alms and forest-bordered foothills. The

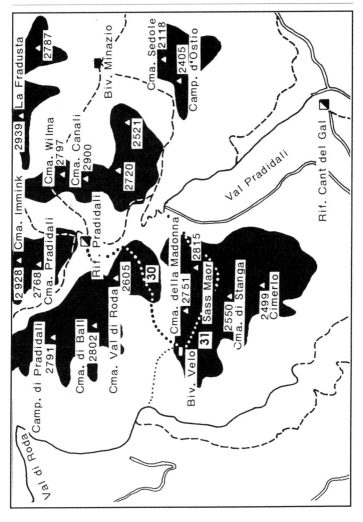

The Via Ferrata del Velo. On the left is Sass Maor

Route 30

elegance of the symmetrical massif can be admired especially impressively from a little rock saddle between Cima di Ball and Sass Maòr. Over it leads the Via Ferrata del Velo as a welcome short-cut approach for climbers. This protected section of path from the Pradidali Hut to the pass also provides for reasonably experienced mountaineers a round tour worthy of recommendation, with a maximum of excitement and variety.

Approach: A) From the hotel colony S.Martino di Castrozza, a favourite summer and winter sports centre south of the Rolle Pass, you take the chair-lift to the Col Verde and change there into the Rosetta cableway. It goes in 7mins up to 2609m, to the south-west edge of the Pala plateau. The short detour to the Rosetta summit 2742m is absolutely rewarding. Thanks to its outlying situation it is a first class view-point. By the neighbouring Rosetta Hut 2578m at the beginning of the gigantic undulating bare and rocky plateau, you take waymarking 702/715 in the direction of Passo di Ball. First it leads 200m down a steep shelf. By a boulder No.702 goes down to the valley and keeps lying to the right. The continuation of No.715, magnificently along under the bulging west wall of Pala di San Martino, which is flanked by its smaller, pretty sister, the Cima Immink. Through the middle of a slabby rock wall on the right of the broken Val-di-Roda ridge a path no wider than the human foot has been curved out

*The Ivan Dibona High Level Path on Monte Cristallo -
Queues are not uncommon! Photo: G.Sellers*

which is protected with wire rope in steep sections and leads to a basin. From here without difficulty up to the Passo di Ball 2449m - over snow and scree fields according to the time of the year. This crossing - named in honour of the English Dolomite pioneer, John Ball - gives a magnificent open view to Sass Maòr and the organ-pipe structure of Cima Canali. (Nearby, to the south, on the same level, the Campanile-Pradidali.) At the base of the Cima di Canali stands the neat Pradidali Hut, 2278m, open for walkers needing rest! It is reached from the Ball Pass in 15mins descent (eastwards). (1½hrs from the Rosetta Hut.)

B) From San Martino or Fiera del Primiero by car into the Val Canali as far as the Rif. Cant del Gal, 1160m; adequate car park, overnight lodgings, restaurant. Here you follow Path No.711, which leads up easily and only moderately steeply to Pedemonte, a classic resting place with benches. A vehicular road, fallen into disrepair in places and closed to private cars, also leads to this point from Fosne. On Path No.709 (Long-distance Footpath 2) steeply and laboriously but safely on a grassy rock outlyer on the western cliff of the Cima Canali to the Rif. Pradiadali.

Ascent: At the Rif. Pradiadali a small sign points to the west on the unwaymarked but clearly trodden-out Path No.739. First up a little hill, then in serpentine bends very steeply down via a steep and splintered slope into a rocky ravine filled with scree. There is a short snowfield to be crossed here which can be hard in late summer. Now down over rock and scree to a rocky structure and over to the big red star on the rock wall which is visible even from the rock ledge before the snowfield. The via ferrata (called the *Via Ferrata del Portòn* as far as the Portònscharte) begins with two airy, vertical pitches of iron staples, and leads - in a fascinatingly fine route adequately protected by wire rope, and mostly very to moderately exposed - up across the almost vertical walls of the Cima di Ball. Here the route leaves the walls via a poorly protected ledge, and leads into the deep rock ravine between Cima di Ball and Sass Maòr. (If you want to return the same way you must impress the very badly waymarked exit from this wall very precisely on your mind. In mist you can very easily get on to rough terrain here.) Faint trackways, sometimes running in parallel, now lead very steeply and laboriously up through the scree ravine, endangered by stonefall and always gloomy and cold, until a loose rope, faulty in its upper part, helps you up over the last difficult bit. In a few steps right, on the

A fine upper pitch on the Paternkofel, De Luca-Innerkofler protected war-time path. Photo: G. Sellers

narrow scree-path, you reach the rocky saddle of the Portònscharte, 2480m. The exit on to the wind-gap can present great difficulties and be dangerous when there is snow or icing, and no complete protection is available. The track on the far side of the gap leading directly down into the valley through the Val della Vecchia direct to San Martino is, however, hardly used, as otherwise you miss half the enjoyment of the via ferrata. (And see Descent B)).

From the gap on a clear but inadequately waymarked track in broad curves to the left, at first gently downhill, then almost level, and finally up easily through broken rock. The section of via ferrata which follows now across the cliff-structure of Cima della Madonna - here somewhat more level - has recently been protected in an exemplary manner and leads downwards, in parts excitingly airily, over the vertically dropping lower cliff-structure of the north side over to the west side of Cima della Madonna with the Rif. Velo della Madonna, 2358m.

Descent: A) If you must return to the starting-point at San Martino, follow the newly-established Path No.713, which leads down directly from the hut, first into a broad depression, then - well protected and in places blasted out of the rock - through the western cliff-structure to the cliff-foot. The older via ferrata here is abandoned. After 2hrs descent you reach Path 724 in the forested zone; now on the vehicular track to the valley station of the goods cable-way. Here continue to the right and past the deserted Malga Sopra Ronz with its ruined alm huts to the first villas of San Martino. If you keep consistently to the right here on the narrow asphalted road you will get back again to the valley station of the chair-lift on Col Verde without any particular detour or loss of height.

B) *Descent via Path 713.* This descent shortens the Velo Via Ferrata appreciably but destroys much of its enjoyment and is therefore hardly used. Go down immediately west of the Portònscharte and, following the red waymarks, on easy crag, scree and between big boulders, quickly down to a rock platform with protection. The waymarking to this platform, though, is very inadequate and cannot be found when there is mist or new snow. Continue down into the big corrie until you strike Path No.713 after half an hour.

C) *Descent via the Sentiero Cacciatore.* For anyone who has reached the Rif. Pradidali from the south, from Val Canali, the Sentiero Cacciatore is the best descent. The route is distinguished by narrow ledges, a wild, rocky ravine, meadows full of edelweiss and, almost always, complete solitude. From the Rif. Velo della Madonna first on a scree path and afterwards through steep, rocky terrain, adequately waymarked, up to Cima Stanga, 2550m (Path No.742). Now very steeply down through broken rock which narrows to a rock groove, to where the path branches and Path No.747 ["Sentiero D.B."] goes off to the right. Straight on here - that is to say, keep to the left - down the rock groove to where grass begins. Now continue left and via a steep step to the floor of the corrie. There is usually a small rock-hard snowfield here. Down left in easy curves to another rock platform; a vertical rock groove some 10m high is protected with wire rope and presents no problems.

Continue downwards on grassy ledges into a really romantic rock ravine with big jammed boulders - always plenty of drinking-water. A narrow grass ledge leads almost horizontally out of this impressive rock basin: some airy spots above the yawning depths of the ravine are protected with wire rope. The wide, grass-covered rock-spur which stretches out to the south is an ideal place for a rest, secure from stonefall and with a unique panoramic view of the rock walls and towers which soar up on all sides: from here to the right you can even spot the Rif. Pradidali. Ledges, sometimes wide but sometimes very narrow and airy too, adequately protected by wire rope where necessary, now lead down to the foot of the cliff. Down following sparse waymarks in a dry stream-bed to the path between Pedemonte and Fosne (Signpost here: "Sentiero Cacciatore 749"). In 5mins go left towards Pedemonte and from here in ³/₄hr to the Rif. Cant del Gal.

D) *Descent via the Dino Buzzati Via Ferrata.* See next route in reverse direction.

Altitude Difference: Rosetta Hut 2578m - Fork in Path 702/715 about 2300m - Passo di Ball 2450m - Rif. Pradidali 2278m - Portònscharte 2480m - Rif. Velo della Madonna 2358m - San Martino di Castrozza 1460m (Rif. Cant del Gal 1160m)

Time Required: Rosetta Hut - Pradidali Hut 1¹/₂hrs, Portònscharte 1¹/₂hrs, Portònscharte - Rif. Velo della Madonna 1¹/₂hrs.

Descents: Portònscharte - San Martino 2¹/₂-3hrs. Rif. Velo della Madonna - San Martino 3-3¹/₂hrs, Rif. Velo della Madonna - Rif. Cant del Gal via the Sentiero Cacciatore 3hrs, via the Dino Buzzati via ferrata 3¹/₂-4hrs.

Difficulties: The via ferrata sections of the Via Ferrata del Velo are relatively short; but the first section (near the Pradidali Hut) leads in places over very airy traverses. Damaged protection must be reckoned with on this section: therefore it is only for experienced climbers. Snow or indeed ice before the Portònscharte increases the difficulties appreciably. When there is mist, orientation on the non-ferrata sections is very problematic. Descent A) is free of problems in all weathers. Descents C) & D) are free of problems in good conditions, but problematic in mist. You are most strongly advised *not* to attempt Descent B) in mist.

Bases: Rif. Rosetta, 2578m, CAI, 66B.& M.; wardened from the end of June to the end of September; Rif. Pradidali, 2278m, CAI, 70B.&M., wardened from the end of June to the middle of September; Rif. Velo della Madonna, 2358m, 70B, wardened from about 20 June to 30 Sept.

Note: In the Pala Group, as in the Brenta, there is frequently persistent thick mist, especially in autumn!

   Descents A) and D) are not shown on any map.

31.   The Dino Buzzati Via Ferrata
Pala Group   (Group c)

This via ferrata, set up in 1978, will admittedly hardly achieve the popularity of the two famous vie ferrate of the Pala Group, but at any rate it provides a superb alternative descent to the 'classic' climbing-paths available, and opens up new possibilities for varied round-trips between the Pradidali, Velo della Madonna and Cant del Gal huts. Although admittedly very strenuous in ascent the route is only moderately difficult in good conditions. It leads out of the alm country through mature forest and latschen to the rock-towers and series of vertical rock-walls of Cimerlo and on to the ridge of Cima Stanga via a short but surprising rock pitch.

   This lonely path has been named after the local poet and mountaineer Dino Buzzati. If you want to experience a day far from the famous, much-used routes, you will find that the round-trip of the Sentiero Cacciatore and the Via Ferrata Dino Buzzati provides a day's objective that is really solitary.

Approach: By car from San Martino or Fiera del Primiero into the Val Canali as far as the Rif. Cant del Gal. From here continue by car on a good, sandy road, first to the signpost to the Rif. Piereni, then up to the right in the direction of Fosne at the first branch in the road (signpost). The first signpost 'Sentiero attrezzato Dino Buzzati 747' is at the next crossroads.

Drive another 200m from here to limited parking at Fosne, an alm with mountain pastures set in an idyllic situation (altogether 2.4km from the Rif. Cant del Gal). (see map p95)

Ascent: Follow the clear signpost, at first on an easy alm path, past a ruined alm, to the next branch in the path: about ½hr. Turn sharp left and go west for about 10mins through mature forest. At the next sign the path - now newly trodden out - leads almost directly up the slope, at first through shady, timbered forest, then through a short belt of latschen, and finally over scree and between isolated, soaring little rock-towers to the first rock wall. A firm wire rope provides help up a crack with good holds. (A misleading red waymark - perhaps older - points here to a little chimney and a wall.) After the crack, go up left (wire rope, a bit difficult to find), then via some sections of wall to a small gap. Go right here into a ravine and on a scree-path to a steep flank of broken rock. Up this - very well protected. Now comes the big surprise: a wire rope in a steep rock fissure less than a man's breadth, leads to two narrow iron ladders which bring you up into daylight again. You must take off your rucksack in places - be warned against carrying too big a pack! Your efforts are rewarded by a fine viewpoint. The route continues over inadequately waymarked grassy terrain to a grassed shoulder on the wide west ridge of Cimerlo. From here in a few minutes to the small summit boulder, 2499m. A wide scree-ledge leads right from the shoulder to a little, protected way through rock; from here through a wide little gap on to the east flank again, where you climb down on protected ledges of broken rock to the wide grassy ridge between Cimerlo and Cima Stanga. Over to the 'Sentiero Cacciatore' on a level path, and now steeply and laboriously, but without problems to the ridge of Cima Stanga. From here first on broken rock, then on a scree-path to the Rif. Velo della Madonna, already easily visible from the ridge.

Descent: A) Sentiero Cacciatore. See Descent B) of previous route.
B) See Descent A) of previous route.
C) Via the Via Ferrata del Velo to the Rif. Pradidali (see previous route in reverse). From there on the normal route down to the Rif. Cant del Gal: see Ascent B) of previous route in reverse.

Altitude Difference: From Fosne to the ridge of Cima Stanga about 1250m.

Time Required: Fosne - Rif. Velo della Madonna 4hrs.

Difficulty: Without difficulty apart from some technically demanding places, but very strenuous in ascent. Not recommended in mist on account of the inadequate waymarking on the high pastures below Cimerlo, especially in descent.

Bases: Rif. Velo della Madonna 2358m (see Route 30).

32.   Cima di Val di Roda 2790m, Sentiero attrezzato Nico Gusella Pala Group   (Group c)

The Cima di Val di Roda is an isolated summit in the heart of the Pala Group, easily accessible, with overpowering and instructive views down from it. The Sentiero Gusella is a little used path which is not "forced out of the rock" but which follows the natural ledges and grooves of the terrain: not a route for great sporting ambition, but the peaceful enjoyment of a landscape which in parts consists of dramatic rock scenery. Admittedly it is not a wholly independent route: its ascent and descent lead over other vie ferrate which are appreciably more demanding. But the Sentiero Gusella can also serve as a welcome way of by-passing the difficult Via Ferrata del Ponton: it allows an appreciably easier and scenically richer crossing from Rif. Pradidali to the Rif. Madonna del Velo.

Approach: As A) or B) for Via Ferrata del Velo. (Route 30)

Ascent: From the Rif. Pradidali, 2278m, north-west on an easy path gradually ascending into a basin filled with huge rock-rubble, and then soon on to the grassy Passo di Ball, 2450m, where a superb view opens up to the north. It also commands a view of almost the whole of the ravine into which the Sentiero Nico Gusella, which begins here, leads. Across gentle snowfields and scree-covered paths, diagonally at first, then in a few short curves up to the base of the rock where the first rope begins. Over easy, moderately steep rock (protected), then via a short bulging rise. Now you by-pass the lower, steeper part of the snow-filled groove on the rope; then on good, practicable rock to the upper third of the groove, which is narrower and gentler here. Mostly, good tracks lead up without problems. However, when the snow is hard an ice-axe or light crampons are strongly advised! A rope, which leads out over a short section of wall, begins again here under a big overhang. After a few metres of scree, a groove leads to the gentle ridge, to the Forcella Stephen, 2680m. From here an easy little path leads in hardly more than 15mins to the North Summit (big new cross made of steel tubing). The extensive view includes fascinating glimpses into the depths below! In two or three minutes you reach the somewhat higher South Summit by going south over the easy ridge: particularly fine view of the Passo di Ball. After this mini summit-traverse you can climb down via small rock steps to the cliffs on the south side and traverse back to the ascent path following foot-marks. From the Forcella Stephen the Sentiero Nico Gusella waymarks lead fairly steeply south over easily practicable rock terrain with good holds, down to the foot of the north wall of Cima di Ball. A section of rope gives assistance up a short, usually damp rock groove. The traverse of the western rock-base of Cima di Ball, which towers up vertically here, is distinctly more exciting. Ropes lead over rather smooth, sloping places. After a few steps uphill you are standing on the col on the south-west side of Cima di Ball. Waymarks lead down over steep grass. In the bouldery terrain which follows, the route goes briefly to the left. After a grassy hump come a gentle, grassy little gully and a short traverse half-left. Suddenly you are on an edge where the view of Cima della Madonna opens up. In a few minutes you reach the Portòn Pass over steep grass.

Descent: From the Portòn Pass see Via Ferrata del Velo (Route 30):
A) thus the very demanding Via Ferrata del Portòn, which leads back to the Rif. Pradidali is a possible return route.
B) It is less demanding to continue the route using the Via Ferrata del Velo, with the possibility of climbing down via the Sentiero del Cacciatore to the Rif. Cant del Gal. See Via Ferrata del Velo, descent C).
C) If adequate time is allowed, it is also possible to go down using the Via Ferrata Dino Buzzati from the Rif. Velo della Madonna.
D) Descent via Path 713. See Descent B) of Sentiero Dino Buzzati. (Route 31)

Altitude Difference: Rif. Cant del Gal 1160m - Rif. Pradidali 2278m - Passo di Ball 2450m - Forcella Stephen 2680m - Cima di Val di Roda 2790m - Forcella Portòn 2480m - Rif. Velo della Madonna 2358m.

Time Required: Rif. Cant del Gal - Rif. Pradidali 2$^{1}/_{2}$hrs, Rif. Pradidali - Cima di Val di Roda 1$^{3}/_{4}$hrs, Cima di Val di Roda - Forcella Portòn 1$^{1}/_{2}$hrs, Forcella Portòn - Rif. Velo della Madonna 1$^{1}/_{2}$hrs.

Difficulty: In good weather and with good snow-conditions, no difficulty. When there is hard snow in the ravine, only with ice-axe.

Bases: See Via Ferrata del Velo.

33.   Croda Grande 2837m, Via Ferrata Fiamme Gialle
   Pala Group   (Group e)

Croda Grande is the second highest summit in the southern part of the Pala Group. Its impressive northern aspect can be seen from the head of the Valle d'Angheraz. As well as the normal ascent from Gosaldo, you can undertake a strenuous but interesting route to the summit from the much-used ascent to the Passo Canali: two vie ferrate lead through the rock-chain between Vallon del Coro and the almost completely barren plateau on which the Reali Bivouac has been erected as a base and emergency accommodation. The Fiamme Giale via ferrata is admittedly not particularly long, but exciting and demanding throughout. The descent via the unprotected ledges of the Vani Alti requires a certain amount of experience on rock. Onsets of mist are to be feared, and one of these can easily cause route-finding problems. But in good conditions one experiences the serious, severe character of the Pala on the high-lying sections of this route - and usually in complete isolation.

Approach: From Primo di Fiera (Fiera di Primiero) 3.1km east in the direction of Agordo, then off left into the Val Canali and another 3.5km as far as the Rif. Cant del Gal, 1160m. From there a narrow road leads further into the inner Val Canali. But you can only drive a further 1.2km on asphalt. There is a convenient car park at about 1300m.

Ascent to the Reali Bivouac: you walk further along the road and in about 15mins reach the footbridge over the mountain stream; from here after climbing for a further 45mins on a moderately steep, winding path through mature forest, you reach the cosy Rif. Treviso 1630m. Now the character of the path changes. It goes for a short distance through open pine-woods, then the view of the great scree basin, surrounded by rock, opens up. On the right stand walls and towers, still in shade in the morning; on the left is the summit, already in sunshine on the far side of the valley. You soon cross the first level snowfield (still there in early summer) and then climb more steeply on the right-hand side of the high-lying valley, close along under the vertical walls, over scree slopes strewn with gigantic boulders and still grassy in the lower part. After a wild mountain-stream you find the sign 'Vanti Alti' (your descent route) between two scree-slopes, snow-covered until well into the summer. The branch route to the Reali Bivouac follows soon after: it is hard to find as there is no sign. The path goes up very steeply and laboriously and in early summer leads over an extensive snow-field in its upper part. Below the foot of the cliff, left on a big rock-terrace (about 2340m), a unique ledge with a view, which invites you to have a final rest. From here left once again to the first fixed ropes, which lead diagonally across steps on the rock wall on narrow ledges into a gloomy ravine. Airily on its right edge up on a rope to a rivulet. A short dièdre follows which leads out to the right on to an exposed section of wall - but with good holds. Up on the rope - exposed! A narrow, scree-covered terrace affords a short breathing-space; then the route goes to the right into a shallow little chimney. A well-protected ledge leads into the final steep funnel of the ravine. It is almost always filled with old snow which covers the steel rope. According to snow conditions its traverse varies from easy to tricky. A stepped, but in the end very steep wall is climbed strenuously on the rope in the fall-line, then, to your surprise, you are standing at the exit (Forcella del Marmor). In a few minutes via easy rock steps to the tiny Renato Reali Bivouac, 2650m.

Ascent of the Summit: From the bivouac refuge across the level snow-field to its south-east edge, where the waymarks for the descent via the Vani Alti begin. From here you have a view of the lower part of the summit ascent. This should only be attempted in good visibility and under no circumstances in mist. First with no path down into the wide saddle (Forcella Sprit) before the summit massif. (The saddle is often still snow-covered.) East through the corrie on clear traces of a track or on tracks over snow up to the summit wall and diagonally up on a wide, natural rock ledge to the scree-slope below the actual sudden rise in the rock leading to the summit. From there very steeply and arduously over scree to a little wind-gap. Then on the south-east flank on traces of a path over easy rock terrain to the summit with its comprehensive panoramic view.

Descent: Back again to the start of the branch route to the summit where the waymarking "Vani Alti" begins. (The ascent to the summit and the return take altogether about 2hrs.)

From the start of the waymarking easily upwards for about 10mins. On the only slightly inclined south flank the waymarking leads down on to a rock plateau on whose western edge the branch paths 'Gosaldo' and 'Rif. Treviso' are painted on the rocks. The path which leads from here on to the stepped west wall uses ledges and dièdres which have been left in their natural state and are only moderately steep, and winds in broad curves into the corrie. There is no protection; anchorages for rope have simply been placed at appropriately wide intervals from each other. Some of the middle sections are somewhat airy. Experienced climbers can be protected with a rope, using the anchorages. Only at the exit from this section are four 'irons' set so closely that one can climb down a somewhat difficult bit in via ferrata style. The continuation through the corrie - very steep at first - is laborious; in early summer the waymarks are hidden under a snowfield the first half of which one must climb down carefully. The tracks lead chiefly in the fall-line along with faded waymarks and always remaining just as steep down to Path No.707. If you cannot find the waymarks you can climb down the snowfield instead. This 'goes' even in the narrow, rather steep sections. Do not on any account miss the tracks of Path 707 crossing the snow. The rest of the descent follows the ascent route.

Altitude Difference: Rif. Cant del Gal 1160m - Rif. Treviso 1630m - Bivacco Reali 2550m - Croda Grande 2837m. Height of via ferrata about 150m.

Time Required: Rif. Cant del Gal (Car park at 1300m) - Rif. Treviso 1hr. Rif. Treviso - Bivacco Reali 3hrs. Bivacco Reali - Croda Grande 1$^{1}/_{2}$hrs. In descent appreciably shorter times.

Difficulty: Via Ferrata Fiamme Gialle is short, but difficult and exposed. The Vani Alti path demands sure-footedness and freedom from vertigo on unprotected rock ledges. On the plateau in the summit region, there are navigational difficulties in mist.

Bases: Rif. Cant del Gal, 1160m, fully wardened. Good starting-point; Rif. Treviso, 1630m, fully wardened, overnighting possible; Bivacco Renato Reali 2650m, emergency accommodation, sleeps 4, always open, no water.

Note: The plan to protect the Vani Alti path in the style of a via ferrata is obviously not going to be carried out for a long time!

34. Forcella dell'Orsa 2330m, Sentiero attrezzato del Dottore (Via attrazzata dell'Orsa)
Pala Group (Group d)

This short but difficult via ferrata constructed in 1925 is not likely to be the principal reason for visiting this remote corner of the Pala. Rather it is the appeal of the peaceful northern 'flip-side' of the popular Via Ferrata El

Dorado which can offer a series of scenic surprises. Monte Agnèr does not appear so aloof, so unapproachable and massive from any side as from the north, where it falls steeply with vertical pillars and walls into the idyllic Valle di San Lucano. Old snow does not lie so late in any Pala rock-basin as in the peaceful head of Valle d'Angheraz, where at about 1300-1400m lush and profuse vegetation exists in contrast with permanent ice in the corries and ravines never touched by the sun. The descent from the north side of the Forcella di Miel finally "pulls out all the stops" of the scenic beauty of the Pala so impressively that this route through every grade of alpine plant life leaves a more lasting impression than many a celebrated via ferrata.

Approach: From the fork in the road in Taibon (Agordino) drive 7.9km to the Col di Prà. From there on a narrow, gravel-surfaced road up straight ahead and, ignoring the 'No Entry" sign, just 2km further to a bend at about 1050m where there is a memorial tablet to Cesare Benvegnu; under it is a path-sign. The parking is very limited. There is another small car park about 200m further up.

Approach: to the Dordei Bivouac: First on a narrow path through thick forest from the bend in the road, about on the level, to a vehicular track which comes up from Col di Prà. It is steep in places and finally narrows to a path which leads to a wide, dry stream-bed but very soon swings to the right again into dense deciduous forest. You come to another, narrower, stream-bed in which you can climb further into the corrie at the valley head. The fork left to the bivouac is signed, but in 1985 the path through fallen timber in the young deciduous wood was almost impassable.

Ascent: The start of the via ferrata is certainly marked, but inconspicuously and difficult to find. The wide, conspicuous, smooth vertical wall on the western side of the valley basin is a good help in finding your way. In front of it, to the left, there is a block of rock only about half its height. The start of the climb is to the left of this, somewhat hidden, at about 1550m. Long, swinging ropes, without intermediate anchorages, with three short steel ladders in between, lead up on the edge of a dièdre, almost vertically, on the steep, gloomy rock precipice. A similarly somewhat slackly stretched rope leads diagonally out to the right. You are now in the middle of the wide ravine, exactly above the smooth wall seen from the valley basin. The waymarking leads a few metres up on easy rock, then to the right through dwarf pine (latschen) to a second rivulet, leads a short distance high on its right side and traverses to the left again. Up on the right-hand edge of the left-hand rivulet over scree- and grass-paths; you cross the rivulet to the left at the top under a steep step. Up on the left edge of the ravine. Before a basin, the path leads into the rocks, which give a stimulating climb (Grade I). The rivulet is now crossed for a second time; then the route goes up left to a grassy bit with scanty waymarking. A rock spike with the inscription Miel stands in the middle of a flat snow-field, which is nearly melted away by late summer. The inscription indicates the direction into the little ravine on the right-hand edge of the basin, from whence the path traverses up very steeply again to the left over grassy slopes interspersed with rock and rich in flora. You get into a wide basin - usually snow-filled - from which the further course of the route can be seen. Up left on a scree-covered ledge below a steep step, then a few metres on easy rock to a final scree-ledge under the vertical east wall. A short rope protects the narrowest place. After that you are standing in the notch. The indication of altitude 2472 refers to the summit towering up north of the notch. From the Forcella dell'Orsa you climb down a few metres through a scree-groove and very quickly reach path 705 on which you reach the Passo di Canali, 2469m, in about 20mins. (The Path 708 to the Rif. Pedrotti branches off here.)

Descent: From the Passo di Canali you follow the 705 waymarks due north. Navigational skill is needed on the karstic plateau. A re-ascent leads to the sprawling Forcella di Miel, 2538m. Only here is the highest point of the round trip reached. Path 707 (waymarked) also joins here from the left. The further course of the route is appreciably more clearly waymarked. A very long descent to the north follows, which leads through a barren zone of grass interspersed with rocks: no track at all, but with clear waymarks. The large, flat meadow with the old herdsman's hut (Casera, 1866m) which you see from above when it is still distant, forms a scenic contrast. From here an always discernible path leads through lush alpine flora. After crossing the mountain stream which pours out of the east wall, an unforgettable scenic experience follows: on an open ledge you have a unique view into the heart of the Valle d'Angheraz, above which tower up the bold north walls and rock pillars of the rock ridge south of Monte Agnèr. Now you are soon swallowed up in the dark, cool mixed woodland which accompanies the path right down to the road. A short stroll along the road, which drops down gently here, finally leads to your starting-point.

Altitude Difference: Possible parking at the 4th curve in the road at the start of the route, about 1050m - Forcella dell'Orsa 2330m - Forcella di Miel 2520m. Height of via ferata about 200m.

Time Required: Starting-point - Forcella dell'Orsa 3¾-4hrs. Forcella dell'Orsa - Forcella di Miel 1hr. Descent described, 2½-3hrs.

Difficulty: Via ferrata sections at the start of the ravine (about 200m ascent) difficult; danger of stone-fall. All remaining parts without difficulty, although very sparsely waymarked. Do not attempt in mist! In particular the ascent to the Forcella di Miel is then very difficult to find.

Bases: Dordei Bivouac, 1380m, emergency accommodation, sleeps 9; open all the year round. Water can be obtained from streams only during early summer.

35. Monte Agnèr 2872m, Via Ferrata Stella Alpina Pala Group (Group f)

In complete contrast to posh San Martino di Castrozza with its chic hotels and international hustle and bustle the unassuming villages in the Valle Sarzana give an initial impression of having hardly anything to offer, especially in the way of vie ferrate. But Monte Agnèr has become a touchstone for the more daring lovers of vie ferrate because of the Ferrata Stella Alpina, set up in 1977. At least in the Pala the Stella Alpina has outclassed all other vie ferrate. Anyway, together with the Rino Pisetta, the Tomaselli, the Costantini and the Cesare Piazetta, this ferrata is considered one of the most difficult and demanding: several largely smooth, very steep walls, which would be rated Grade V unprotected, must be climbed on a somewhat too thin rope, either without any footholds or with very poor ones, and in the whole 300m-high wall there is scarcely one place which could be described as 'not exposed'. The continuation of the climb over the sparsely waymarked flanks of Lastei d'Agnèr and finally the actual summit ascent on the shady north side, with its exposed ledges and unprotected ribs, pull out all the stops of an exciting rock route, richly seasoned with dizzy glimpses into the depths below and a comprehensive summit panorama.

Approach: Frassenè, 1083m, situated on the road that crosses the pass between Agordo (10km) and Fiera di Primiero (23km). (Chair-lift traffic to Rifugio Scarpa ceased in 1985. Reconstruction of the obsolete installation was begun in 1988.)

Ascent to Rif. Scarpa if the lift is still available. In the middle of the village follow the sign and drive up the narrow road, always keeping left, (at the first crossroad follow the clear sign "Albergo Belvedere") to the end of the asphalted section. Very limited parking here. At the end of the asphalted surface, a sign "Rif. Scarpa", Path 771. You follow the old, steep path to Malga Losch, which is paved with big stones, using the historic technique of path construction. (Take NO NOTICE of the misleadingly waymarked branch left just 100m after the beginning of the path: straight on here!) This paved path is waymarked red-white-red with the addition of mustard-yellow crosses. It leads consistently steeply straight through the deciduous woods. About half-way up you cross a shallow ravine: the old arched bridge carrying the paved path collapsed long ago. You reach the alpine pastures 20mins before the hut, at the lower station of a chair-lift.

Ascent to the Biasin Bivouac: From the Rif. Scarpa you follow the sign "Via del Nevaio 4h", traverse below the rocks above the old alm hut (Malga Losch) with a white memorial plaque, visible from a distance, and stroll across flowery meadows to the fork to Ferrata Stella Alpina at 1885m, which is very inconspicuously marked - with good reason. Below a short ravine a little yellow arrow points upwards. If you follow the yellow spots you will see the note *Difficile* on the rock at 2045m. Up the left edge of the ravine to half its height; then the yellow spots lead right, on to the wall. Up to the right (Grade II) and out of the ravine on a ledge. A few metres up on well-stepped rock (Grade II) until a clear path on a grassy spur leads in 10mins to the start of the rope-protection. The next 300m up are almost vertical and call for a lot of strength. About half-way up you traverse left, very airily; then the route once more goes almost vertically up. At the exit three iron bolts provide help up over the last completely vertical section of wall. From the end of the rope-protection at 2310m you traverse left a short distance (Grade II) and then climb up through a groove. A grassy path leads to the sign: *Guardate e non toccate*. Here, amid rare alpine flora you see the bivouac for the first time diagonally above you - but it is soon lost to sight again.

Grassy paths now lead up diagonally right for some time. At the first shallow rivulet (usually dry) the route goes at first up to the left, then over slanting slabs and wide, dried-up rivulets to somewhat more difficult rock again. Below a prominent cleft in the ridge the waymarking leads up more steeply and then leads down again to the right on a wide ledge below slabby rocks. At the end of a longish, rather exposed traverse the bivouac comes into sight again, this time within reach. An easy ledge leads into a ravine on whose edge you climb up to the first gap where, for the first time, you can see to the north. A "Sentiero alpinistico non attrezzato" *[An unlaid alpine path. Translator]* leads from here to Col di Prà in 3hrs. You are most strongly urged not to attempt this unprotected descent! (There is a route-description in the bivouac.) In a few steps via steeper, easily practicable rock to the bivouac-box at 2645m.

Ascent to the Summit. From the bivouac north up to the first rope-protection. At first, airy, sparsely protected ledges lead almost on the level towards the north side. Then up in a shallow groove and on a wide, slanting scree-ledge and up diagonally on a broad, slabby ledge with a good grip. Via a deep, narrow cleft and up on an edge about 15m high. Then about 40m to the left on an easy ledge (cairn). Now up again in the fall-line - NOT left into the steep snowfields - and via steps on the wall with good foot- and hand-holds (Grade I) to a shallow chimney, which is climbed. After that the waymarks lead easily on well-stepped rock to a level path which leads to the highest point (wooden shrine with crucifix). The iron summit-cross is about 50m lower down and is reached via easy rock in 5mins. The panoramic view is hard to equal. Even the bivouac-box can be seen from the most south-westerly point of the summit terrace.

Descent: A) "Via del Nevaio". From the summit reverse the ascent route to the bivouac. From there down via a wide ledge; then further on track-marks, and once more down via a short ramp. Then the path leads down over easy scree-covered platforms and steps. A wide dièdre follows, and eventually the waymarking leads on to the eastern edge of a huge ravine. Here you find the only problem-free place to climb down on a low rock ridge. From there the path leads down to the right to the end of the big ravine. Down 10m on a thin rope through a vertical chimney with good foot-holds, then immediately up right for 2m. Now a thin little rope leads over an easy natural ridge, almost on the level at 2130m, into the snow-filled corrie in front of the vertical walls of the funnel-like gorge. From here it is still 300m to the waymarked hut path.

B) "Via Normale". At 2420m a waymarked track branches east from the "Via del Nevaio" and leads in wide curves back to the Rif. Scarpa somewhat monotonously through ordinary terrain.

Altitude Difference: Frassenè 1083m - Rif. Scarpa 1742m - Monte Agnèr 2872m. Height of the via ferrata on the Via Ferrata Stella Alpina about 300m.

Time Required: Frassenè - Rif. Scarpa 2hrs (in descent: 1 1/4hrs). Rif. Scarpa

- Biasin Bivouac via the Via del Nevaio 2^{1}/$_{2}$hrs (in descent: 2hrs), via the Via Normale 3hrs (in descent: 2hrs), via the Via Ferrata Stella Alpina 3-3^{1}/$_{2}$hrs, Biasin Bivouac - Summit 1hr (in descent ^{3}/$_{4}$hr).

Difficulty: The Via Ferrata Stella Alpina is extraordinarily fatiguing and exposed in places for about 300m of climb. There is a danger from stone-fall if several parties are on the route. Via del Nevaio is more or less free of difficulties, but still with danger from stonefall. Not recommended in mist. Via Normale simple but long-drawn-out and rather lacking in attraction. Summit climb exciting, airy in parts, only partly protected and sparsely waymarked.

Bases: Rif. Scarpa, 1742m, wardened in summer, very good accommodation; Giancarlo Biasin Bivouac, 2645m, emergency accommodation (sleeps 9), always open, water to the left below on the rocks.

Note: Only tackle the Via Ferrata Stella Alpina when the rock is dry. Suitable gloves are most strongly advised because of the somewhat too thin ropes.

The Eastern Dolomites

It is difficult even for the outstanding connoisseurs of the Dolomites to give a clear answer to the question whether they would prefer to be on foot in the Western or Eastern Dolomites. Both parts of this great mountain area of the southern limestone alps appear to consist only of superlatives. If the Western Dolomites claim the Marmolata as the highest Dolomite summit, the proud Antelao, the second highest, soars into the sky in the Eastern Dolomites. If the 1600m north wall of Monte Agnèr in the Pala Group (Western Dolomites) is one of the mightiest precipices in the Eastern Alps, the regal Civetta wall (Eastern Dolomites) also belongs without doubt to this exclusive circle. It is not to be wondered at if the vie ferrate also seem to compete with each other.

The Prags/Enneberg Dolomites with Fanes (Fanis), the Sexten Dolomites with the Cadin Group, the Ampezzo Dolomites (Tofana, Cristallo/Pomagognon, Nuvolau, Croda da Lago, Pelmo, Antelao, Sorapis, Marmarole) and the Zoldo and Belluno Dolomites (Civetta/Moiazza, Tamer Group, Boscanero Group and Schiara) form the Eastern Dolomites. The Gader, Abtei and St. Kassian Valleys, and the Cordevole Valley separate them from the Western Dolomites. In the north the Pustertal determines the boundary with the Central Alps (Deferegger Berge), in the north-east and east the Sexten Valley, Val Canelico and the Piave River separate the Eastern Dolomites from the main Carinthian range and the Carinthian Volalpen.

Large parts in the north of the Eastern Dolomites were theatres of mountain warfare in 1915-1917. Especially in the region of the Fanis Group, on the Tofana and in the Sexten Dolomites, those who like protected paths will always be meeting vestiges of the war which have survived the passage of time. Many mountaineers will recall after successful climbs being shocked by these serious impressions. They should be a memorial to remind us that such mass murder must never occur again!

For the user of climbing-paths the Eastern Dolomites are the highest heaven of his expectations. In the Via Ferrata Costantini and the Via Cesco Tomaselli, he finds the most difficult challenges; the Schiara paths on the other hand look in vain for their equals in scenic impressions, while the routes of the Civetta or the Tofana offer attractive ascents to the so-called 'great Dolomite summits'. Some of the paths are reminiscent of the Brenta, like the Alpini Way or the Cengia Gabriella in the Sexten Dolomites. Others again could be counterparts to the often exaggeratedly abundant protection of many vie ferrate in the northern limestone alps (Alpspitz-Ferrata - Via Ferrata Merlone!)

Apart from the sporting value of overcoming one difficulty or another, it is above all the continually changing impressions of the Dolomite scenery which, for instance, make a holiday in the Eastern Dolomites so fascinating. There is still much to discover; many a solitary spot is indeed not far from the noisy busyness of the 'high spots'. It is just from this point of view, in my opinion, that the visitor to the Eastern Dolomites is richly rewarded. He may look out with open eyes beyond all the wire rope, brackets and ladders to the experience of the landscape. And he will find more on many (ferrata-free) detours than he had dared hope. 'Nuff said!

36.   Hochalpenkopf (Cima dei Colli Alti) 2542m, Olanger Via Ferrata Prags Dolomites   (Group d)

The Hochalpenkopf is one of the most northerly of the Dolomite mountains. It is a summit within the picturesque chain south of the Olang and above the Pustertal. in 1984 the local section of the South Tirol Alpine Club constructed a nice via ferrata with only wire-rope protection, on the northern flank of the Hochalpenkopf. Admittedly it demands long approach routes, but they are also scenically attractive.

Approach: A) South from Ober Olang into the Brunstbach valley, follow waymarking No.20 as far as the Brunst Alm. In the lower part the path runs alongside and on a natural toboggan-run and shortly before its end leads left into the forest. From here it goes up, very steeply and laboriously in places, to the Brunst-Alm. Following waymarking No.20 in curves along the troughs of the area around the source of the Brunstbach, passing on the west under the Durrakopf, and finally somewhat laboriously up on to the Kühwiesenkopf, 2140m (also known as Franz-Josephs-Höhe and Monte Pra della Vacca). From there you follow the grass covered crest to the west and finally - in places it is narrow and a bit airy - reach the sudden rise of the east ridge of the Hochalpenkopf. The path crosses over on to the north flank. Friable broken rocks and scree lead to the start of the wire rope.

B) From the Pragser Wildsee Hotel also on the path waymarked No.20,

114

up the Kühwiesenkopf from the south-east - somewhat shorter and less strenuous. Continue as A).

Ascent: At first follow the rope through earthy grooves, then steeply and in places very exposed on rather smooth rock to the exit on the north-west ridge of one of the Hochalpenkopf towers. Now on to the south side again and over the grass slope below the crest, without any difficulties, to the summit cross.

Descents: At first on track-marks to the gap between the Hochalpenkopf and the Maurerkopf.

A) To Ober Olang: on a narrow path below the Maurerkopf west to the Flatschkofelscharte. From there north on Path No.6 via the Lanzwiesen Alm into the village.

B) To the Pragser Wildsee. On track-marks down south from the gap between the Hochalpenkopf and the Maurerkopf until you meet Path No.61, which leads, almost on the level in an easterly direction on the south flank of the Hochalpenkopf on to the approach Path No.20 once more.

Altitude Difference: Oberolang 1083m - Hotel Pragser Wildsee 1494m - Hochalpenkopf 2542m.

Time Required: Oberolang - Hochalpenkopf 5¹/₂hrs, Pragser Wildsee - Hochalpenkopf 3¹/₂-4hrs, Hochalpenkopf - Oberolang about 3hrs, Hochalpenkopf - Pragser Wildsee 2-2¹/₂hrs.

Difficulties: Beautiful but strenuous mountain walking with a short, relatively demanding, via ferrata section. Fitness is necessary.

37. Heiligkreuzkofel 2907m, and Zehnerspitze 3026m, Protected Path Fanis (Fanes) Group (Group b)

The Heiligkreuzkofel, Zehner and Neuner are the summits of a huge crescent-shaped rock wall which falls steeply to the north and west, and characterises and dominates the Abtei Tal. A surprisingly simple approach to the karstic plateau of the Kleine Fanesalpe leads from this valley over the Varella Saddle (Val Medisc Joch) from which both summits can easily be climbed by their south sides. But the approach-route also offers a cultural experience. A Via Dolorosa in 14 Stations of the Cross leads to the Heiligkreuz (Holy Cross) Church of Pilgrimage, one of the most sacred shrines in the South Tirol. There is documentary evidence that this Gothic church, lying 2045m above sea level, was consecrated by Bishop Conrad in 1484. It was enlarged about 1650 and the massive tower added. The present-day inn was erected in 1718 as lodging for the sexton and for pilgrims; the barrel-vaulted hallway with similarly vaulted lunettes, and the panelled rooms, are worth seeing. In 1782 under the Emperor Joseph II the shrine was closed, de-consecrated and used as a sheep-pen. It was only because peasants and pilgrims insisted on revering it that in the end a reconsecration was carried out in 1840. Today the superbly restored church is still the scene of solemn processions and high festivals.

Approach: Best to use the chair-lift from Pedraces, 1324m, in the Abtei Tal to its top station, 1829m. The ride leads over a piece of mountain-farming landscape worth seeing for its cultural interest: two ancient, remote farms, sheep-pastures that are well cared for, weather-beaten alm huts. Then for half an hour you walk the 14 Stations of the Via Dolorosa up to the Church of Pilgrimage. Right in the middle is an unusual and surprising cross with the so-called "Coat of Arms" of Christ's Passion.

Ascent: At the fork in the path a few paces above the church, go right. At first, almost horizontally through dwarf-pine (Latschen), then on scree to the rocks. You soon get on to the broad ledge, for the most part very easy, that leads diagonally on the west flank of the wall, up to the ridge. At the start the route goes up a wide groove, later up scree-covered ledges, protected in places but never exposed, and several times up little rock spurs. The steepest of these is climbed with the assistance of a steel rope. At a prominent ledge you enjoy the first morning sun as well as the splendid view. After a horizontal section a further, only moderately steep, wire-rope section follows. Since 1985 you can climb up here easily instead of struggling through the corrie in steep bends on scree, as one had to previously. At the Kreuzkofelscharte (wind-gap), 2612m, the karstic plateau is stretched out, framed on the north side by a border of rock with fairly steep, jagged summits. The way to the Kreuzkofel is a comfortable stroll which leads up in one place literally "on the edge of the abyss". Here, at an indentation in the vertical west wall, you are conscious for the first time of the total verticality of this rock-fortress. The summit of the Kreuzkofel is quickly reached on a moderately steep scree-path.

Traverse to the Zehner: The branch path to the Zehner is about 50m below the summit, to the south. A very exciting section leads at first along by the base of the summit, which falls towards the south like a step-pyramid. Now the path - level once again - crosses a broad, gentle scree-slope and, climbing over boulders, you approach the final section of the route. The short but very airy west ridge of the Zehner presents you with 10mins of stimulating Grade II climbing. The rock is well stepped and has plenty of good hand- and footholds everywhere. But the ridge is not protected, though iron anchors for rope have been set at a certain distance apart, and these serve as handholds in places - and also as intermediate belays and belays from stances if you are using a rope.

Descent: As ascent. If you go to the Zehner first in ascent you can climb the Kreuzkofel on your way back, pathlessly up its gentle, rocky north side, and achieve a small mountain traverse.

Altitude Difference: Pedraces 1324m - Top Station 1829m - Rifugio San Croce 2045m - Heiligkreuzkofel 2907m - Zehnerspitze 3026m.

Time Required: Pedraces - Top Station of the chair-lift on foot 1$^{1}/_{2}$-1$^{3}/_{4}$hrs, Top Station - Rif. San Croce $^{1}/_{2}$hr, Rif. San Croce - Heiligkreuzkofel 2$^{1}/_{2}$-3hrs. Continuation to the Zehner 1hr. Descent appreciably shorter.

Difficulty: Easy one-day route. Ridge to the Zehner summit Grade II.

Bases: Rif. San Croce, 2045m, fully wardened in summer. Restaurant.

38. Cunturinesspitze 3064m, Protected Path
Fanis (Fanes) Group   (Group e)

High above the St Kassian (S.Cassiano) Valley stand the Centurinesspitze, 3064m, and La Varella, 3055m, which reveal from this side, the west, forbidding, greyish-yellow cliffs. Both mountains can be climbed comparatively easily from the Gr.Fanes Alp through the Vallon de Lavares, the Cunturinesspitze being the more difficult. Even though baulks of timber make the ascent of the summit massif easier for short stretches, the Cunturinesspitze is anything but a via ferrata mountain. Rather it is one of those rewarding Dolomite three-thousanders which are made accessible to experienced and proficient mountain walkers through sparse climbing aids.

Approach: From the Fanes Hut [This can be reached by a jeep-taxi from Pederü at the head of the Rau Tal (Valle di Tamores), which is reached from St Vigil], via the Limo Joch, 2172m; or from Peutelstein (on the road between Schluderbach and Cortina) through the Fanes Tal to the Gr.Fanes Alp, 2104m.

117

Ascent: From the Gr.Fanes Alp easily south-west to the Tadega Joch, (Passo Tadega) 2157m. [This may also be reached from the St Kassian valley via the Alpina Hut, 1730m, accessible by private car, and the Col Loggia, in about 1$\frac{1}{2}$hrs.] Now west through the Vallon de Lavares over scree and slabs (waymarked tracks), passing above Lake Cunturines until under the ridge running between La Varella (on the right) and the Cunturinesspitze (on the left). South on track-marks on to the summit massif of the latter. Airily with the help of baulks of timber somewhat awkward to climb and via easy ledges to the highest point.

Descent: The same route.

Altitude Difference: Fanes Hut 2060m - Limojoch 2172m - car park in the Fanes Tal about 1300m - Grosse Fanesalp 2104m - Tadegajoch 2157m - Cunturinesspitze 3064m.

Time Required: Fanes Hut - Grosse Fanesalp $\frac{1}{2}$hr, car park in the Fanes Tal - Grosse Fanesalp 2$\frac{1}{2}$-3hrs, Grosse Fanesalp - Cunturinesspitze 3-3$\frac{1}{2}$hrs, Alpina Hut - Cunturinesspitze 4-4$\frac{1}{2}$hrs.

Difficulties: A big, demanding mountain trip rather than a via ferrata. Fitness, climbing skill and freedom from vertigo are needed. For less experienced climbers, use a rope on the summit massif. The Cunturinesspitze is one of the Dolomites' outstanding summit viewpoints.

Bases: Fanes Hut, 2060m, privately owned, 39B, 40M, telephone, wardened from the end of June to the end of October; La-Varella-Hut, 2045m, situated on the Kleine Fanes Alp a little to the west of the Fanes Hut, privately owned, 33B, telephone, wardened from the beginning of July to the end of October.

Tip: The neighbouring La Varella, 3055m, is also to be recommended as a climb: After coming down from the summit massif of the Cunturinesspitze follow the track-marks into the northern wind-gap. From there in a northerly direction over broken rock and a rock ledge to the western summit, then via a ridge on to the main summit. About 1hr from the Cunturinesspitze.

39.　Via Ferrata Barbara　Fanis (Fanes) Group (Group c)

A little via ferrata route with no summit - unless you wish to combine it with the next route, Monte del Vallon Bianco. However, the Via Ferrata

Giovanni Barbara is also worth while for its own sake. Just the thing for an "active rest-day" when perhaps you don't feel like a big route and the weather is too good for *dolce far niente.*

Approach: The Fanes Tal (Valle di Fanes) is reached from the Schluderbach-Cortina road a few kilometres south of the Peutelstein ruins (sign at the road junction). On the narrow, asphalted road north all the time along by the Boite River to a car park at about 1300m. Here there is a barrier and the way to the via ferrata is clearly indicated. First follow the signs across meadows, then through forest. Soon cross a scree-shot and then on easily through the forest until the little path becomes very narrow. It leads to the edge of a ravine. Track-marks lead to a viewpoint from which you get a splendid view of a huge waterfall. The via ferrata leads to this.

The Via Ferrata: Back a few metres from the viewpoint and through a steep, earthy groove (occasional wire ropes) downwards to the south. The fixtures of the path lead in zig-zags towards the bottom of the ravine with its raging stream. You reach it, traversing on wire ropes and cross the stream in front of the waterfall already mentioned, on a metal gangway. On the wall on the far side, partly on ledges, partly over short protected steep steps to the western edge of the ravine and through forest on to the Fanes Tal Path, waymarked No.10. Back to the car park on this.

Altitude Difference: Car park about 1300m - western edge of the ravine about 1450m; Via Ferrata Barbara about 100m down and up.

Time Required: Altogether 2-2$^{1}/_{2}$hrs.

*Difficulties:*Comparatively simple, but scenically very attractive via ferrata. Half-day outing or rewarding addition to an ascent of the Monte del Vallon Bianco on the "Friedensweg".

40. Monte del Vallon Bianco 2687m, Via della Pace (Friedensweg) (Path of Peace)
Fanis (Fanes) Group   (Group a)

Undoubtedly the mountains around the two Fanes Alps, the "Pale Mountains", are among the most curious, if in parts untypical, landscapes of the Dolomites. The Monte del Vallon Bianco is one of their peripheral mountains. It can be climbed quickly, without difficulty, yet very interestingly on the Via della Pace (Friedensweg: Path of Peace), a wartime path constructed in 1915/17 and newly repaired.

Approach: From the Fanes Hut, 2060m [This can be reached by jeep-taxi from Pederü at the head of the Rau Tal (Val di Tamores) which is reached from St Vigil] via the Limo Joch, 2172m; or from Peutelstein (on the road between Schluderbach and Cortina) through the Fanes Tal to the Gr. Fanes Alp, 2104m.

Ascent: First you follow the Dolomite High-Level Route No.1 until the bottom of the Vallon Bianco. There you leave it and climb east straight to the Furcia-Rossa-Spitzen. You cross the Vallone del Fosso and then walk on a good path to a fork in the path. The via ferrata to the right leads over the Furcia-Rossa-Spitzen (see next route). The Via della Pace leads in an easterly direction, and later on the north side of the Monte del Vallon Bianco on easy ledges towards the summit. A well-built bridge over a ravine is the most attractive point. Many remains of the mountain war are to be found in the summit area.

Descent: On the same route.

Altitude Difference: Car park in the Fanes Tal about 1300m - Fanes Hut 2060m - Limo Joch 2172m - Gr. Fanes Alp 2104m - Monte del Vallon Bianco 2687m.

Time Required: Car park in the Fanes Tal - Gr. Fanes Alp 2^1/$_2$-3hrs; Fanes Hut - Gr. Fanes Alp ^{1}/$_2$hr; Gr. Fanes Alp - Monte del Vallon Bianco 2hrs; Monte del Vallon Bianco - Fanes hut 1^1/$_2$hrs; Monte del Vallon Bianco - Car park in the Fanes Tal 3hrs.

Difficulty: Beautiful, basically easy mountain walking, which cannot really be described as a via ferrata. Nevertheless there are artificial climbing aids (sections of path blasted out; bridges). A long day's outing when the approach through the Fanes Tal is included. If the Fanes Hut is chosen as the starting-point, the Monte del Vallon Bianco can be combined with the via ferrata on the Furcia-Rossa-Spitzen.

Bases: See Cunturinesspitze, Protected Path.

41. Southern Furcia-Rossa-Spitze 2792m, Protected Path Fanis (Fanes) Group (Group d)

Like the Monte del Vallon Bianco (see Route 40) the Furcia-Rossa-

Spitzen (Northern, 2665m; Middle, 2703m; Southern, 2792m) are part of the Fanes Ridge, which also includes such prominent heights as the Southern Fanisspitze (see Route 42) or the Cima Scotoni - famous among rock-climbers - and ends with the Kleiner Lagazuoi (see Route 43) above the Falzarego Pass. There are no fewer than four vie ferrate on this ridge - if we may actually call the Via della Pace one - and it seems to be only a matter of time before the whole length of the ridge from Monte della Vallon Bianco in the north to the Kleiner Lagazuoi in the south can be traversed on protected climbing-paths. Mountaineers who are convinced that artificial aids should not be used in the mountains may regret this - and justifiably, but in view of the enthusiasm there is for opening up vie ferrate, this gigantic via ferrata project may not remain utopian for very long. The via ferrata up the Southern Furcia-Rossa-Spitze is a reconstructed military path which was again made usable by the "Friends of the Dolomites" on the initiative of Walther Schauman.

Approach: See previous route.

Ascent: As for Monte del Vallon Bianco (see previous route) as far as the fork in the path above the Vallone del Fosse. There you follow the waymark "FR" to the right and use a rock ridge, overhung in parts, to a wind-gap with the remains of military structures. Now on exposed wire-ropes running vertically in places, and iron staples, finally over scree on to the Southern Furcia-Rossa-Spitze.

Descent: South very steeply down to the foot of the cliff on ladders protected by wire-rope; then on tracks waymarked to "Bivacco della Pace/ Monte Castello" directly by the precipitous summit massif of Monte Castello, 2817m, which is only accessible by rock-climbing. Here you once more join the Dolomite High-Level Path No.1. North on this path (Path No.17) through the Vallon Bianco between the Furcia-Rossa-Spitzen and the Campestrinspitze back to the approach route and down to the Grosse Fanes Alp.

Altitude Difference: Car park in Fanes Tal about 1300m - Fanes Hut 2060m - Limojoch 2172m - Grosse Fanes Alp 2104m - Southern Furcia-Rossa-Spitze 2792m.

Time Required: Car park in Fanes Tal - Grosse Fanes Alp 2^1/$_2$-3hrs; Fanes Hut - Grosse Fanes Alp ^{1}/$_2$hr; Grosse Fanes Alp - Southern Furcia-Rossa-Spitze 3^1/$_2$hrs. Descent via Bivacco della Pace/Monte Castello and the Vallon Bianco to the Fanes Hut about 2hrs.

Difficulty: Very exposed in places, but a very well protected via ferrata, comparable in difficulty with the upper section of the Via Michielli-Strobel on Punta Fiames (q.v.).

Bases: See previous route.

Note: The protected path up the Southern Furcia-Rossa-Spitze can well be combined with climbing Monte del Vallon Bianco.

42. Punta Sud (Südliche Fanisspitze) 2989m, Via Tomaselli Fanis Group (Group f)

The Dolomite rock wilderness around the Falzarego Pass was the focus of the fiercest encounters between the Austrian Imperial Riflemen (Kaiserjäger) and the Italian Alpine Soldiers (Alpini) in the First World War. Mountain walkers, causal strollers at passes and users of vie ferrate are still confronted today - whether they like it or not - by the remains and traces which the merciless struggle in the high mountains has left behind: rusty barbed wire, splinters of shrapnel, ruined trenches, sections of paths, dug-outs, shell holes, the ruins of barracks, tunnels made with great effort, and rock caverns which stare from cliffs and towers like dead eyes.

Similarly, old war-time paths, well waymarked, lead to the 'Hohen Fanis' (High Fanis), built in the style of a castle amid bygone remains of war. Magnificently situated, it serves as a memorial to the brave sacrifices on both sides. Since a via ferrata was set up in July 1969, alpinists come here from all over the world. Of course, as a protected path, the Via Tomaselli cannot be classified in the standard of normal 'ferrate'. The route remains in a natural state without artificial ladders, brackets and holds, fitted only with 800m of thin guide-ropes which lead the way via finger-broad ledges, walls with small holds and vertical corners, to the almost 3000m - high summit. Not an undertaking for beginners to earn their first rock-climbing spurs on, but an elegant treat for the experienced.

Approach: By cable-car from the Falzarego Pass, 2105m, up the Kleiner Lagazuoi, 2728m. From here climb down, northwards, to the Lagazuoi Pass (Forcella Lagazuoi), waymark No.20, and a short distance east to the Travenanzes Pass (Forcella Travenanzes). This point can also be reached on foot from the Falzarego Pass (No.402, 1¹/₄hrs). You change now on to No.20B, which leads up over a small saddle (a rocky knob with

122

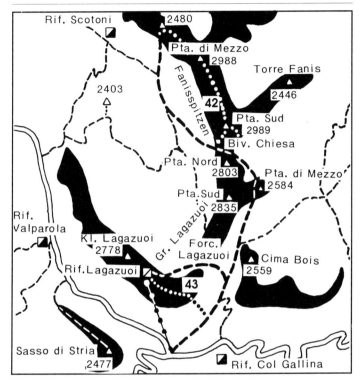

interesting caverns on the right), keeping along the east foot of the Grosser Lagazuoi to the Forcella Grande (Grosse Fanisscharte) 2650m. After a few steps downhill to the west a wartime tunnel provides access to the level site of a former Austrian gun emplacement. Today a bivouac stands here which bears the name of the brave Lieutenant Gianni della Chiesa. Unfortunately, this is said to be 'a filthy tip' at present - better to bivouac.

Ascent: The first rope of the route - named after the journalist Cesco Tomaselli - is fixed somewhat above the bivouac hut and leads up very steeply near old wartime ladders. An extremely airy traverse to the left follows, then you climb round a corner and strenuously obliquely up left

123

Route 42

Cavern

Bivouac Hut

The Punta Sud with the Via Tomaselli in the centre. Right is the variation which avoids the first difficult section. Left is the variation through the cavern

to sloping areas of crag. Over these on a wide, comfortably practicable ledge that is followed to the right to a spacious platform. Now straight up, not very steep at first but soon steeper, vertical now and then, and strenuously on to an area of scree. Here a chimney begins. Strenuously (slightly overhanging) into this and steeply up to the final wall. To the left, extremely airily up the ridge and over its crags to the summit. Panoramic and close views of surrounding mountains; the various Fanis Towers, the three Tofane and the Lagazuoi massif are incomparable.

Descent: From the summit, a short distance back on the ascent route, then left following the wire ropes over sloping rock down into the N.E. wall.

After a short airy traverse to the right (in descent) you reach a narrow little pass. To the right (in descent) vertically down (crux), then, after a more level area, down through a very steep chimney. To the right, easier again, to a rock ledge which leads towards the left (in descent) on to the Fanis Saddle, 2730m. From here downwards to the east via a very steep passage of scree, and lastly to the right under the cliffs on to Path No.20B again. (About 1¼-1½hrs to here.) Via this either back to the Grosse Fanisscharte or via the Travenanzes Pass to the Falzarego Pass.

Variation: (Detour avoiding the first, difficult section of the Via Tomaselli.) From the lower end of the steep scree-passage described above, west via a steep slope of scree and boulders (tracks) up to ledges which lead under steeply falling rock to the spacious platform mentioned above.

A further Variation begins before the difficult final phase of the Via Tomaselli (at the end of the less steep section, protected by wire rope, which follows the spacious platform). By a double red arrow to the left, traversing west (ropes), you reach a passage under a roof, a couloir, and move further on distinct tracks, always without difficulty, to the mouth of a cavern. Through this 100m long tunnel (torch!) you slip over to the north side and come out on a rock ledge above the Fanis Glacier. You climb down to the permanent snowfield via a steep protected step, cross the snowfield towards the east (tracks, caution when iced, stonefall frequent) and gain the Fanis Saddle and the protected route through the N.E. flank described in Descent.

The really pretty **Alta Via Fanis, L. Veronesci** as a digression on **The West Shoulder of the Middle Fanisspitze** begins on the south side by the rock tunnel (gallery). So instead of slipping through the mouth of the tunnel, you go further via a ledge fitted with wire ropes, west, about level. At the end you arrive completely without problems on the Cima Scotoni, 2676m. About 35mins from the mouth of the tunnel.

The Scotoni summit is so to speak the forward west shoulder of the middle Fanisspitze and provides a fine view of all the mountains in the upper Abtei valley.

Over easy crag terrain you climb down to the right to a scree field which leads comfortably to the Forcella del Lago (2480m) between Cima Scotoni and Torre del Lago. Further via scree down southwards to the Rifugio Scotoni near the romantic little Lake Lagazuoi.

Altitude Difference: Grosse Fanisscharte (Bivouac) - climbing-path to summit. 330m Fanis Saddle - summit 250m.

Time Required: Kleiner Lagazuoi cable-car station - bivouac hut 1¼hrs, via the Tomaselli climbing-path to summit 1½-2hrs. Protected descent via the N.E. side to the Fanis Saddle ¾-1hr. Back to the top station or to the Falzarego Pass 1¾hrs. Variation via tunnel - Fanis Saddle 2hrs. Via the route on the N.E. side to the summit 1-1¼hrs. Descent, Alta Via L. Veronesi to the Rifugio Scotoni about 1¾hrs.

Tip: For anyone for whom the protected northern ascent is also too difficult, the Tunnel Variation (leaving out the summit) with a descent from the Fanis Saddle, as previously described, likewise offers an exquisite and satisfying Dolomite experience.

Bases: Hotels at the Falzarego Pass, 2105m; Mountain hut on the Kleiner Lagazuoi, 2728m, Bivouac, 'G. della Chiesa', 2650m; Rif. Scotoni, 2040m, 12B, open from the end of June to the end of September.

Difficulty: The Via Ferrata Tomaselli is one of the most demanding of this kind; only for really experienced rock-climbers.

Note: The difficulties are naturally heightened when there is bad weather or icing. A climbing rope is advisable in any case.

43.   Kleiner Lagazuoi 2778m, Rock Tunnel
Fanis Group   (Group a)

As is well known, the area around the Falzarego Pass was one of very close fighting during World War I. The Cengia Martini in the south wall of the Kleiner Lagazuoi achieved special fame half a century ago. The hostile outposts stood within a few metres of each other on this narrow, exposed strip of rock-rubble. The Austrians twice undermined the Alpini positions and blew them up. The lighter colouring of the rock where the damage occurred is still visible. The large fields of rubble at the foot of the wall - about 130,000 cubic metres of rock - derive from the blasting and tunnelling. In 1917 Italian Pioneers worked for six months on an 1100-metre-long tunnel, which led from the Cengia Martini up to underneath the Kleiner Lagazuoi summit, which was occupied by Austrian Imperial Riflemen (Kaiserjäger). The final chamber was packed with 33,000kg of gelignite which was exploded on the 20th June, 1917. But the Austrians up there, warned by the noise of the drilling, had already evacuated their positions. The Italians did indeed occupy the crater caused by the explosion, but could penetrate no further into the enemy front line.

Route 43

*The Kleiner Lagazuoi,
with the hidden line of the Felstunnel*

The Falzarego-Lagazuoi cable-car company has equipped the tunnel (which is slabby and slipery and very steep in parts) with wire ropes throughout its entire length. Old leather gloves are recommended for using it, and a pocket-lamp in good working order is essential. To enhance the interest and fun, real torches can moreover be obtained at the top cable-car station. NB. This route is extremely popular.

Approach and Descent: Immediately by the top station of the cableway on the Kleiner Lagazuoi, 2728m, the waymarking begins, red/white with a black 'G' (Galleria) in the middle, which leads along a path on the south side, and which disappears into the interior of the mountain after 10mins. The tunnel winds downwards for 350m of height, passing occasional 'windows' and side caverns. You come into daylight again on the lower third of the wall on the Cengia Martini, with an old watertrough of masonry. Always following the waymark 'G', a ravine is crossed. Then through a 25m tunnel and to the remains of military huts. Via scree on the new ski-piste to reach the Falzarego Pass, 2105m. Descent of the tunnel ¾hr, to the Flazarego Pass, altogether, 1¼hrs.

Note: Of course, you can also use the Lagazuoi Rock Tunnel in ascent but this is not recommended. Very fit and experienced users of vie ferrate can also add on the Via Tomaselli (Route 42) as a continuation.

44.   Col Rosà 2166m, Via Ettore Bovero
Tofana Group (Le Tofane)   (Group e)

Col Rosà is the most northerly summit of the Tofana massif comparatively modest in height (over 1000m lower than the principal Tofana summits), but simply on that account a useful alternative for the via ferrata user if unfavourable conditions preclude routes on high mountains. Even though it is thickly covered on its north side with areas of dwarf conifer (Latschen), Col Rosà towers above the Albergo Fiames (starting-point for Route 52) as a bold peak, and together with its 'appendage', the Campanile Rosà, provides altogether a wild Dolomite picture.

Approach: The starting-point is the campsite "Olympia" about 1½km south of the Albergo Fiames, which is reached by car from the main Cortina/ Toblach road by a bridge west over the River Boite. Now north on a forestry road, moderately up and down for about 2km, until a clearly signposted branch to the west points to the via ferrata. Through forest pleasantly in tight zig-zags, always following the waymarks No.408, up to the Passo Posporcora, 1711m, which provides a way over into the Fanestal (Valle di Fanes). From the pass, northwards, still in steep zig-zags at first, then avoiding the first rocks on a narrow path to the west, in the S.W. flank of the mountain, and through craggy terrain overgrown with latschen to a metal plaque (in memory of Ettore Bovero, whose name the path bears). (See map p142)

Ascent: Follow the route to the right to a scree-covered ledge, then left to the first wire rope, which leads up very steeply for about 10m. The steep step that follows is very airy and strenuous. Then a short traverse to the right on to the edge and up it - difficult and airy - for a few metres. Then up to the right of the edge through a chimney-like groove, a traverse of about 5m to the left (very exposed) and then continue on the edge very finely up to the exit rocks. Once more really difficult over these (little footholds) to the end of the via ferrata. A path now leads to below the summit rocks. Here protection begins again and leads on to the broad summit plateau. Many remains from the mountain war.

Descent: On the waymarked Path No.447 first north through alpine-rose bushes and latschen, then in curves to the east and later south-east through forest to a sandy slope down which you climb, at first on its

Start of the top set of ladders on the Toblinger Knoten.
Photo: G.Sellers

The exposed top traverse on the via ferrata Zacchi.
Photo: G.Sellers collection

orographic left edge, and then cross to the right. Continue on the path east down into the valley of the Boite. You meet the forest road mentioned at the beginning, which leads back to the campsite and car after about a 4km walk in the southerly direction.

Altitude Difference: Campsite about 1200m - Pass Posporcora, 1711m - Col-Rosà-Summit, 2166m. Pure via ferrata about 320m of height.

Time Required: Campsite - Passo Posporcora about 1½hrs, Paso Posporcora - Col-Rosà-summit about 1½hrs. Descent to starting-point about 1½-2hrs.

Difficulty: Very airy in places, but for short sections and less serious than the vie ferrate on the Tofana. Purely from a technical point of view quite comparable with the Via Cesco Tomaselli. (Route 42). "A steep and sharp little route on excellent rock."

45. Tofana di Rozes, 3225m, Via Giovanni Lipella
   ## Tofana Group   (Group e)

The conchoidal, scree-covered summit dome of Tofana di Rozes, or Tofana I, stands exactly 3225m in the sky. The smallest sister of the triple constellation in the Ampezzo Dolomites keeps an alpine dainty in readiness for every mode of mountaineering: Mountain walkers walk round it comfortably and experience panoramic views and magnificent rock scenery. For 3000-metre-baggers it is more accessible than Tofana II and Tofana III. For 'extreme' rock-climbers, the goal of all their gathered climbing desires is the orange-coloured South Wall. And for lovers of protected rock routes, an attractive 'iron way' using 1400m of wire rope was installed on the ledged north-west flank in 1967. It bears the name of an Italian who fell in the war, Giovanni Lipella, and is traced back to the initiative of the Banca Commerciale Sub-Section of the Milan CAI.

Approach: 8km from the Falzarego Pass in the direction of Cortina a good little road branches off left to the private Rifugio Dibona, 2025m (Car park). West on the waymarked path No.404 along the south plinth of Tofana di Rozes, as far as a ladder and the entrance to a tunnel, 2420m (1hr). Signboard.

Ascent: A pocket-torch is an essential piece of equipment for the adventurous, 800m-long Alpini Tunnel! After a long ascent in the dark you come, on the right, to an exit protected with rope and guarded on the

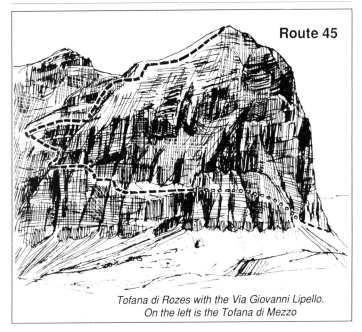

Route 45

Tofana di Rozes with the Via Giovanni Lipello.
On the left is the Tofana di Mezzo

outside by an old concrete wall. (The tunnel itself leads a further 15m or so like a spiral staircase up to its actual end. A guide-rope begins there which leads again to the height of the exit mentioned first. It is therefore sensible to use this first exit straight away.)

The Fanis Group lying opposite is superb - the view accompanies the whole of the well waymarked route. Over easily sloping scree terrain to rocks, not difficult, with the first protection. Another horizontal scree section, which ends at a pretty smooth wall with small holds. A guiding rope leads diagonally up and surmounts this most demanding pitch of the lower section.

More easily up to the right and following the ropes straight up on to a wide ledge. Follow this to the left (fine view of the Fanis Tower) round some rocky corners, cross a ravine, usually wet, on rope protection (danger of stonefall from climbers in front) and climb a short way behind the first corner after the ravine steeply up to the right on to the system of

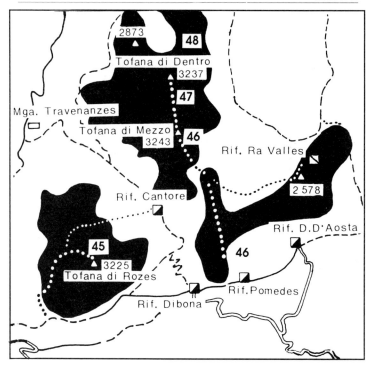

ledges lying higher up. Some steep rock platforms with very fine and airy via ferrata sections lead to a ledge with a division in the route: to the left a black arrow indicates the route to the Rif. Giussani. It goes round a rocky projection and from an indentation you suddenly see the two other Tofane and the bizarre rock-sculpture of the Tre Dita (Three Fingers). An ideal place at 2700m to rest and look at the view after 2hrs ascent.

For those who are tired or if bad weather threatens a good possibility is offered by the traverse to the Rifugio Camillo Giussani, 2600m, near the old Cantore House, by the Forcella Negra (¾hr).

At the parting of the ways mentioned above, a second black arrow and the word 'Cima' point right to the protected summit-route. Those in training climb on wire ropes through the rock amphitheatre of the final section of

131

the N.W. Wall vertically up to the fore-summit. These 300m of height are exposed, tiring, and problematical when there is new snow or icing.

At the memorial tablet to Giovanni Lipella you meet the normal route. On this over scree along the steep final dome, to the cross, 3225m. The view and the satisfaction of reaching the summit are of correspondingly high quality.

Descent: The north flank is traversed via the sparsely waymarked normal route over scree-covered rock steps, and often snow-fields as well, by the foot of the Punta Marietta to the new Rifugio Giussani. From there through the broad Vallon scree-corrie on route No.403 to the Rif. Dibona.

Altitude Difference: From the beginning of the climbing-path to the summit, 800m.

Time Required: Via ferrata as far as Tre Dita 2hrs from the start of the tunnel, as far as the summit 3$^{1}/_{2}$hrs altogether.
Descent to Rif. Giussani 1$^{1}/_{2}$hrs - Rif. Dibona $^{3}/_{4}$hr.

Difficulty: The Lipella climbing-path demands endurance, surefootedness, agility on rock, and natural freedom from vertigo. Some sections are endangered by stonefall.

Bases: Hotels at the Falzarego Pass, 2105m; Dibona Hut, 2025m, private, 30B, 6M, wardened all the year round; Rif. Giussani 2561m, CAI, 53B and M, wardened beginning of July to end of October.

Note: In cold weather the rocks, running with water during the day, are often covered with verglas in the morning and so increase the difficulties. Similarly the final swing up to the summit, which is often covered with snow, can present problems when there is icing.

46.   Tofana di Mezzo 3244m, Via Ferrata Giuseppe Olivieri
Tofana Group   (Group f)

The highest, very attractive Tofana II, called 'di Mezzo', has had its via ferrata since 1957. But in 1972 a variation via the Punta Anna was planned which is now the normal ascent. For some time the Tofana de Mezzo has been linked with Cortina by cable-car, much to the regret of 'pure' Alpinists. On the east side the 'Himmelspfeil' (sky-arrow cable-car) rushes up with a pleasing sensation of height to just below the summit cross. No place for shorts and sandals. On the other side, fortunately, we

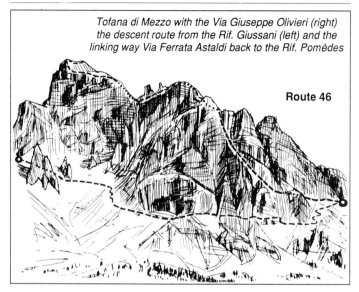

Tofana di Mezzo with the Via Giuseppe Olivieri (right) the descent route from the Rif. Giussani (left) and the linking way Via Ferrata Astaldi back to the Rif. Pomèdes

Route 46

can use one of the most fascinating iron ways in the Dolomites undisturbed.

The Via Ferrata Giuseppe Olivieri is long, extremely airy, mostly provided with nothing but guide-ropes, and demands both endurance and familiarity with rock-climbing. The old route has been abandoned, old protections are mostly broken and its use is strongly to be discouraged.

Approach: As route No.45 to the Rifugio Dibona, and in ½hr climb up on Path No.421 to the Rifugio Pomèdes, 2280m (privately owned) and a better starting point. Also to this point by chair-lift from Col Drusciè or the Rifugio Duca d'Aosta, soaring up over the celebrated ski-run, Canalone delle Tofana. (Not always operating in summer.) (See map p131)

Ascent: From the Pomèdes Hut, steeply up zig-zags over coarse scree towards the rocks which the Punta Anna throws off. Shortly before this point - fork in the path; to the right, the old, abandoned route.

The Via Ferrata Giuseppe Olivieri leads left diagonally up on the crest of the ridge. Now follows a series of guide-ropes which reach as far as Punta Anna. This section is extremely airy and spectacular, but good hand- and footholds on sound rock are to be found everywhere. The

133

glimpses downward and the view of the peaks which rise steeply up all round are inspiring. It is essential to belay weaker ferrata-climbers, and also to use sling-and-carabiner self-belay on this exposed ascent.

From the Punta Anna down into a wind-gap. An inscription "Cima" points on to the right flank of the ridge, across which a sloping ledge, protected with rope, leads upwards. At the end of the horizontally-running ledge, you reach a moderately sloping scree-flank where a descent to the middle station of the Ra Valles cableway branches off right (the Sentiero Olivieri, not to be confused with the Ferrata Olivieri to Punta Anna).

You climb left to the summit on a path through the scree-flank to the ridge, where the protection begins again. A ladder provides help up a jagged knife-edge ridge. Later you leave the ridge left (west) and reach the wind-gap before the Torre Gianni via an easy ledge. Very strenuously up the vertical wall of the tower (one place tends to push you off) to a ledge. Where the rope divides, keep right (not straight up to the top of the tower: impossible to get down on the other side!). Via a ledge to the corner of the wall of the tower. On a double rope, very airily and with a tendency to be pushed off, horizontally to the right on small footholds into a corner and up to a ledge on two iron bolts. Now follow the wire rope down into the wind-gap above the "Bus de Tofana", a cyclopean window in a knife-edge ridge, framed by a magnificent rock arch (Forcella del Foro, 2910m).

From the 'Bus' you can get to the Rifugio Giussani or to the Rifugio Dibona on the opposite, south-west side via a field of boulders and rock debris, steep at first. Another possible descent is on the N.E. side via a partly snow-covered corrie down to Ra Valles, the middle station of the Tofana cable-car.

After going through the cyclopean window you continue the ascent to the summit of the Tofana de Mezzo on the N.E. side, left on the upper edge of a snow-field (distinct tracks usually, care if iced). The iron avalanche barriers show ways through. You reach a ledged rock platform with protection, which leads from left to right to a small terrace. You climb a black, bulging wall via two iron ladders and now stand in front of the final upward swing.

The glimpse down to the left to the streams of scree around the Forcella Negra, out of which the north flank of the Tofana di Rozes rises, is unique. A last ladder brings you to a broad ledge. The protection is now at an end. It is advisable to keep strictly to the red waymarks, especially when visibility is poor. They lead over crags and easy walls, zig-zag to the forward summit and immediately after to the highest point, 3243m.

Magnificent panoramic view: the outer circle, which includes all Dolomite groups, above all the Marmolata, Civetta, Pelmo and Antelao, extends from the Gross Glockner via all the snow-peaks in the north, to the Ortler, Adamello and Presanella. Cortina lies far below.

Descent: The cable-car (5mins below the summit) to Ra Valles - col Druscié - Cortina d'Ampezzo, offers the most comfortable, possibility for the descent. Via the climbing-path down again as far as the Forcella del Foro. You go through the 'Bus' and climb down to the S.W. side via the scree combe - steep at first. To get to the Rifugio Giussani you bear right at the foot of the rock and reach the hut via a short ascent. If you want the Rifugio Dibona keep on waymark 403 and descend further down the Vallon combe on a now good path. About half-way a signpost left says 'Via Ferrata Astaldi'. This surprising finale should not be avoided. The Astaldi Way turns out to be extremely original. It leads, well protected, via airy, extraordinarily brightly coloured rocks of clayey 'Raibler' Strata (named from Raibl, a village). Apart from that, a pretty linking route, with a short ascent at the end, to the Rifugio Pomèdes. If you have parked by the Rifugio Dibona, turn off to the right on waymark 421 before the final ascent, and thus get there direct in 20mins.

Altitude Difference: Rif. Pomèdes - Tofana di Mezzo, 1000m.

Time Required: Climbing-path to summit 4¹/₂-5hrs. Descent: summit - Bus di Tofana - Rif. Dibona 2¹/₂hrs. Variation via the 'Via Astaldi' to Rif. Pomèdes, 1hr longer.

Bases: Rif. Pomèdes, 2280m private, wardened; Top station of the 'Freccia nel Cielo' cable-car (Himmelspfeil; Sky-arrow), 3223m, Restaurant; Rif. Giussani 2561m, and Rif. Dibona, see Route 45.

Difficulty: Familiarity with rock on exposed terrain is necessary for the Via Ferrata Giuseppe Olivieri, via the south ridge of the Punta Anna. One of the most difficult Dolomite Vie Ferrate.

47. Tofana di Dentro, 3238m, Via Ferrata Lamon
Tofana Group   (Group c)

Even the Tofana di Dentro (Hintere Tofana), which was still quiet until a few years ago, is now included in the via ferrata network. By using the Via Ferrata Lamon and the Via Ferrata Formenton (Route 48) you can even traverse the mountain.

Approach: Either on the Via Ferrata Giuseppi Olivieri over the Punta Anna to the summit of Tofana di Mezzo (see Route 46) or on to that mountain using the cable-car from Cortina d'Ampezzo.

Ascent: From the top station of the cable-car on Tofana di Mezzo follow the route to the summit upwards for about 5mins. Here the protected descent into the saddle between the two mountains branches off to the right (waymark "Tafana III"). From the fork via a rock step a few metres high on to the ridge, and on its far side down via a narrow ramp covered with scree (continuous wire-rope). Shortly before the deepest indentation the ropes lead right on to the ridge which connects with Tofana di Dentro. On the airy knife-edge of the ridge, sometimes to the left of the ridge, sometimes to the right, to the massif of the Tofana di Dentro mountain. Via ledges and steeper rock steps on the Ra-Valles side up to a ruined military shelter, visible from a distance. Here to the left and, following the wire-ropes, further up to the roomy summit.

Descent: A) It is best to reverse the ascent route to Tofana di Mezzo. But if you want to go down to the Rif. Giussani, leave the via ferrata at the point when it goes up again to Tofana di Mezzo and go down via a snowfield and some scree-gullies (footprints) into the Forc. Fontana Negra and to the hut.
B) Via the Via Ferrata Formenton (see Route 48).

Altitude Difference: Descent to the saddle 160m, ascent to Tofana di Dentro 150m.

Time Required: From Tofana di Mezzo 1hr.

Difficulty: Continuous, faultless wire-rope protection. Somewhat airy on the connecting ridge, but otherwise no problems.

48.   Tofana di Dentro, 3238m, Via Ferrata Formenton
Tofana Group   (Group c)

The sharp form of the south ridge of Tofana di Dentro is conspicuous even from the road between Schluderbach and Peutelstein. It makes a particularly striking impression in early summer: a fine, knife-edge snow ridge, which immediately arouses the desire to climb it. The Via Ferrata Formenton runs along this ridge and in good conditions makes a comparatively simple traverse of the Hintere Tofana possible, using the

Via Ferrata Lamon (see Route 47) for descent.

Approach: Go up from Cortina on the Tofana cable-car - Freccia nel cielo - as far as the second station (Ra Valles, 2470m). (See map p131)

Ascent: First go down for a short distance from the Rifugio Ra Valles on Path No.407 in a northerly direction towards the Forcella Ra Valles, then along north-west on scree and limestone pavement below the steep eastern cliffs of the Hintere Tofana. At its lowest point the protected path leads up to the Formenton military post of the 1915-1917 mountain war, and to the "Baraca degli Alpini" bivouac, 2922m. From there south on the ridge to the summit of Tofana di Dentro. Though waymarked and not very steep, this is somewhat airy in places.

Descent: On the Via Ferrata Lamon on to the saddle between the Hintere and Mittlere Tofana and follow the previous route in reverse to the top station of the Tofana cable-car. Very easily back to Cortina on the "Freccia nel cielo" (Ger: Himmelspfeil; English: Sky-Arrow).

Altitude Difference: Rifugio Ra Valles 2470m - Tofana di Dentro 3238m.

Time Required: Rifugio Ra Valles - Tofana di Dentro 2$^{1}/_{2}$hrs. Tofana di Dentro - top station of the Tofana cable-car (via the Via Ferrata Lamon) 1hr.

Difficulty: The route is well protected and without technical problems, but somewhat airy in some places. In early summer and until about the end of July/beginning of August, the ridge from the Bivacco Baraca degli Alpini to Tofana di Dentro is a knife-edge snow ridge which demands experience of that kind of terrain. This section of the ascent is difficult when icy and is to be recommended only to good mountaineers.

Note: To combine the ascent of Tofana di Mezzo on the Via Ferrata Giuseppe Olivieri with the crossing to Tofana di Dentro on the Via Ferrata Lamon and the descent on the Via Ferrata Formenton gives a splendid via ferrata traverse of the Mittlere and Hintere Tofana: but it is long, difficult, and demanding from a mountaineering point of view. Without doubt it is one of the most rewarding objectives of this kind for mountaineers with stamina and who are equal to the demands of this route.

49. Col di Lana 2462m, Protected Path
Buchenstein Mountains (Group b)

Col di Lana, which lies half-way between the Marmolata and Fanes Groups, achieved notoriety in the First World War: in April 1916 about a hundred soldiers were killed on the summit of this "Bloody Mountain" when it was undermined and blown up. A tiny church a little below the highest point, and the long military trenches, in which, typically enough, forget-me-nots grow, are a reminder even today of the horrors of that mountain war. Moreover, this mountain, formed of volcanic rock, is a first-class viewpoint. Why it now appears here in a via ferrata guidebook is quickly explained: some sections of the traverse from Monte Sief to Col di Lana are protected with wire-rope. Like the Hexenstein (see Route 50) Col di Lana has been included in the present work for the sake of completeness. Not a via ferrata, but an unforgettably fine mountain walk!

Approach: From the Rifugio Valparola, somewhat north of the top of the pass (see also Route 50), splendid walking south-west below the cliffs of Settsass on Path No.23 to the Siefsattel.

Ascent: From the saddle (Siefsattel) south on the crest, partly in military trenches, on to Monte Sief, 2425m (Memorial Plaque). Further on the ridge, or below it (some protection) on to Col di Lana.

Descent: As ascent.

Altitude Difference: Rif. Valparola 2168m - Monte Sief 2425m - Col di Lana 2462m.

Time Required: Rif. Valparola - Col di Lana 2$^{1}/_{2}$-3hrs. Col di Lana - Rif. Valparola 2hrs.

Difficulty: Splendid walking with magnificent views of the Marmolata, Civetta, Pelmo, Sella, Fanes and Tofana Groups. Sure-footedness needed in places. Not a via ferrata in the true sense in spite of occasional protection where appropriate.

50. Hexenstein 2477m, Protected Path
Buchenstein Mountains (Group b)

The area around the Valparola Pass and the Falzarego Pass was one of the most dramatic scenes of the 1915-1917 mountain war. No matter whether you undertake routes on the Fanisspitzen, Tofana, Kleiner Lagazuoi (this is the "Col Alto" in Luis Trenker's *Mountains in Flames)* or even Col di Lana - everywhere you encounter vestiges of this 'lonely war', which seem to be a silent memorial and admonition. The Hexenstein also (or Hexenfels - Italian:Sasso di Stria), which falls away to the south in precipitous cliffs on which there are some rock-routes, was one of these contested summits. Today it is the goal of a quick mountain walk which can easily be taken in when crossing from the Abteital into the mountains around Cortina. A fine view of many Dolomite groups turns this detour into something completely rewarding.

Ascent: From the top of the Valparola Pass follow the waymarked path on the north-west flank until just below the summit rocks. Now via a steep step to a narrow rock-cleft. Through this and up two short ladders, reaching the summit cross in a few minutes.

Descent: As ascent.

Altitude Difference: Top of Valparola Pass 2197m - Hexenstein 2477m.

Time Required: Top of Valparola Pass - Hexenstein 1¼hrs.

Difficulty: A short route, only worth recommending in good weather, because it is primarily worth while for the view. Sure-footedness and freedom from vertigo are necessary for the summit rocks.

Note: Hexenstein and Col di Lana (see Route 49) can easily be climbed on the same day.

51. Averau 2647m, and Nuvolao 2575m. Protected Paths
Nuvolao Group (Group a)

Between the Falzarego Pass and the popular Nuvolao rises the massive Averau. It presents from every side steep, forbidding, rugged cliffs. Only on the north-west side is there a single, easily accessible "weak spot": easy rock ledges and a gloomy chimney. Short rope-protections lead to the beginning of the great trough-shaped corrie on the east side. From there the summit can be climbed without problems on tracks on rocky terrain, with rock-steps and ledges, and without difficulties. If you extend the half-day outing by a bare half-hour and stroll further south to Nuvolao you are treading on historic ground, in an alpine sense. The Rifugio Nuvolao was built as early as 1883 and was at that time called the

"Sachsendankhütte" (The "Saxon's Thanks" Hut) - so-called from a curious epigrammatic verse written on the hut wall, and now barely legible. There is also a modern bronze sculpture celebrating Riccardo dalla Favera's 800th(!) ascent of Nuvolao. If you climb Nuvolao from the Passo Giau - ie. from the south - you have another nice, short via ferrata section on the ridge - surprisingly narrow here - just below the summit. This ascent on the south side provides an experience of nature both solitary and rewarding.

Approach: A) From the Falzarego Pass a few kilometres down to the east and on a steep, narrow, but asphalted little road (Gradient 15%) uphill for 4.3km to the Rifugio Cinque Torri, 2137m.

B) Falzarego Pass, 2105m.

C) Passo Giau, 2333m.

Ascent: A) From the Rifugio Cinque Torri on a wide, vehicular road, climbing steadily, past the Torre Grande, the famous 'climbing-tower' of Cinque Torri, to the Rifugio Scoiattoli, 2280m, top station of a chair-lift. (This point can also be reached by chair-lift from the valley station Rifugio Bai de Dones.) Still on the road, to the Nuvolao Saddle, where the new, small Rifugio Averau, 2413m, stands. A waymarked path leads diagonally up on the east side into the corrie and to a small col. Go left there and in a few minutes you are at the rocks. The first rope leads left to a short, gloomy, vertical chimney which you climb through on good hand- and footholds, surprisingly free from problems. A wide ledge leads right to a second steep rock step which leads almost disappointingly quickly to the exit. The summit cross is already visible from here. On clear tracks, first through the corrie, and then without problems over easy rock steps to the summit. Care in mist - no waymarking at all!

B) You can get to the Nuvolao Saddle from the Falzarego Pass by a somewhat longer ascent on waymarked Path No.441.

C) From Passo Giau you can reach Rif. Scoiattoli on Path No.443 or go over Nuvolao on Path No.408 (Long-distance Footpath No.1). The ascent of Nuvolao by the south side is comparatively long, but scenically very beautiful. The final section of ridge before the summit is protected by wire-rope. The Rif. Nuvolao 2575m, built as early as 1883, stands on the summit. From there, however, you have to descend 160m to the Nuvolao Saddle.

Descent: The via ferrata is the only easy route to the summit, *and* for descent!

Altitude Difference: From the Rif. Cinque Torri 510m; from the Falzarego Pass 542m; from the Passo Giau 470m (with 160m intermediate descent and a corresponding re-ascent on the way back). Height of the via ferrata: about 50m.

Time Required: From the Rif. Cinque Torri 2³/₄hrs; from the Falzarego Pass 3¹/₂hrs (to include Nuvolao, add 20-30mins ascent, and 15mins descent); from the Passo Giau over Nuvolao 4hrs. Descents in each case about ³/₄hr shorter.

Difficulty: Via ferrata sections short and not difficult. Chimney somewhat more demanding. Suitable for beginners. Via ferrata sections on the south side of Nuvolao very easy.

Bases: Rif. Averau, 2413, simple catering; Rif. Scoiattoli 2380m; if necessary Rif. Nuvolao, 2575m also (on ascent C)), catering and overnight accommodation; at the start, Rif. Cinque Torri 2137, easily reached by private car; catering and overnight accommodation.

Note: If you are fit enough this simple half-day's outing can be followed by the ascent of the Southern Fanisspitze (Via Ferrata Tomaselli) as an afternoon bonus.

52. Punta Fiames 2240m. Via 'Michielli Albino Strobel' Pomaganon Range   (Group d)

In 1964 the Cortina mountain guides fixed a very fine climbing-path along the west flank of the Punta Fiames in memory of their friend Strobel who was killed in a fall. Punta Fiames is the western corner pillar of the Pomagagnon Range and not an imposing summit in comparison with the other monarchs of the Cortina Dolomites. Nevertheless it enjoys a great vogue. What makes the Via Ferrata Strobel so attractive is: it is in the immediate vicinity of Cortina and can be done as the 'first and last route of the year', as Ugo Pompanin, a Cortina climber of the 'Scoiattoli'-Guild once put it. On account of it facing west, inclined to sun and warmth, it remains relatively free of snow, an advantage also made use of by climbers on the classic south-wall routes, who use the iron way in early spring and late autumn months as a convenient descent. Of course the north side to the Forcella Pomagagnon is then covered in snow or iced up. The protected section is fitted with 500m of steel rope and a climbing ladder, and utilizes the terrain very skillfully.

141

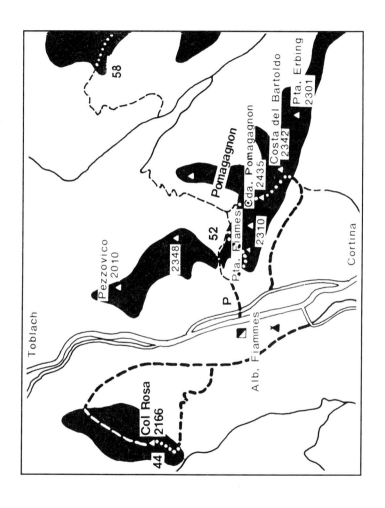

Approach: A) From the Hotel Fiames, 1200m (see Route 44), across the road. By the building opposite, signpost and the start of a narrow path which soon crosses the motor-road running parallel with the main road. This motor-road runs south to the old Fiames Railway Halt on the disused Cortina/Toblach line. The waymarked path climbs fairly steeply to the south-east at first, but soon turns east and leads in a steep ascent towards the walls of Pezzories. Later laboriously east straight up a section of scree towards a deep ravine between Pezzories and Punta Fiames. South of the ravine, the start of the climbing-path (sign). About ³⁄₄hrs from the Hotel Fiames.

B) By the 16km stone on the main road from Cortina to Toblach a dirt road branches off half right on which you reach the Fiames Station of the old light railway (1340m) after about 1km. You can park here. You continue on foot in a northerly direction on the old railway track to a sign for the ferrata. Branch off right on a little forest path, where you meet route A).

Ascent: First about 400m to right on a moderately steep ledge, then, following the waymarkings and the first wire rope, obliquely up left to a ledge (about 80m, very steep, rocks, good hold nevertheless). A few metres without difficulty to the left on a ledge, then following the ropes, first straight up, on airy traverse left, and further, following the protection into a sloping area of dwarf conifer and crag, which you surmount without difficulty on tracks. Thus you reach a very exposed pulpit on the edge of a ravine which divides the rock curtain up which the climbing-path runs, from the Punta Fiames south wall. Very steeply, but very delightfully up the brow of the curtain (wire ropes, iron rungs) in about 15m to level terrain which leads to an almost vertical step. You surmount this at first with the help of a ladder, subsequently following rungs, brackets and ropes, and get to a sloping terrace under the summit crags (80m altogether, the most difficult but also the finest section of the climbing-path). On tracks to the last wire ropes, which lead without difficulty on to the level north roof of Punta Fiames. Via its highest section to the summit.

Descent: First north on a distinctly trodden little path, then east, first into the narrow gap between Punta Fiames and Punta della Croce. Further, following the path, into the Forcella Pomagagnon, 2178m, between Punta della Croce and Croda di Pomagagnon. From here via the big scree area ('Grava') below the principal Pomagagnon summits, Testa and Costa del Bartoldo, partly on tracks (Waymark No.202), downwards, south towards the hamlet of Chiave (north of Cortina). Before the end of the scree, to the

143

Route 52

Punta Fiames from the south

right under the rocks of the Campanile Dimai and the Punta Armando and continue down over the scree.

Keep to the right-hand branch of the scree-run, which soon becomes a streambed. Continue down this. Near the edge of the forest conspicuous waymarking to the right. Here on a narrow, steep little path down through the forest (keep right when it branches), finally in or near a streambed on to the old railway track, which leads right (north) to Fiames Station.

Altitude Difference: Hotel Fiames 1280m - Fiames Station 1340m - Punta di Fiames 2240m. Altitude Difference of the climbing-path about 600m.

Time Required: Hotel Fiames - start of the climbing-path ³/₄hr, climbing-path to summit 2hrs; descent via the Pomagagnonscharte to Hotel Fiames 1¹/₂hrs.

Difficulty: Except for an 80m high, vertical, exposed climbing section in the upper part, not very difficult, though very airy in parts.

Base: Cortina d'Ampezzo, 1210m.

Tip: Possible even early in spring as a training route. In the heat of high summer an early morning start advisable.

Note: Anyone who does not feel that his mountaineering needs have been satisfied after the Strobel via ferrata may be recommended to try the so-called 'Third Ledge' on the south wall of the Costa del Bartoldo. You reach it (in this case without effort) from the lower part of the scree-slope ("Grava") of the Pomagagnon Scharte descent (clear tracks lead to the beginning of the ledge). You now climb up this "Third Ledge" airily and with intermittent protection, sloping to the right, upwards across the south walls of Costa del Bartoldo and Punta Cestelis. At the notch between this and Punta Erbing the route goes over to the north side and, after a steep descent, ends at the Forcella de Zumeles, 2072m. From there south on Path No.204 to the hamlet of Chiave bei Cortina. Altogether 3$^{1}/_{2}$-4hrs.

53. Monte Cristallo. Ivano Dibona High-level Path
Cristallo Massif (Group c)

The Dürrensee (Lago di Landro) courteously holds up its mirror to the beautiful form of Monte Cristallo, 3216m. There the cyclopean group of giant, snow-trimmed ashlars, with blunted corners and level roof, appears at its most attractive, and very photogenic. The deeply indented Cristallo Pass joins it to the no less changeless neighbour summit, the Piz Popena, 3152m, a fine specimen of a wild, defiant Dolomite tower. Into this dismembered north side with its compact stone shelves and ravines are wedged, as a high-alpine characteristic, two heavily crevassed little glaciers. In contrast with the forbidding rock architecture on the north side of the Cristallo Massif, the south side presents a more compact, largely snow-free rock front. Cortina d'Ampezzo profits from its wind-shadow.

In the long sector from the Cristallo Pass to the Col di Stombi and Schönleitenschneide (Cotabella) there was bitter fighting in the first world war. For the Alpini the defence of the Ampezzo Valley basin was at stake and for the Imperial Riflemen the Höhlensteintal (Valle di Landro) with the Landro Fort, which protected the Purstertal. From 1915 to 1917 the south side of the Cristallo swarmed with Austrian and Italian alpine troops, who dug themselves into the rocks and built barracks, cableway for materials, casemates, caverns, trenches, barbed-wire entanglements and gun-emplacements. More than seventy summers and winters have passed since this alpine war, conducted on both sides with heroism and great sacrifice. But its traces, though falling into ruin, are still not obliterated. In 1969-70 mountain guides and mountain lovers of Cortina laid out a well protected high-level route through this rocky region so full of memories. The interesting and scenically very impressive route leads along rock

145

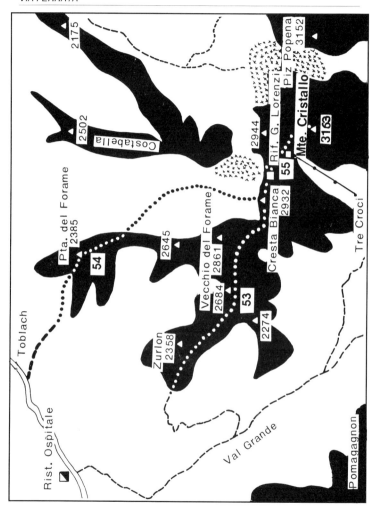

walls with cables on good paths, over ridges and gorges, through ravines, over wooden bridges and iron ladders, without too many difficulties and without laborious ascent - the gondola-lift undertakes this, to a height of 2918m. It bears the name of the mountain guide Ivano Dibona who inexplicably fell to his death with his client in 1968. He was grandson of the famous pioneering rock-climber Angelo Dibona, who in 1909 climbed the N.E. Ridge - the Dibona Ridge - of the Grosse Zinne, where the young Ivano Dibona met his fate six decades later.

Approach: From Cortina on the Dolomite road (Strada di Valbona) in the direction of the Tre-Croci Pass as far as the bottom station, 1680m (5km) of the double chair-lift from Rio Gere to Son Forca, 2240m. This is continued a few steps downhill from the half-way station, by a gondola-lift to the Forcella Stauniès. The extremely laborious 3½hr ascent in the scree combe is not to be recommended. Axe and crampons needed most years.

Descent: The route begins directly by the top station of the gendola-lift in the Forcella Stauniès. Immediately up via a convenient ladder to the left, then following the wire rope on the N.E. side of the rocks and via a wooden gangway to a short tunnel (Galleria del Cecchino). Through the tunnel on to the south side, then right (west) via two more wooden gangways to a deep rift in the rock. A 27m suspension-bridge leads across this, the Ponte Cristallo, till now the longest suspension-bridge in the Dolomites. On the far side of the bridge via two iron ladders on to the ridge. You now reach the highest point of the whole route, 2985m. Following the ridge down you reach the waymarked diversion to the Cristallino d'Ampezzo, 3008m (the route is likewise well protected and requires about 25mins there and back). Further down along the ridge. After an iron ladder and some rock steps (often iced) you reach the Forcella Grande (³⁄₄hr from the Forcella Stauniès).

Fork: To the north-west the Via Ferrata Renato de Pol branches off. See route 54. (The descent to the Son Forca hut is no longer feasible).

The actual Ivano-Dibona-High-level Route now begins. It leads along keeping to the south side of the Cresta Bianca (summit can be reached by an easy diversion) via a series of ledges and wooden gangways, protected with wire rope in some exposed places, to the Forcella Padeon, 2760m. (Descent south to Son Forca possible but not recommended: at the end of the scree, keep right until you meet the tracks at the foot of the Torrione Padeon. Beware! This descent now very doubtful.) Now south round Col Pistone, 2862m (Ascent to summit possible) and on wide ledges, protected in places, to the Forcella Alta, 2689m (1¾hrs from the Forcella Grande). From the Forcella Alta south down scree until after about 200m the red waymarking leads west. (On the right, looking out. Easy to miss. On no account try to reach valley direct from here.) You cross the south ridge of the Vecchio del Forame and reach the Forcella Bassa, 2467m. (Descent to Valgranda feasible - 'Sentiero difficile'.) After a short climb the route leads steeply down again in serpentine bends to an iron ladder, after which you arrive on the Zurlongrat, 2379m. Keeping always on the ridge, by-passing a spur to the south to the Forcella Zurlon, 2363m (last wire rope), 1hr from Forcella Alta. From the gap, down about 100m of height and to a scree couloir which leads to the Testaccio. Now down zig-zags, over crag and grass to the most westerly summit of the Cristallo massif, the Col dei Stombi, 2168m (¾hr). From here a broad wartime path twists down through latschen and forest into the Valgranda, where you meet the road from Malga di Padeon (about 1700m. ¾hr). On the road out of the valley to Ospitale, ½hr. (This road is closed to vehicles.)

Altitude Difference: Forcella Stauniès, 2918m - Ospitale, 1474m.

Time Required: Reckon 6hrs for the total length of the high-level route.

Difficulty: Purely technically there are only trifling difficulties. Nevertheless for undertaking the second half, that is from the Forcella Grande, a high degree of sure-footedness and freedom from vertigo is required, as the route leads in parts through very steep craggy terrain and is no longer continuously protected with wire ropes. In snow conditions or when there is icing the use of the route is unconditionally not to be recommended.

Base: Cortina d'Ampezzo, 1210m; Tre Croci Pass, 1809m; Rifugio Capanna G. Lorenzi, 2932m, near the Forcella Stauniès (14B, running hot and cold water); Emergency accommodation (war-time barrack) on the Forcella Padeon, 2760m. (Buffa Di Perrero bivouac.)

Note: First lift: weekdays, 9.00am Sundays and Holidays 8.30am.

54.   Monte Cristallo:Climbing-path, Via Ferrata Renato (René) de Pol Cristallo Massif   (Group d)

As a companion-piece to the much-frequented Sentiero Ivano Dibona which leads from the Forcella Stauniès through Italian combat positions of 1915-1917 the Via Ferrata Renato de Pol was opened in August 1974. It leads through very interesting former Austrian war installations and front paths. The climbing-path was built by his Cortina mountaineering friend in memory of the young Renato de Pol, who fell on the Jori-Kante of Punta Fiames in the summer of 1973. The active hut warden and mountain-guide Beniamino Franceschi from the Capana-Rifugio Lorenzi assisted energetically and the Cristallo Cableway Company gave financial support.

Approach: As for Route 53 (Sentiero Dibona). (See map p146)

The Course of the Route: From the Forcella Stauniès via the iron stair behind the cableway station into a little gap on the north side of the Cristallino d'Ampezzo. There are now two possibilities:

a) Left via iron ladders, wire ropes and the Ponte Cristallo on the 'Ivano-Dibona-High-level Route' as far as the Forcella Grande, ³/₄hr (see Route 53). From here you first climb down steeply over snow and coarse scree towards the north into the Gravon del Forame scree-basin. Where the steepness decreases, you keep left straight to the Forcella Verde.

b) To the right fairly steeply down to the little Cresta-Bianco glacier (Dangerous when iced! Ice-axe and crampons advisable! Not recommended.) Below the snow-field you join route a).

You cross over the Forcella Verde, traverse on the west side of the Torrione, 2380m, and reach the Forcella Gialla via a protected section. Further, exposed, over steep grass and crag terrain, in part directly on the ridge, as far as the Selletta divisoria saddle, and from there to the Punta Ovest del Forame, 2385m. The route now leads with more difficulty from the summit down over three large rock steps. Wire ropes and pegs take the edge off dangerous places. At the upper rock step (Salto Superiore) there is still an old well. After a scree ledge (Cengia Superior) the middle step (Salto Inferiore) follows to the lower ledge (Cengia Bassa). Now it goes still further down over the 'Pareta Nera' (Schwarze Wand: Black Wall); then the route leads further west. (The route book has been housed in a cave marked *Libro Firme*.) It now goes down a comfortable path between dwarf conifers into the Bosco del Formae de Fora forest, 1669m, and finally via a last steep shelf into the Val Felizon. In about 20mins you reach Ospitale on the old railway line. From here bus or taxi to Cortina.

Altitude Difference: Forcella Stauniès, 2918m - Ospitale, 1474m.

Time Required: From Forcella Stauniès reckon about 4¹/₂-5hrs.

Difficulty: An ice-axe is generally really useful for the Cresta-Bianca

Glacier. Probably orientation difficulties when visibility is poor. Confidence on rock and crag terrain, as well as freedom from vertigo essential for the second half.

Bases: Cortina d'Ampezzo, 1210m; Tre-Croci-Pass, 1809m; Rifugio Capanna G. Lorenzi (Forcella Stauniès), 2932m.

55. Cristallo Central Summit (Cima di Mezzo) 3163m, Climbing-path 'Marino Bianchi'
Cristallo Massif (Group d)

In the summer of 1973 mountain guides from Cortina together with the Scoiattoli Climbing Guild laid out a new via ferrata from the Forcella Stauniès to the central Cristallo summit (Cima di Mezzo, 3163m). Equipped with 800m of wire rope held in place by 140 pegs, and with two metal ladders, the rock-route bears the name of the Cortina mountain guide Marino Bianchi, who fell in the Fanis group in 1969. (See map p146)

Ascent: The route begins directly at the south-east end of the large sun-terrace of the Rifugio Lorenzi. Always following the wire rope it goes sometimes left, sometimes right of the ridge to the Cristallo North-west summit. Through a groove down to a little gap between the North-west summit and the middle summit. Exposed. Up again on the other side to the first ladder. Shortly afterwards a scree-ledge leads right, to the foot of the yellow wall. Here it goes straight up (hardest pitch) to the second ladder. Over black rock to a large slab and through a cleft on to the ridge. An easy descent along on the north ridge to the last upward swing. Away up this on to the ridge and the summit. The summit book lies beyond the end of the wire rope, to the left under the cairn.

Descent: The same way.

Altitude Difference: Forcella Stauniès, 2918m - Cristallo Central Summit, 3163m.

Time Required: $1\frac{1}{4}$-$1\frac{1}{2}$ hours for the ascent; descent 1hr.

Difficulty: The route is exceptionally rewarding. In spite of the almost continuous wire-rope protection it is tricky from time to time in unfavourable conditions [snow, ice], which are not rare on the Cristallo.

Bases: Cortina d'Ampezzo, 1210m - Tre-Croci-Pass, 1809m - Rifugio Campanna G. Lorenzi, 2932m.

The climbing path Marino Bianchi

Route 55

Tip: If you spend the night in the private Lorenzi Hut on the Forcella Stauniès (first lift not until 9.00am; Saturday and Sunday 8.00am, from Rio Gère) you can, by making a prompt start, climb the Cristallo central summit and then complete the Sentiero Ivano Dibona. Good goers thus experience in one day a first class summit, together with the scenically finest Dolomite traverse.

56. Monte Piano 2305m, Hauptmann Bilgeri Gedächtnissteig Sexten Dolomites (Group d)

Note: The Monte Piana massif has two summits. The northern summit is called Monte Piano (2305m) and the southern Monte Piana (2324m). The whole is now usually just called Monte Piana. Monte Piano, field of merciless battle in the mountain war of 1915-1917, is now an open-air war museum. Hardly anyone who visits the summit can avoid the depressing mood

151

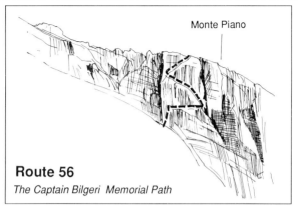

Route 56
The Captain Bilgeri Memorial Path

which overcomes you when you walk along the great summit plateau by former trenches and machine-gun emplacements. The Captain Bilgeri Memorial Path is likewise a reminder of that war, as hard-fought as it was senseless. The short via ferrata leads on the north-west wall to the 'Historic Circuit' and on to the summit, which, by the way, can almost be reached by car (the Bosi Hut, to which a road leads, stands near the rounded south summit: see Route 57).

Approach: From the car park just north of the Dürrensee (Lago d.Landro) at the entrance to the Rienz Tal (approach drive from Toblach in the Puster Tal through the Höhlenstein Tal) follow the waymark No.6, cross the level latschen and scree fields at the beginning of the Rienz Tal and follow the easy path upwards on the north-west side of Monte Piano. After a few pieces of wire-rope protection a flat platform is reached. A little higher you encounter a line of soldiers' graves where the ascent routes divide. The via ferrata leads to the right up towards the precipitous walls.

Ascent: From the start follow the thin wire-rope over short rock-steps and ledges, through a short chimney and finally through a ravine to the exit. You reach the east side and thus the 'Historic Circuit', over which the summit is quickly reached.

Descent: Back to the junction of the little path that leads over from the Captain Bilgeri Memorial Path, and go to the right on the south side; finally along by the walls of the summit massif to the graves already mentioned. Then on the ascent route back to the car park on the Dürrensee.

Altitude Difference: Car park north of the Dürrensee 1407m - Monte Piano 2305m.

Time Required: Car park - Monte Piano 2¹/₂-3hrs, Monte Piano - Car park 1¹/₂hrs.

Difficulties: A "quick" via ferrata, not so much difficult as historically interesting, with airy sections; the chimney demands a rather stronger effort.

Note: Can be combined with the next route, the Heeresbergführersteig.

57. Monte Piana 2324m, Heeresbergführersteig, (Path of the Army Mountain-Leader) Sexten Dolomites (Group d)

The Heeresbergführer Path runs south from the Hauptmann-Bilgeri-Gedächtnis Path and can well be combined with it, especially if the Rifugio Bosi is chosen as starting-point.

Approach: The Rif. Bosi, 2205m, can be reached on a single-track wartime military road, (narrow in places, and not made up in the upper section,) which branches off in a northerly direction from the road to the Auronzo Hut (see Route 58) very near its beginning (sign). Only people experienced in mountain driving are recommended to drive up this road. From the Rif. Bosi on the 'Historic Circuit', waymarked No.6a, which leads along above the south precipice on ledges, narrow in parts, until below the simple wooden cross on Monte Piana (picturesque view of Monte Cristallo). Further downwards into a saddle to which the ascent from Schluderbach leads up. From here follow the waymarks to the east into the Forcella dei Castrati and on Path No.6 until in front of the rounded north summit (Monte Piano - see Route 56). You follow the path branching off to the left (Waymark No.6) down as far as a shoulder, from which you can see the Hauptmann-Bilgeri-Gedächtnis Path to the right. Here follow the waymarking left (south) to the "Heeresbergführer" Path. Cross on a tiny little path in the latschen, then down and along below the west walls of Monte Piana. The first wire-rope protection follows after a scree-slope. Then laboriously to the start.

Ascent: Up to the left airily by a ravine, then in it, and finally left of it again through a chimney-like groove to the exit. From there on waymarked tracks up over a grassy slope to the 'Historic Circuit'.

Descent: Over Monte Piana back to Rif. Bosi.

Altitude Difference: Rifugio Bosi 2205m - Monte Piana 2324m - Start of the "Heeresbergführer" Path about 2200m.

Time Required: Rifugio Bosi - Monte Piana - Forcella dei Castrati - Start of Via Ferrata 1¼hrs. Heeresbergführersteig ½hr. Return to Rif. Bosi ¾hr.

Difficulties: An interesting, rewarding short via ferrata round-route of medium difficulty. Danger of stone-fall on the Heeresbergführersteig.

58.   North East Cadin Spitze 2790m, Via Merlone Sexten Dolomites   (Group d)

South of the Drei Zinnen (Tre Cima de Lavaredo) rise the bizarre towers and teeth of the Cadini di Misurina, a small dolomite group which has always been regarded as the private preserve of rock-climbers. Since the end of the sixties it also means something to via ferrata users: The Via Melone leads (in the truest sense of the word) up the North East Cadin Spitze, which is also the second highest summit of the Cadin Group. It is one of the controversial 'iron ways' - although it merits this description as does hardly any other protected route. A system of colossal Firemen's Ladders leads up the steep west wall, interrupted by a few sections protected only by wire-rope. Without doubt suitable for newcomers to via ferrate; can be done easily in a day.

Approach: You drive up about a kilometre on the toll-road to the Auronzo Hut until a narrow little road branches off to the right (Signpost: Rif. Fonda Savio). Via the Pian degli Spiriti (Geisterplatz: Place of Spirits) on the easy path waymarked No.115 to the hut.

Ascent: From the hut south on a waymarked path below the cliffs of the North West Cadin Spitze whose foothills are crossed on broken rocks (sure-footedness needed). Then left to the start of the via ferrata. Over a short preliminary section on broken rock (50ft no protection, then cable) to the first ladder, which leads up extremely airily to a more friendly zone of the wall. Near the summit a scree-filled (sometimes snow) demands careful walking (danger of stonefall for those following).

Descent: The same - as are the difficulties. Beware crossing on ladders - care needed.

154

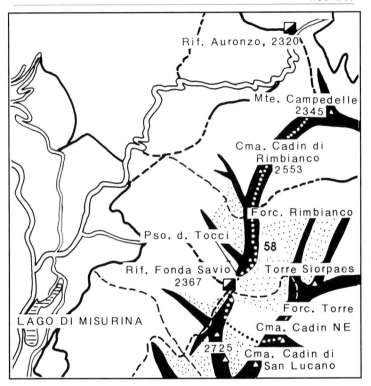

Altitude Difference: Misurina 1752m - Pian degli Spirit 1900m - Rif. Fonda Savio 2367m - North East Cadin Spitze 2790. Actual via ferrata about 280m.

Time Required: Ascent to hut from car park about 1hr. Rif. Fonda Savio - North East Cadin Spitze 1½hrs. North East Cadin Spitze - Rif. Fonda Savio 1½hrs.

Difficulties: The Via Merlone is technically without difficulty but demands absolute freedom from vertigo. Its short approach and summit ascent make it suitable in autumn as well, after the huts have closed down. Beware stonefall.

Note: Can well be combined with the next route.

Route 58

*Northeast Cadinspitze with Via Merlone.
On the right is Cima Cadin di San Lucano;
in the foreground the Rif. Fonda Savio*

59. Monte Campedelle 2346m, Bonacossa Way
Sexten Dolomites   (Group b)

The Bonacossa Way, which joins the Cadin Group to the Drei Zinnen (Tre Cima) is a protected high-level path rather than a via ferrata. That is to say, those less experienced get fun out of this, too, and - unlike the Via Merlone with its demand for freedom from vertigo - they can really enjoy the wild Dolomite scenes which are here presented in abundance.

Approach: To the Rif. Fonda Savio. See Route 58.

The High-Level Path: From the hut follow the waymark No.117 and descend some 200m in a northerly direction. After that, to the Forcella Rimbianco, 2206m - a fairly steep ascent. (From there it is possible to go down west to the toll-road.) Near the gap there are remains of the 1915-

1917 mountain war and a branch path, No.119 into the Valle Campedelle. Further north-east; finally up a small iron ladder into a wind-gap below and to the west of the summit of Monte Campedelle. Here there is an especially fine view of the Drei Zinnen (Tre Cima) on one side, and the Cadin Group on the other. Follow Path No.117 further north to the Auronzo Hut.

Descent: By the Zinnen road back to the car park. (Best to try to hitch-hike back to your car.)

Altitude Difference: Rif. Fonda Savio 2367m - Forcella Rimbianco 2206m - wind-gap below the summit of Monte Campedelle 2320m - Auronzo Hut about 2300m.

Time Required: Rif. Fonda Savio - Auronzo Hut about 2hrs. Auronzo Hut - car park for the Rif. Fonda Savio about 1hr.

Difficulty: Scenically splendid ¹/₂-day walk: can be managed even if you are not very fit. Sure-footedness necessary. Also suitable for middle/end October when the huts are closed but there are often days of settled weather.

60. Paternkofel (Monte Paterno) 2744m, Protected Wartime Path, De Luca - Innerkofler
Sexten Dolomites   (Group d)

In two years' laborious work Alpine soldiers of the Brigata Cadore together with men from the Pustertal Mountain Rescue Service, mountain guides from Sexten and Alpinists from Padua, cleared out the wartime tunnel through the Paternkofel and so far put it in order that it can be used since 1975 without danger by every mountaineer. At the same time various wartime paths to the east were improved and protected as climbing-paths. The new route was called De Luca - Innerkofler in memory of Piero de Luca and Sepp Innerkofler, the two recognised protagonists of the wartime events on these Dolomite peaks over 70 years ago, and who were awarded the Golden Order of Honour.

Approach: There are several possibilities of varying at will the combinations of ways through the various systematically laid-out paths. Anyone who wants to undertake the 600m-long tunnel ascent in the interior of the Paternkofel (pocket-torch essential!) starts best from the Drei-Zinnen Hut

(Rifugio Locatelli). You reach this hut most conveniently from the Rifugio Auronzo, waymark 101, via the Paternsattel, and from there almost level along the west walls of the Paternkofel (about 1$^{1}/4$hrs); or from Moos (S.Giuseppe) or Sexten (S.Veit) by car to the Fischleinboden, 1451m, big car park, via the Talschluss Hut, 1540m, waymark 102, 3hrs.

Ascent: Past the well-known 'Frankfurter Würstl' (Frankfurter Sausage) you reach the entrance of the tunnel in 7mins. At first climbing moderately you move in semi-darkness and from time to time can enjoy the view of the Drei Zinnen through the enlarged side-windows. You must have the help of a pocket-torch; the continuation is dark and becomes steeper and damp. Almost at the end you go through a 10m-long corridor with two cemented windows. A red arrow points to the left and you slip out into daylight at a height of 2520m. Wire ropes (missing 1989) indicate the continuation which leads over craggy sections, an easy chimney and - according to the time of year - via a snow - or scree-filled groove to the Gamsscharte (Forcella del Camoscio) 2650m. About 50mins from hut. (Cabling uncertain - rope recommended.)

From the Gamsscharte with the help of protection [damaged in places in 1985 and 1986], finally over scree-covered ledges and a short, steep unprotected rock step to the summit.

The grand panorama, - especially the view of the Drei Zinnen - is just as arresting as the memory of the tragic wartime incident on 4 July 1915 in which the legendary 'Standschütze' Sepp Innerkofler from Sexten met his death from Italian occupying forces, just before the summit.

(The Standschützen' were members of Shooting Associations which existed in the Tirol and Vorarlberg from the 16th Century until 1918 and were dedicated to the defence of their land. Translator's Note.)

Descent: Back to the Gamsscharte. Now you have three choices:

A) Return on the ascent route through the tunnel.

B) On the Schartenweg to the Büllelejoch (see Route 61 in reverse).

C) Via the Passportenscharte to the Paternsattel (again see Route 61).

Altitude Difference: Zinnen Hut, 2405m - Paternkofel, 2744m - Paternsattel, 2457m; Gamsscharte, 2650m - Büllelejoch, 2528m.

Time Required: Zinnen Hut - Gamsscharte (ascent of tunnel) 50min - Summit 20mins; Descent Gamsscharte - Paternsattel 1$^{1}/4$hrs; Gamsscharte - Schartenweg - Büllelejoch 1$^{1}/2$hrs. Zinnen Hut 1hr - Paternsattel 45mins; Rif. Auronzo - Lavaredo Hut - Paternsattel 1hr.

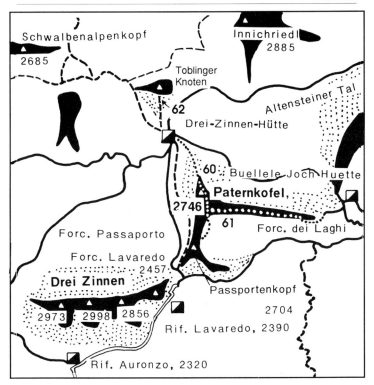

Base: Hotels and guest-houses in Misurina, 1756m; Hotels and Guest-houses in St. Veit and Moos in Sexten, 1340m (car park Fischleinboden, 1451m); Auronzo Hut, 2320m, CAI, full service mid-June to end of September; other times limited winter service, 60B, 40M, large car park; Lavaredo Hut, 2325m, private, wardened mid-June to mid-October, 30B, 15M; Drei-Zinnen Hut 2405m, CAI, wardened 20th June to end of September, 50B, 100M; Büllelejoch Hut, 2528m, private, wardened mid-July to 20th September, 12M.

Difficulties: The ascent of the tunnel in the Paternkofel is without problems so long as there is no icing through the strong draught in certain weather conditions.

159

The summit ascent from the Gamsscharte is without difficulties when the protection is in good condition; if it is not there is Grade I climbing in places.

61.   Paternkofel 2744m, Schartenweg (Percorso delle Forcelle). The Wind-gap Path
Sexten Dolomites   (Group d)

Undoubtedly the Paternkofel stands in the shadow of the world-famous Drei Zinnen (Tre Cima) and even from its summit those three stone giants dominate every aspect of the outlook. Nevertheless the Paternkofel (Italian: Paterno) is a striking and finely shaped mountain, especially when seen from the Drei Zinnen Hut. It is also famous in military history, as noted in the previous route. Sepp Innerkofler, the legendary mountain guide and rock-climber, met his fate upon this mountain. There are several versions of how he fell but no one knows precisely how Sepp actually met his death. It is certain that he fell down the Oppel Chimney in the course of a skirmish.

Apart from the rock-tunnel described in the previous route, the Schartenweg justly enjoys great popularity and is extremely rewarding for the ascent as well as a variation in descent. Combined with the descent via the Passportenscharte it makes a very fine circular route which is impressive because of fascinating scenic and rock pictures, although, of course, it does avoid the famous rock tunnel.

Approach: From the Drei Zinnen Hut (see Route 60) go east above the picturesque Bödenseen (Böden Lakes) to the Büllelejoch. Now you go south along below the Bödenknoten on a scree-path and reach the Forcella dei Laghi, 2600m. At first the path leads on, still without difficulty. Then you find yourself standing where the path breaks off: start of the via ferrata.

Ascent: The protection leads in a delightful switch-back via ledges and short rock steps to the Gamsscharte below the summit massif. (Here it is joined by the previous path, viz. the De Luca-Innerkofler protected wartime path). Continue as described there. (Route 60)

Descent: From the Paternkofel summit back to the Gamsscharte. From there south, following the waymarks down over scree and easy rock until fine ledges - reminiscent of the Brenta High-Level Route - lead below the

The Paternköfel with the
Drei-Zinnen Hut. From the
Gamsscharte the Schatrenweg
goes to the left

G = Gamsscharte
S = Tunnel Entrance
F = Frankfurter Sausage

Route 61

south ridge of the Paternkofel to the Passportenscharte, from which there
is a fascinating view of the Drei Zinnen. Here the via ferrata goes over to
the west flank of the Passporten Kopf and leads via ledges and through
a tunnel - a short, unpleasantly polished place - to the exit above the

161

Patern Saddle.

Altitude Difference: Drei Zinnen Hut 2405m - Büllelejoch 2528m - Paternkofel 2744m.

Time Required: Drei Zinnen Hut - Büllelejoch 1hr. Büllelejoch - Paternkofel 1hr. Paternkofel - Paternsattel (via the Passportenscharte) ³/₄hr-1hr.

Difficulties: A short, rewarding, scenically magnificent via ferrata route, technically moderately demanding. Some sections are really airy, however.
Bases: See Route 60.

62. Toblinger Knoten (Torre Toblino) 2617m, Reconstructed Military Path
Sexten Dolomites   (Group d)

From the Patern Saddle the Toblinger Knoten (Torre Toblino) is seen as a delicate, three-pointed tower west of the Drei Zinnen Hut, which seems to grow out of the Sextenerstein (Sasso di Sesto). From the Paternkofel the Knoten appears as a twin rock peak which is joined to the Sextenerstein by a long very level humped ridge. In the First World War the Toblinger Knoten became the key-point of the Austrian line of defence at the time of the Italian attack in August 1915. The vertical south walls prevented its capture by the Italians. Only a break-through through the positions on both sides could bring down this artillery observation post.

The great strategic importance of the Toblinger Knoten rested above all upon the fact that here Austrians and Italians were facing each other only 300m apart. In April 1916 the Italians blew up the Col di Lana and three months later the Schreckenstein (Castelletto). As the Italians were very active in developing dug-outs and tunnels on the adjacent Sextenerstein it was feared that they would also attack the Toblinger Knoten by mining it. The credit for developing the summit of the Toblinger Knoten as an observation post and a fighting position is due to the celebrated and highly decorated Padre Hosp. The reconstructed path following the normal route was called the Padre Hosp Path in his honour. As early as Spring 1917 the Austrian "Standschützen" (Tirolese and Vorarlberg Shooting Associations) had begun building a route with ladders through the north chimney. Four historic wooden ladders, twenty-four historic iron pitons and the other remains are still a reminder of this engineering activity. In contrast with the so-called 'normal route', over which the change of guard could be successful only by night or in mist, this route, which was not in the line of the Italian snipers, made it possible to change guard safely by daylight; indeed, the soldiers regarded it as amusing climbing practice. This route, which illustrates in such a graphic way the mountaineering and military achievements of the "Standschützen" and militia, was allowed to fall into disrepair for sixty years. In 1978 the Club of the Friends of the Dolomites decided to put it into good repair. A team of five needed only seven working days to fix the 17 steel ladders and continuous ropes for protection.

Approach: To the Drei Zinnen Hut - see Protected Wartime Path 'De Luca - Innerkofler.' (Route 60)

Ascent: Behind the Drei Zinnen Hut a sign-post points past the new chapel, directly north along a path waymarked with red triangles to the flat saddle between the Sextenerstein and the Toblinger Knoten. Under the south wall of the Toblinger Knoten to its west shoulder, then further at the same level on to the north side, and after a short ledge, on which you must crawl, to the start of the via ferrata (Marble Plaque). Through a dièdre with small holds and up via short sections protected by wire-rope to the first ladder. Pass the first of the four historic wooden ladders to a wide scree-ledge. Now up steel ladders through the first series of north chimneys until just below the wind-gap between the two summit towers. You cross a narrow ledge on fixed pitons, to the left into the second series of north chimneys. After four ladders it is possible to go into a machine-gun dug-out. Further on the left edge of the chimney and over a small overhang with a last, very airy, ladder to the former military post on the summit, a fissured series of rock slabs with a splendid view on all sides - a real observation post!

Descent: A few metres to the south of the last ladder on the ascent a rope leads down again on to the so-called Normal Route. This via ferrata through the east flank to the former Adlerwache (Eagle Watch) leads down again without difficulty over moderately steep rock and back to the hut. The Adlerwache and the entrance to the Maendl-Gallery lie immediately on this normal way.

Altitude Difference: Drei Zinnen Hut 2405m - Toblinger Knoten 2617m. Height of actual via ferrata 110m; length 160m.

Time Required: Drei Zinnen Hut - Toblinger Knoten ³⁄₄hr. Descent ¹⁄₂hr.

Difficulty: The route on the north wall is very airy but completely protected.

Only for those completely free of vertigo and with climbing skill. Descent via the normal route is without problems and this is recommended to the inexperienced as the ascent route also.

Note: The Toblinger Knoten and one of the vie ferrate on the Paternkofel (De Luca-Innerkofler or Schartenweg) can easily be accomplished in one day.

63. Sextener Rotwand (Croda Rossa di Sesto) 2939m, Protected Path Sexten Dolomites (Group b)

In the celebrated Sexten sundial - Neuner, Zehner, Elfer, Zwölfer, Einser (9-o'clock, 10-o'clock, 11-o'clock, 12-o'clock and 1-o'clock peaks) - the 'Zehner' was Sexten's peak of destiny in the first world war. Latterly, of course, the name Sextener Rotwand (Croda Rossa di Sesto) has replaced it. The massif, almost 3000m high forms a mighty screen above the valley.

One should not let oneself be misled into using the many ruined wartime paths and gangways; it is better to follow the well-established red waymarks. The complicated ascent route is crammed full from start to finish with scenic surprises, which are no exception in the magnificent rock world of the Sexten Dolomites. The route was officially inaugurated in July 1973. The whole ascent is free of difficulty, never exposed, always well waymarked, and wire ropes are fixed in necessary places. The waymarking is said to be 'ailing' at present. There is considerable exposure on this route.

Approach: By the 'Rotwandwiesen' chair-lift, whose valley station stands at 1362m, south of Moos in the Sexten valley, in 15min to the Rotwandwiesen, 1925m, just above the edge of the forest. (See map p172)

Ascent: By the restaurant 'Zum Rudi' as far as the south-east edge of the alm-meadow (sign). Branch left here (Waymarks 15A & B), following the waymarks red-white-red, No 15B (right) after about 200m, over scree and easy crag in ¾hr on to the rock ridge of the Burgstall (Castelliere) 2260m: on the far side a view down in the direction of the Kreuzberg Pass. A short way up a rib interspersed with grass, then right, into easy rock (first wire rope) out of which a steep groove leads to a narrow gap (in groove beware of stonefall when several parties are on the move). Behind the gap there opens out a semi-circular, gloomy rock basin with a small glacier. The serpentine path leads to the top via scree and shallow grooves and turns south to a 'ghost barrack-town'. The path leads to the edge of the basin, loses a little height, leads over a little saddle and goes through the middle of old military positions, to reach the Rotwandscharte soon after.

A war-memorial stands on a level piece of rock, and somewhat further up, remains of the Austrian Command Post with its cableway station. Both are now in a poor state.

Over slabs to a steep rock step and up over that with the help of a wire rope without particular difficulty; then over stepped rock (remains of snow in early summer), and later over scree and broken rock through a shallow ravine which runs out into the Obere Rotwandscharte (Forcella Alta di Croda Rosa) on the summit ridge. Left on to the east side, and in a few minutes on to the summit. The cross does not actually stand on the highest point but corresponds with the spot-height 2939m, the so-called 'Trapeze'. The panoramic view from here is unequalled.

Descent: As ascent or use the Via Ferrata Zandonella, Route 64.

Descent Variations: On the small level area of rock immediately below the war-memorial at the Rotwandscharte there begins an unwaymarked, trodden-out little path that leads left (in descent) through a boulder-filled, partly green hollow. Then over scree and rubble to a narrow rock ledge which changes to a short groove that ends at the permanent snow-field which leads down from the Sentinella Scharte at the end of the Alpini Way. Descend the scree - to waymarking 124. But follow No.124 only for a short time to a stream-bed and the junction with Path No.100. Climbing easily to the right, No.100 has yet another junction after a few minutes: left almost on the level through the Steinernes Tor (Stone Gate) along on the west side under the Rotwandköpfe, to the Rotwandwiesen. (An unpleasant descent.)

It is prettier and more interesting to ascend about 100m of height to the right. Now in cheerful to and fro over the 'Köpfe' ('heads') thickly covered with dwarf conifer. From the last top, in a number of zig-zags down through forest to the Rotwandwiesen.

Since the summer of 1976 there is a further, very rewarding Ascent (or Descent) Variation on the Rotwandköpfe. On the Rotwandwiesen a notice to the right 'Klettersteig Rotwandspitze'. The protected route, waymarked with a red triangle on a white band, and equipped with ladders and wire ropes, leads via the south-west ridge of the upper Rotwandköpfe (magnificent view down into the Fischleintal) into the large, semi-circular rock combe. Now you go left, along the lower edge of the scree-basin, until, shortly, you join the normal route which comes up from the Burgstall (about 2hrs from the Rotwandwiesen).

Altitude Difference: Rotwandwiesen - Rotwandgipfel, about 1000m.

Time Required: From the top station of the cableway to the summit, altogether 3-3¹/₂hrs. Descent 2-2¹/₂hrs, with the variation over the Rotwandköpfe, somewhat longer.

Difficulties: For footsure walkers, free of vertigo, none.

Base: St Veit and Moos in the Sexten valley, 1340m; Rotwandwiesen Hut, 1924m (Rif. Prati di Croda Rossa) a few minutes south-west from the top station of the gondola lift, private, 24 sleeping places; wardened from 1st July to 1st October.

64. Sextener Rotwand (Sexten Red Wall) 2939m, Via Ferrata Mario Zandonella
Sexten Dolomites   (Group e)

In 1978 the routes of the Italian front on the Sextener Rotwand had begun to be converted into vie ferrate. So this summit, once so strenuously fought over, can equally well be climbed on a via ferrata from the Berti Hut, the Via Ferrata Mario Zandonella, called after an Italian climber who fell to his death in 1975 on Monte Pelmo. Of course, the Zandonella Via Ferrata, like its south-east variation, is distinctly harder than the via ferrata on the Sexten side. The south route, which is better for the ascent, demands a lot of the climber and is comparable with the Bolver-Lugli Via Ferrata on the south shoulder of the Cimone della Pala (Route 29). Done in conjunction with descent via the South-East Variation it provides one of the most rewarding traverses of this kind in the Dolomite area - and this is also true of the views: Elfer, Zsigmondy Ridge and Hochbrunner Edge can be seen from the Via Zandonella from the most attractive side.

Approach: As Route 65 as far as the Rif. Berti.

Ascent: From the Berti Hut go west *[rather north-west: Translator]* on waymarked path No.101 into the Vallon Popèra. At about 2550m leave this path, which leads to the Sentinella Scharte, and go right, towards the southern precipices of the Rotwand (clearly waymarked fork). Follow a narrow path to the start of the climb near a large natural cave. Now to a built dug-out and further right until wire-ropes lead up left over a ramp-like ledge. Follow the ropes and the red/green waymarks to a very steep sharp rise in the rock which is overcome with the help of ladders. Further, very airily and steeply on to the big rock ledge at about 2800m, which you reach near a former Italian military post. Here right (east) and up to the summit ridge. You cross this via a wind-gap - below the spot-height 2939 - and soon meet the final bit of the previous route.

Descent: The wire-ropes, which lead down south-east via a short subsidiary ridge, begin directly on the summit by a red/green triangular waymark. Now down very steeply and airily into a corrie lying east of the Rotwand and usually snow-covered. From here a short ascent to the south to the wind-gap (Forcella A) between Gugli and the Torre Pellegrini, 2757m. From the wind-gap either through a scree-groove to the Selletta di Sasso Fuoco, in curves ('Canalone 1') down to the Vallon Popèra and on to Path No.101, OR *(More attractively):* From Forcella A west via a steep step in the rock wall (protection) up to a broad ledge which leads horizontally across the south precipice of Gugli. You follow this north-west to its end (splendid view of the wildly shaped mountains round the Vallon Popèra) and climb through a groove with wire-rope protection on to the scree-slope of the so-called 'Canalone 2' and down on to Path No.101.

Altitude Difference: Berti Hut 1950m - Rotwand Summit 2939m.

Time Required: Berti Hut - Rotwand Summit 4hrs. Rotwand Summit - Berti Hut about 2hrs; by the variation via the ledge below Gugli 2$\frac{1}{2}$-3hrs.

Difficulties: The Via Ferrata Mario Zandonella is one of the most demanding. In addition to sure-footedness and absolute freedom from vertigo, rock-climbing skill (for the descent, too) and stamina are advantageous.

Bases: See Route 65.

65.   Via Ferrata Aldo Roghel - Cengia Gabriella
Sexten Dolomites   (Group e)

In the summer of 1968 an area of the Popèra group in the southern Sexten Dolomites, which until then had been relatively unfrequented, was admirably opened up by the Padua Section of the CAI with two complementary protected climbing paths. The first part, the Via Ferrata

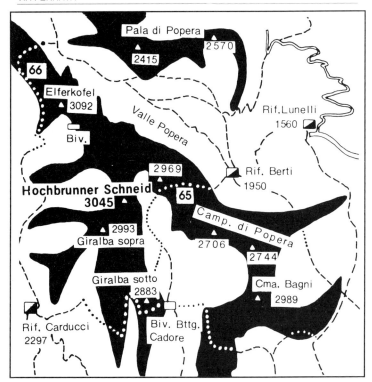

Aldo Roghel, forms the connection between the Rifugio Berti in the Vallon Popèra (Arzalpe) and the Bivacco Battaglione Cadore in the Cadin di Stallata via the Canalone dei Fulmini and the Forcella dei Campanili. The second section reaches from the bivouac via the Cengia (ledge) Gabriella to the Carducci Hut in the upper Val Giralba between the Zwölferkogel and the Monte Giralba.

This semi-circle is not an artistic climbing-path; it more or less follows the route indicated via rock ledges which encompass Monte Popèra (Hochbrunnerschneide) and Monte Giralba at half their height. The views are scenically magnificent, wild and inspiring even for connoisseurs of the mountains.

The length of the route (at least 6-7hrs), the somewhat exhausting switchback, several technically not entirely easy pitches, in parts extremely exposed, demand fitness and some rock experience.

We spoke above of a semi-circle. The circle can, of course, be finally completed on a second day: From the Carducci Hut, via the Giralba Joch one quickly gains the connection with the Alpiniweg - described in Route 66 - which has been famous for decades.

Approach: The shortest approach to the Rif. Berti is from the Selvapiana in the upper Comelico Valley. For those approaching from the north: From the Sexten-Kreuzberg Pass drive down about 8km to where, by a sign-post 'Valgranda' and 'Rif. Selvapiana' (5km) a narrow but good little road branches off at a sharp corner. From the Selvapiana alm and hut (car park - beware thieves) a beautiful ascent, No.101, begins to the Rif. Berti, enthroned on a rock pulpit, (1hr). To avoid error: on old maps one still finds the abandoned and more highly sited Rif. O. Sala or Rif. Popèra. The Berti Hut, 1950m, belongs to the Padua Section of the CAI; it sleeps 100 and is well equipped, even with a telephone, 04 35 / 6 88 88 Pieve di Auronzo (Advance Bookings). The route is long; it is an advantage to stay overnight and make an early start next day.

The Route: From the Rif. Berti an arrow Via Ferrata Roghel points due west. Descend into a little valley lying some 50m lower, then ascend the moraine slope directly opposite the hut as far as the highest patch of green. Isolated red waymarks point to a snow tongue, to a large boulder at the foot of the Guglie di Stallata and to the start of a rock and scree couloir not visible from below. By a little sign 'Via Ferrata Aldo Roghel' to the right, fairly steeply via moraine humps and scree up the Canalone del Fulmini towards the north-west. The ferrata which is furnished with 26 metal ladders and 110m of wire rope, begins at a height of 2350m. The exposed ladder-system soars rapidly up the left (orographically right) overhanging rock wall, and ends in a small ravine, usually snow-filled, between the Fulmini, running from the Cima Popèra, and the Guglie di Stallata. Another short section of rope protection which ends at the Forcella dei Campanili, 2565m. From the hut, 2-2½hrs.

From the narrow notch, the steep groove leads into the broad hollow of the Cadin (Combe) di Stallata. Red waymarks here again. These lead, via a branch left, to the Bivacco Battaglione Cadore (Sleeps 9, cooking utensils).

To the right a direct approach, established in 1970, leads up via a rocky top to the Cengia Gabriella. But it is worth while to take the detour to the left, involving some loss of height. The bivouac shelter stands on a rock shelf falling steeply into the Valle della Stallata (Descent not recommended. Difficult.) and is a charming rest-place, surrounded by rippling streamlets and with views of the Marmarole and Antelao. Shortly before this, a smoothly cut-off boulder with the inscription: 'At. Variante via Ferrata Roghel 200m' to which one must afterwards return, 5min from the bivouac hut.

Warning: Around the Bivacco there are also other signs and numbers, which must all be ignored. According to the warden of the Carducci Hut they are in part wrongly put up and lead to confusion.

From the aforementioned boulder, near a stream-bed, up 200m via a slope, to several red ladders, which lead finely up 190m to the start of the Cengia Gabriella, together with the junction of the direct approach already mentioned. From now on the path branching off to the left is excellently signed. Red triangles with No.109, ropes for protection and the words 'Carducci Hut' additionally confirm that one is on the right route. The route leads along, full of tension and variety, with splendid views away and below, under overhangs, via bends and an amusing crawl along a ledge. In easy switchbacks via crag and short, steep grass slopes (care when wet) as far as a high ravine.

It continues up to the right via a well protected, stepped wall, then two airy ledges which lead round a rock corner. For variety, a nice chimney, and once more steep grass slopes. Now begins a long, sloping scree ledge, scarcely as wide as a foot, which is to be undertaken with some care on the edge of the abyss. The hut comes into sight, apparently near, but one isn't there as quickly as that! The descent begins: via a slabby wall with big steps, which ends by a little notch and the last rope. A gloomy ravine, directed to the north and brimful with scree and snow is the last hurdle before the big combe that borders Monte Giralba, whose south walls is traversed at half height. Via a good track to the hut path which comes up from the Giralba Valley. Still a final ascent, then one stands in front of the inviting Carducci Hut and admires its splendid situation.

Altitude Difference: Selvapiana 1560m - Berti Hut 1950m - Start of Climbing-path 2350m - Forcella dei Campanili 2565m - Bivacco Battaglione Cadore 2251m - Start of the Cengia Gabriella 2320m - Carducci Hut 2297m.

Time Required: Selvapiana - Berti Hut 1hr - Forcella dei Campanili 2-2¹/₂hrs - Bivouac Hut ¹/₂hr; Cengia Gabriella to Carducci Hut 3-3¹/₂hrs. (Up to 10hrs in all possibly.)

Difficulties: The route should only be undertaken by really experienced and trained climbers. Its length and difficulties lie above the average of other vie ferrate. Not recommended in uncertain weather.

Bases: Rif. Italo Lunelli (Selvapiana), 1560m, wardened in summer; Rif. Antonio Berti, 1950m CAI 46B, 50M, wardened mid-June to end of September; Rif. Carducci 2297m, CAI, sleeps 30, wardened end of June to end of September.

Tip: Of course one can descend from the Carducci Hut to Sexten via the Giralba-Joch. But one should not miss the magnificent experience of the Strada degli Alpini via the Sentinellascharte and back to the Rif. Berti. (See Route 66.)

66. Alpiniweg. Strada degli Alpini
   Sexten Dolomites (Group d)

The Ferrata Roghel-Cengia Gabriella has in the Alpiniweg a counterpart technically easier but scenically of equal rank. Even though each summer an estimated 2,000 tourists undertake this popular rock path right through the west and north walls of the Elfer, and afterwards revel in superlatives, they must be surefooted and vertigo-free. The Italian 'Strada' (road) is deceptive. In no way is there a question of its being a footpath through high alpine terrain. Especially in early summer and when the temperature is low, one has to cope with snow and ice on the steep flanks on the shaded side. Good boots, warm clothing, a 15m rope for beginners and perhaps a short ice axe are to be included in the standard equipment for Alpiniweg aspirants.

   Its history is interesting: the foundations had already been laid before 1914 by Austrian high alpine troops when they extended a military mule-track a bit to the east from the Giralba Joch. Then in the war Alpini soldiers pushed the way forward - hence its name - from the hard fought over Sentinella Scharte in a westerly direction. Later the Padua Section of the CAI established the connection between the two sections and improved the protected difficult parts. One sees numerous old traces of war everywhere, especially around the Sentinella Pass, the gap which joins

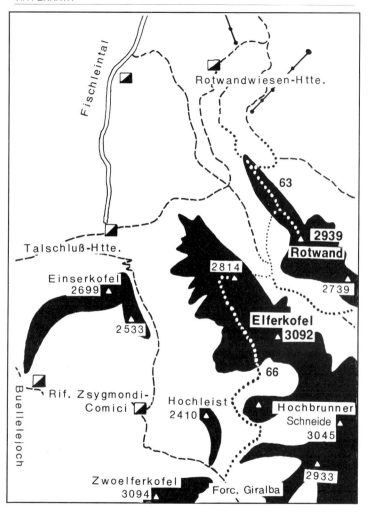

the massif of the Sexten Rotwand to the Elfer and provides the passage from the Fischleintal to the Val Popèra. 'La Sentinella' (Sentry) is the name of an isolated rock tooth at the pass, which the (Austrian) Kaiserjäger christened 'Betenda Moidle'.

The Route: The Giralba Joch is quickly reached in 20min from the Carducci Hut (see Route 65). There the wrinkled, massive Zwölfer Kogel shows itself from its most photogenic side. A few zig zags towards the north (Sexten) down as far as the sign: 'Strada degli Alpini' - 'Alpinisteig'. Then to the right - always on waymark 101, - crossing a broad saddle to which the path from Sexten and from the Zsigmondy Hut also comes up. (This hut makes an alternative starting point.) A minute lake - an 'eye' often 'blinded' by ice (Eissee), the scree-filled basin of the Inneres Loch, the magnificent Salvezza Ledge, notched into walls reaching to the sky, a genuine promenade with rope balustrade, lead to the snow-filled, dark fissure in the mountain, the Busento.

The continuation of the route: through the permanent snow of the Ausseres Loch, then on a well-protected plinth around the Elfer Tower, finally along the ruddy west flank, traversing upwards to the Elferscharte (2-2¹/₂hrs). An incomparable place to rest and look at the view. Absolutely great sight: further over there the Drei-Schuster massif, nearer the Sexten Rotwand, opposite, the ever-fascinating structure of the Zwölfer. The 2600m-high Elferscharte is in some circumstances an important point of decision: in bad conditions a sign gives warning: 'Zur Sentinella-Scharte gesperrt' ('To the Sentinella-Scharte closed'). This warning must be unconditionally heeded. The possibility remains of descending into the combe to path No.124 which comes up from Sexten. The slope is steep to begin with. In early summer hard snow can make the descent more difficult; care is called for; crampons. Path 124 is followed only a short distance to waymark No.100 which introduces the fine, almost level stroll to the Rotwandwiesen, 1924m. There a hospitable hut and lift-station to Sexten Moos (1¹/₂hrs from the Elferscharte).

The Alpiniweg, always No.101, finally turns on to the north side of the Elferscharte. This second section leads along fixed hand-ropes through intrinsically more alpine and somewhat more difficult terrain between rock-foot and combe, sometimes on the upper edges of couloirs of permanent snow (usually with good footing, but care when there is ice or hard snow). Via a high ladder, wooden bridges and again with the help of wire rope, finally via a steep slope of broken rock, the route reaches the

Sentinella Scharte, 2717m (in German: Alderteralpen Scharte).

Far below in the Val Popèra, at the end of the gigantic combe of limestone pavement and scree, stands the Berti Hut. Down to there on a track over scree, snow-fields and rock grooves - at one point an interesting glimpse to the hanging-glacier which is compressed in a fold of the Elfer: finally via comfortingly green patches of high alm in which glistens a little lake.

At the Berti Hut the great circle is complete which one has drawn through the south-east Sexten Dolomites around their culminating points, the Hochbrunnerschneide (Monte Popèra) 3045m and the Elfer (Cima Undici) 3092m. A 'High-Rock-Route' where dolomitic scenery is hardly to be bettered in scenic uniqueness and force of experience.

In his beautiful book on the landscape of the Sexten Dolomites, Karl Springenschmid writes:-

'Uncounted thousands see the fairy-tale land of the Dolomites every year, whether as a fleeting glimpse from the train or in quickly dissolving pictures from the drive on the celebrated Dolomite Road. But they only reveal their whole power and greatness, their highest beauty, to the mountaineer who wins the solitude of their walls, ridges and summits in hard ascent. And this experience, otherwise reserved only for the rock climber, the Alpiniweg gives to the mountain-walker also, in so far as he is experienced, footsure and vertigo-free.'

Altitude Difference: Carducci Hut 2297m - Giralbajoch 2431m - Sentinella Pass 2717m - Berti Hut 1950m - Selvapiana 1560m.

Time Required: Carducci Hut - Sentinella Pass 3-3$\frac{1}{2}$hrs - Berti Hut 2hrs - Selvapiana $\frac{3}{4}$hr.

Difficulties: Hardly any difficulties for reasonably experienced mountain walkers in normal conditions. Freedom from vertigo and sure-footedness are assumed. Difficult and dangerous when there is snow or icing, especially in the neighbourhood of the Sentinellascharte. Beware of falls in temperature or pressure with snowfall in the higher zones. Enquire about the condition of the Alpiniweg in Sexten (Guides' Office), or at the Rif. Berti, the Zsigmondy Hut or the Carducci Hut.

Bases: As for Route 65.

Tip: Anyone not advanced enough for the Ferrata Roghel and the Cengia Gabriella can of course ascend to the Alpiniweg from Sexten: Sexten-Moos, Fischleinboden car park, Talschluss Hut, 1526m, in 2$\frac{3}{4}$hrs through the Bachnertal, No.103 to the Rif. Zsigmondy-Comici, 2235m. From there in a southerly direction towards the Giralba Joch, just below which begins the Alpiniweg, No.101. Descent from the Sentinella Scharte northwards via the long scree combe with steep snowfield (difficult when snow is hard) until one meets path No.100 which leads to the Rotwandwiesen or directly further as far as the Talschluss Hut (1½hrs).

67. The Circuit of the Sorapis Group. Three High-alpine Vie Ferrate   (Group e)

The widely extended Sorapis Group culminates in three summits: the Sorapis, 3205m, which is flanked by the Fopa di Mattia, 3155m, and the Croda Marcora, 3154m. To come to the point at once: all ascents, and the three protected climbing-paths which run round the whole rock massif, are

Route 67

Crodo del Fogo with the Vandelli Climbing Path

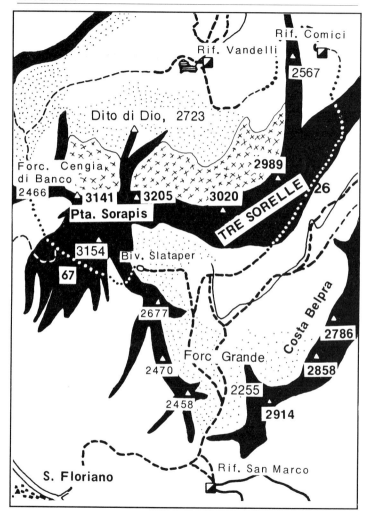

magnificent, long and exacting, the protection laid out very 'sportingly' in Cortina fashion, often even inadequately (for normal users). The waymarks, too, are not always to be relied upon and demand a good sense of direction. Anyone who decides on a Sorapis route cannot be a novice on rock and must also bring along the fitness needed for long climbs up and down in exposed situations. Two huts are situated not very high as starting points: the Rifugio Vandelli, 1929m on the north side, and the Rifugio S. Marco, 1823m at the south foot. In addition there are two bivouac-shelters cleaving to the rocks high above: the Bivacco Slàtaper, 2600m in the south, and the Bivacco Comici, 2000m, on the east side.

Thanks are due to the generosity of the Fondazione A. Berti (an alpine foundation) for setting up this interesting and touristically high-alpine via ferrata as well as putting up the two bivouac boxes. A.Sanmarchi and B.Crepaz co-operated in the work with the support of the Venice and XXX October - Trieste sections of the CAI.

Via Ferrata Francesco Berti (from the Rif. Vandelli to Bivacco Slàtaper)

The Route: From the Vandelli Hut on waymark 215, making a circuit to the west around the pretty Sorapis lake, one climbs through areas of sparse latschen up to a steep moraine ridge. To the left a fine glimpse of the smooth north walls of the 'Finger of God' (Dito di Dio), of Zurlón, Sorapis and Fopa di Mattia, and the fissured western glacier (Ghiacciaio Occidentale). The scenery of the Tondi di Sorapis is without exaggeration unique in the Dolomites and merits a visit on its own account alone. A slabby arena of stone without vegetation, austere, gloomy, on which there are signs of the glacier sliding over it for thousands of years. Almost at the middle-point of the Tondi an important division of paths (to here about 1½hrs).

The right-hand track, No.215, turns upwards in a sharp corner somewhat laboriously through pathless rubble and rock terrain, via steep terraces to the Sella di Punta Nera, 2738m and on the far side down to the hut and top-station of the Cortina - Tondi di Fabria cableway, 2327m 1¾hrs.

Continue to the left to a boulder with the old number 241, from which it later becomes No.242 without notice.

Ascending towards the south, following the red waymarks, between boulders as far as a great slab with arrow and inscription: 'Cengia del

Banco'. A steep scree-field leads up left towards the rocks, with a well visible red rectangle and arrow, somewhat above a bronze plate 'F. Berti' and a notice of the start of the 'Percorso alpinistico attrezzato' (protected alpine tourist-path). There is actually no protection for a long time.

A flat ledge, soon becoming steeper, ends by a wet chimney. One forces oneself over a big boulder up into easier broken crag terrain again and reaches (to the south) a little terrace, about 2600m. Here begins the Cengia del Banco mentioned at the beginning, which runs along on the south-west side of the Fopa di Mattia with no loss of height worth mentioning, but soon becomes fairly airy, rubbly and steep (no rope protection). In addition there is the danger of stonefall. The stones rattle down like shots at all times of the day from the rock terrace (Pian del la Foppa) lying above - from which also a forceful little stream rushes down, fed by a little glacier.

The view and the glimpses down are of course magnificent. Especially the Antèlao ranged directly opposite is splendidly presented and sets the keynote as the second highest Dolomite summit. After about ¾hr the ledge ends on the Terrace of the Croda Marcora, to which a toilsome ascent (in places only footmarks) leads up from the Boite Valley (Dogana Vecchia, 1117m).

The Ferrata Berti continues through the wall - which falls 700m into the depths - of the Croda Marcora, ascends easily to a ledge which ends at the south-east edge of the Croda: an enormous, vertical curtain of rock, whose foot is in a deep ravine, exceptionally liable to the danger of stonefall. One climbs down into this rubble-filled 'stone dish' via a series of ladders on plumb vertical walls. Crossing the steep stone trough as far as possible on its rim to a dièdre up which ladders and wire rope, exposed and not altogether easy, lead up once more. A narrow ledge, protected by wire rope, traverses a towering, precipitous wall to the Forcella del Bivacco. From here one keeps along the left-hand rocks and must beware of some rock-clefts more than a metre wide, to reach shortly afterwards the Slàtaper bivouac-box, 2600m via slabs and scree. From the Vandelli Hut at least 5hrs.

Now one has the possibility of descending south-east to path No.226, which reaches the Rif. S. Marco, 1823m in 2hrs via the Forcella Grande, 2255m.

Tip: At the bivouac the normal ascent (Grades I and II) to the Sorapis summit begins, 3hrs. The route is not altogether easy to find. Here are the main points: From the bivouac, crossing the broad scree-field of the Fond de Rusecco to the right, to a pronounced, somewhat difficult chimney, with a chockstone. Then into a ravine which comes down from a gap in the ridge between Fopa di Mattia and Sorapis. Keeping to the right in the upper part one reaches the summit without further difficulties. Beware in bad visibility: the ravine straight ahead up the Fopa di Mattia, to the left Croda Marcora and to the right up Sorapis.

Protected Tourist Path 'Carlo Minazio'. From the Bivacco Slàtaper to the Bivacco Comici

This section is not expressly a via ferrata but an important connecting-link furnished with few wire ropes but exposed in places, and a fine panorama-route along the Cengia delle Sorelle and the Colli Neri, via the Forcella del Banco to the Comici Bivouac. Unfortunately the waymarks and notices are very sparse here and the tracks are often lost in grass and latschen terrain.

First one descends towards the middle of the great scree-combe, Fond de Rusecco, and keeps in the direction of the foot of the buttress which comes down from the first Sorella (Sister). Ledges of rubble and grass lead easily to a grassy hollow. A further ledge-system at an altitude of about 2300m, with sparse vegetation in places, level at first then falling, makes easy progress possible. (Cenge delle Sorelle). The spurs of the Coston Sorelle are circumvented through two small gorges and one reaches a long, steep ravine.

(Here ends the path which comes up in 3¹/₂-4hrs from the Rifugio Tre Sorelle, private, at the entrance to the S. Vito Valley).

From here obliquely to the right upwards (north) one soon reaches the latschen-covered, beautiful Cengia inferiore dei Colli Neri. This ledge is followed further northwards on 'hunters' paths' to a striking scree-amphitheatre from whose lower ledge a waterfall (usually dry in summer) comes down, which is well seen from the S.Vito Valley. Now two possibilities offer themselves. The shorter, somewhat more difficult route, leads at the same altitude via a steep, weathered slope and an exposed, latschen-covered ridge of broken crag, fairly airily to the Forcella Basa del Banco, 2126m a hardly noticeable notch just south of the Croda del Banco. The other variation is somewhat longer, more wearisome, but technically easier and only sporadically waymarked. It leads first to the left up towards the rocks of the Croda del Banco; through a broad, easy chimney one reaches a sharp notch, the Forcella Alta del Banco (about

100m high). Via the ridge on the far side down to the Forcella Bassa, joining variation No.1. Via grassy ridges one descends further to the north into the Busa del Banco and via the opposite slope shortly up to the Bivacco Comici, 2000m, Variation 1: 3hrs. Variation 2: 3¹/₂hrs.

Via Ferrata A. Vandelli. From the Bivacco Comici to the Vandelli Hut

From the bivouac-box, 2000m, waymarked 280, one turns to the nearby rock walls which surround the Busa del Banco. After surmounting a small rock platform, up a steep, grassy chimney. Traversing to the right at the top, a ledge is reached. This is followed to the north. A rock spur is circumvented along slopes of grass and broken rock, then one turns to the west and reaches a hollow between the rocky north and north-east spur-ridges. Climbing, one keeps up somewhat to the right over steep craggy terrain to a terrace with large boulders. Finally over grassy slopes to the ridge which comes down from the south summit of the Croda del Fogo, 2400m. (Fogo = Ital. Fuoco = Fire).

Here, at this highest point of the Vandelli-Ferrata really splendid views beyond and below await the user of the climbing-path. The great Cristallo Group and the bizarrely broken Cadini stick up into the sky. On the left hand one sees into the no less interesting north side of the Sorapis Rock Circuit with the two glaciers (east and middle).

Now one finally climbs into the back of Sorapis. Traversing somewhat to the left, it goes downwards over large rock steps to the big, pronounced ledge which goes obliquely through the Croda del Fogo. One goes its entire length, during which two rock spurs with no altogether easy sections are made easier with wire rope. Immediately afterwards one stands in the hollowed stone couloir between the Corno Sorelle and the Croda. Traverse this, then climb down a wall which crosses left into a chimney.

From the point on the ridge to here is the technically most demanding section, in which only the really most difficult places are protected. So - not for the inexperienced! (Improvements are planned).

Now down the long but not difficult chimney which is adequately protected with ladders and wire ropes and brings one pleasantly to the end of the climb at the foot of the rock.

The red waymarks show the continuation west via uniquely convex rock ridges and furrowed rock slabs, then dense latschen down to the

180

Vandelli Hut, 1929m, 3hrs.

After this extremely intensive experience of a climbing-path and panoramic views the exciting and beautiful circuit of the Sorapis is completed.

Tip: On account of the beautiful view and the line of the climbing-path it is worthwhile climbing up the ferrata from the Rifugio Vandelli to the ridge as a Hut Route. From there (instead of going down to the Comici Bivouac) over the not difficult, but exposed rocks to the summit of the Croda del Fogo, 2567m. Grade II, 3¹/₂hrs.

Difficulties: Freedom from vertigo, experience on exposed rock and scree terrain, optimal sense of direction and the greatest endurance are unconditionally and necessarily taken for granted. Warm clothing and a few metres of rope together with karabiners for self-belay are unconditionally recommended. Wire rope and ladders are provided only in really necessary places, but it is said that they will be improved. If one wishes to spend the night in one of the two bivouacs, then of course a bivvy-bag and necessary provisions must be taken. Allow 12hrs for the complete circuit.

Sorapis bases and their most important approaches

Rifugio al Sorapis Alfonso Vandelli

1928m, set near the pretty Sorapis Lake. Erected in 1891 as the Pfalzgau Hut of the DÖAV, and later destroyed by an avalanche. Rebuilt in 1924 by the Venice Section of the CAI and called the Rif. C.L.Luzzati, the hut was destroyed by fire in 1959. In 1966 the refuge was rebuilt yet again, enlarged and dedicated in honour of the Venetian CAI President, Alfonso Vandelli.

Approach: Reached most conveniently from the Tre-Croci Pass, 1805m, waymark 215 on an easy path through beautiful woods and latschen terrain, 2hrs. Open end of June to mid-September; 38B, 18M.

Rifugio San Marco, 1823m, of the Venice Section of the CAI.

Approach: From S. Vito di Cadore, 1010m, motor-road as far as Baita della Zoppa, 1429m, then path No.228, 1hr (from S. Vito on foot, 2hrs). Open beginning of June to September; 26B; some sleeping-spaces in an annexe. As the hut is also regarded as a starting-point for an ascent of Antelao, overcrowding must be allowed for, especially at weekends.

Ascent to the Bivacco Slàtaper, 2600m, via the Forcella Grande, 2255m, No.226, 3hrs.

Bivacco fisso (permanent bivouac) Scipio e Giuliano Slàtaper, 2600m, was erected in 1966 by the Fondazione Berti and named after two brave men of Trieste who died in the Second World War. It belongs to the XXX October - Trieste Section of the CAI. The permanent bivouac-box stands on the southern edge of the great scree-combe. Fond de Resecco, near a rock spur. 9 Sleeping places. Perhaps only melt-water. Important base for those climbing Sorapis and using the climbing-paths.

Approach: From the Rif. S. Marco via the Forcella Grande 3hrs; via the protected tourist-path F. Berti from the Rifugio Vandelli 5hrs; via the protected tourist-path C. Minazio and the Bivacco Comici, 3¹/₂-4hrs.

Bivacco fisso (permanent bivouac) Emilio Comici, 2000m, erected by the Fondazione Berti in 1961 in the Busa del Banco near two distinctive, isolated trees, in impressive Dantesque surroundings, amidst the sky-high rock walls of Croda del Fogo, Torri della Busa and Croda del Banco. It belongs to the XXX October - Trieste Section of the CAI. 9 sleeping places, only melt-water, provided the remains of snow are available.

Approach: From Valle Ansiei, Palus S. Marco, 1113m, Path No.227; in the middle section not altogether easy rock terrain, 3¹/₂hrs; via the climbing-path A. Vandelli and the Rif. Vandelli, 3¹/₂hrs; via the protected tourist path C. Minazio from the Bivacco Slàtaper, 3-3¹/₂hrs.

68.   Civetta 3220m, Via Ferrata degli Alleghesi
Civetta Group   (Group e)

The broadly-ledged massif of the Civetta is visible from many Dolomite summits. A giant mountain with fissured ridges, chiselled peaks and pilasters like organ-pipes. The colossal north-west wall is associated with the names of the Munich climbers Solleder and Lettenbauer, who overcame it in 1925 after 15 hours of climbing. In 1963 Toni Hiebeler with companions made a successful winter ascent. From the lovely Tissi Hut on the Col Reàn one looks with a certain awe up the 1200m high wall with the direct route to the summit. It is no less breathtaking to turn one's gaze down the 1200m of altitude to the blue-green Lake Alleghe.

Very moderate mountain walkers stroll on a comfortable, high balcony

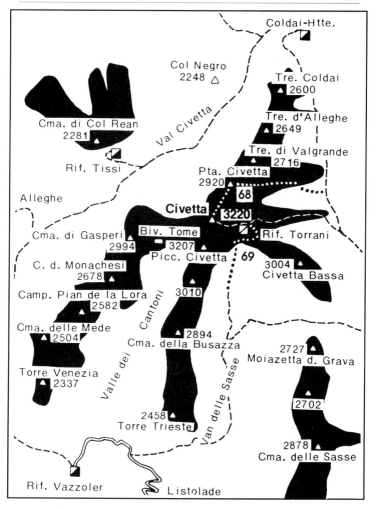

Coldai-Htte.

Col Negro
2248 △

Tre. Coldai
2600

Cma. di Col Rean
2281

Tre. d'Alleghe
2649

Val Civetta

Tre. di Valgrande
2716

Rif. Tissi

Pta. Civetta
2920

Alleghe

68

Civetta 3220

Cma. di Gasperi
2994

Biv. Tome
3207

Rif. Torrani

Picc. Civetta

69

C. d. Monachesi
2678

3004
Civetta Bassa

Camp. Pian de la Lora
2582

3010

Cma. delle Mede
2504

Cantoni

2894
Cma. della Busazza

2727
Moiazetta d. Grava

Torre Venezia
2337

Valle dei

Van delle Sasse

2702

2458
Torre Trieste

2878
Cma. delle Sasse

Rif. Vazzoler   Listolade

183

along the almost vertical stretch of wall. Thus one enjoys alpine beauties of which even connoisseurs assert that they are 'unique in the eastern alps'. For climbers of more rigorous bent there are, especially in the southern part, enough peaks, towers, chimneys, ridges and walls. Those without vertigo have two possibilities to choose from for reaching the imposing Civetta summit: the Via Ferrata Tissi on the south side and the Via Ferrata degli Alleghesi on the east flank. Both are rewarding, airy and long.

The setting-up of the Alleghesi was begun as early as 1950 but was not finally completed until the summer of 1966. The 'Civetta Cat-ladder' goes via iron rungs, pegs, wire ropes, metal ladders, and follows approximately the line of the Hamberger-Merkl route (formerly a Grade IV climb) through the 400m high east wall of the Punta Civetta. When this is passed the north ridge to the summit is reached.

Approach: From the Pordoi Pass or Falzargo Pass via Colle S. Lucia on an asphalt road to the Forcella Staulanza, 1773m, and a few kilometres down the Val Zoldo as far as a ski-lift station. Immediately afterwards a narrow but very practicable motor-road branches off to the right, on which one very comfortably reaches the 'Casèra di Pioda, 1816m, an extensive alm (car parking). One saves an hour's walking and is at the Coldai Hut, 2135m, in 50mins following waymark 556. A good base for the ascent of the Civetta, whether by the normal route or the 'iron' route. The evening view through the hut windows to the redly glowing triptych of Monte Pelmo and down into the green Zoldo Valley is splendid.

Ascent: An early start at daybreak lengthens the day. On the red waymarked path, the Tivàn Way (normal way) one traverses the east side in a swithchback. One leaves the Tivàn Way by a clear notice at the start of the exceptionally well maintained and red waymarked via ferrata (1½hrs from the hut).

From the start, up 10m, then about 10m to the left. On a path to the right and up via a 2m high step. Then about 10m to the right to the start of the 30m high vertical ladder. After this follows a small chimney of which only the first 5m are protected. Then following the ropes to a wide, unprotected chimney about 60m high (Grade II). At its end one traverses left on an exposed ledge and then climbs about 40m vertically up. There follows a 20m high unprotected groove (Grade II in places). At its end, where it changes to a mossy chimney, out to the right. One reaches a horizontal ledge which is followed for about 10m. Then one climbs 5m

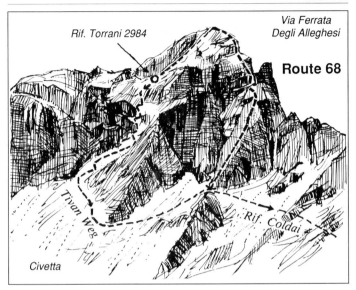

Rif. Torrani 2984

*Via Ferrata
Degli Alleghesi*

Route 68

Tivan Weg

Rif. Coldai

Civetta

vertically up and reaches the ridge of the east spur of the Punta Civetta.

Following the ropes to a 5m high overhanging pitch (rungs), then up without protection and following the next ropes vertically on to the foot of a chimney about 40m high, which is surmounted with the help of iron rungs. Up through a scree-groove, then left and through a protected chimney-groove on to a terrace. Further without protection to a broad ledge which is followed to the left for about 15m. Then directly up to a permanent snow-field. Over this into a gap. From here a short descent to a big ledge with a rock boulder. Behind this to the right through a groove and via a sloping slab horizontally to the left. To the right again, and through an 8m high groove without protection on to the Civetta North Ridge, south of the Punta Civetta. Over the ridge and beside it without protection in places (Grade I) on to the Punta Tissi. From here through grooves and via rock steps, finally immediately on the line of the ridge to the summit cross (north summit) of the Civetta.

Lake Alleghe and the villages of the Cordevole Valley lie in dizzy depths. The panorama is overpowering. Distant glaciers and all the

Ampezzo mountains expose their beauty to our admiration. Yet the Marmolata with its shimmering snowfields exceeds them all; it draws one's gaze irresistibly to itself.

Descent: From the summit first south-east over broken stone and crag to the little Torrani Hut, 2984m, an important base, especially for climbers on the north-west wall. Now via the normal route, following red marks and small cairns, via rubble, gently sloping slabs, often over snow-patches also, down to a not altogether easy, but short, chimney. Via a steep step to the right, a narrow sloping ledge, called Passo del Tenente is reached, which is easily negotiable with wire ropes. A scree-field, another 10m high slab, finally via a scree passage into a combe to a permanent avalanche-cone, which is crossed and the well-made Tivàn Path back north-east to the Coldai Hut thus reached.

Altitude Difference: Casèra di Pioda, 1892m, Rif. Coldai, 2135m, Civetta summit, 3218m. Protected route about 870m in height.

Time Required: Casèra di Pioda (car park) - Coldai Hut 1hr. Via the Ferrata Alleghesi to the summit 4$^{1}/_{2}$hrs. Descent via Rif. Torrani to the Coldai Hut 4hrs.

Difficulties: On account of the length, height and exposure only for those who are in training, are experienced on rock and vertigo-free. Some unprotected passages are up to Grade II. Not recommended when there is new snow or icing.

Bases: Rif. Coldai, 2135m, CAI, 50B, 20M, wardened end of June to end of September; Rif. Maria Vittoria Torrani, 2984m, was badly damaged by storm in 1970. With great effort it has meanwhile been practically restored, enlarged and a helicopter pad laid out. Conegliano Section of the CAI, limited overnight possibilities, Matrazenlager.

Note: From the Torrani Hut one can also descend via the Via Ferrata Tissi to the Rif. Vazzolèr, 1714m, 3hrs (more difficult). See Route 69. (Combining the Tissi and Alleghesi in one day might prove too much - overnight at Torrani).

69.   Civetta 3220m, Via Ferrata Attilio Tissi
Civetta Group   (Group e)

The traverse from the Coldai Hut to the Rif. Vazzolèr is a walk of Dolomite superlatives. It is without qualification preferable to the ascent from Listolade, 682m, in the Cordevole Valley if one wants to reach the Civetta summit on the protected climbing-path from the south. Of all protected paths in the Dolomites the Tissi and the Pössnecker in the Sella Group are reckoned the oldest. The ferrata itself is not too long, but daring and impressive for all that. At its most critical part, a black, overhanging bulge in the lower half, all the metal ropes, holds and missing iron pegs were restored in 1974 under the energetic leadership of Bepi Sararu (Mountain Rescue Service, Agordo). With a bit of skill and a protecting rope one gets over this demanding pitch well.

Approach: From the Coldai Hut (see Route 68) on waymark 560 west over the gap of the same name (¼hr). Up there a dream landscape unexpectedly opens up: lying in the hollow of the combe lies the 10m deep Lake Coldai. Behind rises the profile of a giant bastion which springs up with peaks and needles to the Civetta summit. Go on the rubble-strewn, partly green high balcony with little ascent along under the plumb vertical stretch of wall. If time permits, take the short digression (25min) to the Col Reàn, 2281m, situated on the right. Above stands the fine Tissi Hut, a cosy and comfortable resting-place and a good theatre-box for viewing the north-west wall of the Civetta (1½hrs). For your photographic notebook: for this panoramic walk make a start at the Coldai Hut about midday if possible, as one then has the optimal light-conditions. From Col Reàn the path falls gently down over green meadows, by two alms and various campaniles and towers whose name have a good sound for rock-artists: Pelsa, Su Alto, Brabante, Venezia among others, to the Torre Trieste, the corner pillar of the south ridge of the Civetta. The Vazzolèr Hut nestles here in fine larch woods. (1¾hrs from Rif. Tissi). (Best to overnight here and start early next day.)

Ascent: A mighty difference in altitude of 1600m has to be overcome on this south ascent of the Civetta. Therefore set off early in the morning. First a slight loss of height to the stream-bed of the Val Cantoni. Take the path to the left, No.558, at a sign. Along under the south foot of the Torre Trieste, then up over a latschen slope, and then losing height again to a gully. Follow the somewhat pale waymarking on a well visible path. Broken crag terrain is surmounted in steep zig-zags. To the left a very instructive glimpse of the extremely difficult south-east ridge of the Trieste Tower. Further to a little rock basin, 'Còrol delle Sasse' (last spring) below the Col del Camorz. A short scree field, up several limestone steps -

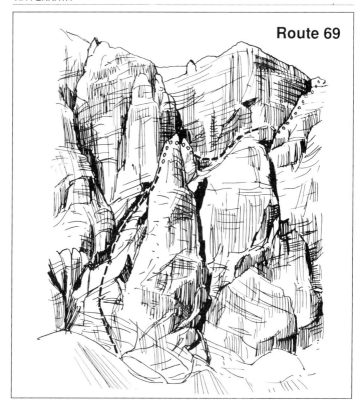

Route 69

'Scalèt della Sasse' - in zig-zags as far as the threshold of the 'Van delle Sasse', about 2420m. A gigantic stony basin, whose edges are formed on the west by the Cantoni della Busazza, on the north by the Piccola Civetta, by the principal summit and the Civetta Bassa. On the east the Moiazza, Cima della Sasse and Moiazzetta della Grava complete the circle of stone. Ascending somewhat towards the north, cross the furrowed limestone pavements and slabs to a tin hut (materials depot). From here to the start of the ferrata best to keep left over scree and snow (tracks), then traverse diagonally to the rocks as far as the highest point of the corrie. A red mark indicates the start at an altitude of about 2500m. The bergschrund can often be very deep.

Pegs and wire ropes lead at first to the left from the start, then up to the right to an overhanging bulge in the wall, whose difficulties are lessened with rungs (allegedly Grade VI!). Then the route turns somewhat towards the left, always indicated by pegs, wire ropes and climbing-rungs, over airy little walls and chimneys to a small gap between the rock massif and the Campanile Psaro. Through a ravine which falls towards the 'Van' (combe), down a bit and again right, up via a groove to an extremely exposed section (Warning! Stonefall possible!) which leads to the next notch. The route has been somewhat altered and improved in this upper part. At first to the right via a ledge provided with wire ropes, then left. By this the often iced exit crags are avoided.

At the last notch between the Civetta and the Civetta Bassa the difficulties are over.

Ascending a snowfield in a fairly big curve one stands shortly after this in front of the Rif. Torrani on the Pian della Tenda (4¹/₂-5hrs). Behind the hut over rock platforms, scree and broken crag without difficulty to the summit (¹/₂hr).

Descent: Via the Tivàn normal way on the east side as for Route 68. To use the Ferrata Alleghesi in descent is not very advisable on account of the length of the protection, except for very fit mountaineers.

Altitude Difference: Rif. Coldai, 2135m, - Rif. Vazzolèr, 1752m - Rif. Torrani, 2984m - Civetta Summit, 3220m. Climbing-path about 350m of altitude difference.

Time Required: Rif. Coldai - Tissi Hut - Rif. Vazzolèr 3¹/₂hrs. Civetta summit 5hrs. descent to Coldai Hut 4hrs.

Difficulties: The Ferrata Tissi is a demanding and exposed protected rock route. A rope can be very useful. Experience on rock, sure-footedness, freedom from vertigo are to be assumed. In addition a helmet is advisable on account of the frequent stonefall, especially in the great dièdre.

Bases: Coldai Hut, 2135m, CAI, 50B, 20M, wardened end of June to end of September; Rif. Tissi, 2262m, CAI, 40B wardened mid-June to end of September; Rif. Vazzolèr, 1714m, CAI, 72B, 24M, wardened end of June to end of September; Capanna Torrani, 2984m.

Note: Care in bad visibility in the Van delle Sasse and in the upper part of the descent from the Rif. Torrani.

Tip: Anyone for whom the Tissi via ferata is too difficult can turn east on Path No.557 approximately in the middle of the Van delle Sasse, to the Forcella della Sasse (also called Forcella della Moiazzetta) 2476m. The whole stretch from the division of paths in the 'Van' to the Rif. Coldai is quite exceptionally well waymarked in red. A very interesting route, hardly used, full of hidden beauties, rare flowers and with a view of Pelmo all the way. Of course it demands sure-footedness and some experience in steep pathless terrain. From the Forcella on the east side about 500m steeply down, then sharply left around the rocks of the 'Tappa del Todesco', one gets in continuous up and down on the permanent snowfield to the Tivàn Way and further to the Rif. Coldai (from Rif. Vazzolèr 6hrs).

70. Palazza Alta, 2255m, Via Ferrata Fiamme Gialle
Civetta Group   (Group f)

The names Monte Alto di Pelsa and Palazza Alta to the south-west of the actual Civetta massif may not convey much even to connoisseurs of the Civetta. Via ferrata specialists have really discovered the Palazza Alta in recent years: the Via Ferrata Fiamme Gialle is without doubt one of the most demanding and at the same time scenically really magnificent Dolomite vie ferrate. The via ferrata itself is comparable with the Via Tomaselli, but significantly longer.

Approach: From Cencenighe, 774m in the Cordévole Tal on a good but narrow mountain road to the hamlet of Bastiani, 971m. (From the northern edge of Cencenighe on a bridge over the river; after the bridge turn right and then left up to Bastiani at the first good opportunity.) Limited parking area.

Ascent: First up on the vehicular road, then, at the waymark "Via Ferrata", left into the forest and up laboriously, following the path into the latschen-belt. You finally get to the start of the via ferrata in a southerly direction, by crossing a sizable rock precipice on ledges, narrow and protected in parts. The via ferrata begins with a vertical rock step about 5m high, and then leads extremely airily and demandingly (only wire-rope protection) to another belt of latschen. Up through this laboriously to the foot of the summit cliffs. From there rope protection leads almost without interruption to the exit somewhat south of Palazza Alta.

Descents: A) From the summit of Palazza Alta, follow the track north, near the cliffs on the west side. The fork to the Vazzolèr Hut keeps right. You get into a wind-gap between Palazza Alta and Monte Alto di Pelsa and climb down to the left (west) in a groove of grass and broken rock (Waymark No.562). Out of this soon to the right, a short re-ascent and on ledges towards the summit cliffs of Monte Alto. Follow the waymarks 562 downwards again to the left. By easy rock-climbing you get into a ravine; out of this (Grade II) into a stream-bed and left into the belt of latschen. Pay attention to the waymarking. The waymarking leads extremely steeply through the belt of latschen (time after time steps of broken rock) into the forest, and meets the approach path far below.

B) Follow the track already mentioned which leads to the Vazzolèr Hut - likewise waymarked No.562. At first it leads south-east, then north-east into the high-level valley between Monte Alto di Pelsa and the actual Pelsa Ridge, which does belong to the Civetta massif. Scenically magnificently along below the impressive rock towers of this ridge and to the Forcella Col Mandro, 2032m (Path No.566 to the Vazzolèr Hut and No.560 to the Rif. Tissi both keep to the right.) North around the outlyers of Monte Alto di Pelsa on the track waymarked No.567, then down to the west towards the Cordévole Valley and south to the hamlet of Collaz. From here a linking-path leads back to the starting-point at Bastiani.

Altitude Difference: Bastiani 971m - Palazza Alta 2255m - fork in the Path No.566 to the Vazzolèr Hut about 1900m - Forcella Col Mandro 2032m. Via ferrata about 700m.

Time Required: Bastiani - Palazza Alta 4-5hrs. Palazza Alta - Bastiani (direct descent) 2$^{1}/_{2}$-3hrs. Palazza Alta - Forcella Col Mandro - Bastiani 3$^{1}/_{2}$-4hrs.

Difficulties: A very difficult via ferrata, consisting only of fixed ropes, which have been laid rather inconveniently in some short sections of the upper part. The route of the via ferrata is very airy in places and really long altogether, thus demanding fitness. The direct descent to Bastiani demands concentration and the ability to climb to Grade II without protection or aid. Anyone who is at all tired after the long via ferrata should choose descent B).

71. Cresta delle Masenade, 2704m - Cima Moiazza Sud, 2878m. Via Ferrata Gianni Costantini
Moiazza Group (Group g)

Friends of vie ferrate who know almost everything in the Alps with 'iron holds' are unanimous: even after the building of the Cesare Pizzetta Via Ferrata and the Via attrezzata Rino Pisetta, the Via Ferrata Costantini is the absolute 'hit' among protected paths: harder, above all longer and more exacting than the Via Cesco Tomaselli, which until now wore the crown - an attractive goal for experienced climbers. In addition there are unique views of the summits: Civetta, Pelmo, Antelao, Tàmer, Talvena, Schiara, Monti del Sole and the Feltren Dolomites dominate the scene.

Here, too, you have a rare opportunity to take a look at the 'Tower of All Towers', the Torre Trieste, which rises in the Cantoni Ridge of the Civetta. The climbing-path experience and the experience of landscape are so united on the Constantini via ferrata as to make a climb on it an absolutely indelible experience.

Approach: From the Rif. C. Tomè on the Passo Duran, 1605m (vehicular approach from Agordo in the south-west or from Forno di Zoldo in the east) on the Dolomite Alta Via No.1 in a south-westerly direction (waymark 549) to the Rif. Carestiato, 1843m at the south foot of the Cresta della Masenade. Now on the Dolomite Alta Via No.1 in the direction of the Rif. Vazzolèr and after a few minutes to where the Costantini Way branches off to the right (sign). North towards the south wall of the Cresta della Masenade up to the start of the climb.

Costantini East Route through the south wall of the Cresta delle Masenade.

On a narrow ledge 30m to the left under a gigantic roof.

Over a cleft 3m wide (bridge), then over slabs (wire ropes) fairly high up towards a mighty U-shaped rock portal in the south wall of the Cresta delle Masenade. A daring traverse on wire ropes over a 10m high, vertical, holdless wall obliquely up to the left (crux; very exacting), and further on pegs and wire ropes straight up to a stance in the U-portal. On its right side up through a vertical chimney (pegs, wire ropes), later through more broken rock obliquely right out to a mighty scree terrace (Inscription: 'Pala del Belia', 2295m). First of all to the right of a chimney up on wire ropes and rungs steeply and exhaustingly, then through a rocky ravine, along continuous wire ropes fairly high up to a secondary ridge. Fine view down to the Passo Duran. On the far side into a ravine running down from the left and on its right boundary over broken rock (wire ropes) up to a gap in the summit ridge (south ridge) of the Cresta delle Masenade (Inscription: 'Cima Cattedrale', 2557m). Further following the waymarks on to the Cresta delle Masenade, 2704m.

Traverse to the Forcella delle Nevère

The path now follows the connecting ridge, nearly 2km long to the Cima Moiazza Sud. At its south-east shoulder the exciting protected rock ledge of the Cengia Angelini begins, which recalls the Bocchette Way of the Brenta. (From the starting point of the rock ledge the summit of the Cima Moiazza Sud, 2878m can be reached by a protected route.) Via the Cengia Angelini one reaches the Forcella delle Nevère, 2601m with the Moiazza-Ghedini bivouac box. (Descent to Vazzoler Hut possible here.)

Descent via the Costantini West Way to the Rif. Carestiato

From the Forcella della Nevère the slabby ravine 'Lavina dei Cantoi' falls steeply down to the south. The Costantini Way runs on the orographically right side of the ravine down into the Van dei Cantoi.

From the gap on the climbing path - always well protected with wire ropes - via steep rock platforms, slabs and scree through the east side of the Cima delle Nevère fairly steeply down; in the lower part on the path with longer traverses further downwards, finally down left to the scree fields of the 'Van dei Cantoi'. This wild combe is bounded on the west by the Torri del Camp, on the north and north-east by the huge walls of the Cima Moiazza Sud and the Cresta delle Masenade. Via the slopes down southwards for 800m to the traversing Alta Via No.1 (waymark 554). Follow this to the left (east) and keep walking along under the south wall of the Cresta delle Masenade, through latschen or via scree fields back to the Rif. Carestiato.

Altitude Difference: Passo Duran 1605m - Rif. Carestiato, 1843m - Cresta delle Masenade, 2704m - Cima Moiazza Sud 2878m - Forcella delle Nevère 2601m.

Time Required: Passo Duran - Rif. Carestiato 1hr. Rif. Carestiato - Cresta delle Masenade 3-3$^{1}/_{2}$hrs. Cresta delle Masenade - Forcella delle Nevère 1$^{1}/_{2}$-2hrs. Forcella delle Nevère - Van dei Contoi 1$^{1}/_{4}$-1$^{1}/_{2}$hrs. Van dei Cantoi - Rif. Carestiato $^{1}/_{2}$hr. (Count at least 8hrs, hut to hut)

Difficulties: The protection in the Via Ferrata Constantini is limited exclusively to wire ropes. Traverses, often slabs completely lacking in hand and foot holds, and ascents over vertical, smooth wall pitches demand special technique and above all the appropriate strength of arm. It is not advisable to attempt this via ferrata when there is ice or lying snow. Anyone finding the first bit hard is advised to retreat.

Bases: Passo Duran (Rif. Cesare Tomè), 1605m, CAI, Agordo Section, sleeps 18, showers, wardened from mid June to the end of September; Rif. San Sebastiano, 1600m, privately owned, 41B, closed from the end of March to 20th June, otherwise open. Both these huts can be reached by car from Agordo, Chiesa or Dont; Rif. Carestatiato, 1843m CAI, Agordo Section, 35M, wardened from mid June to mid September; Bivacco Moiazza-Ghedini on the Forcella delle Nevère, 260lm, CAI, Agordo Section, 6M, open all the year.

The vie ferrate of the Schiara Group

For a long time the Schiara Group was little known on account of its far southerly situation. The waymarked route from the Pustertal to Belluno (Dolomite Alta Via No.1), opened in 1966, through the heart of the group, first turned the attention of mountain walkers to this beautiful area, still in no way overrun or over-developed.

In 1952 the first via ferrata, Col. Luigi Zacchi, was built by mountain troops; in 1959 the Belluno Section of the CAI established the Ugo Dalla Bernadina bivouac-box on its highest point (2320m). In the same year the Via Ferrata Antoinio Berti to the summit of the Schiara was completed. Some years later (1963) the third iron way, the Via Ferrata Gianangelo Sperti was completed, with the bivouac-box of the same name splendidly situated on a grassy projection 2100m high among grey rock walls. Unfortunately there is no water here.

In 1966 the fourth climbing-path, the Via Ferrata Marmòl, was completed. This route branches off from the Via Ferrata Zacchi at an altitude of about 1950m and, climbing to the right, leads through the south wall on to the east shoulder, where in 1967 the Marmòl Bivouac-box, sleeping 9, was set up.

Apart from these three bivouacs there are also two good huts in the Schiara Group (wardened in summer):

A) The Rif. '7° Alpini [pronounced "settimo"] of the Belluno Section, 1498m, in the Pis Pilon high combe. Sleeps 80, wardened from the end
194

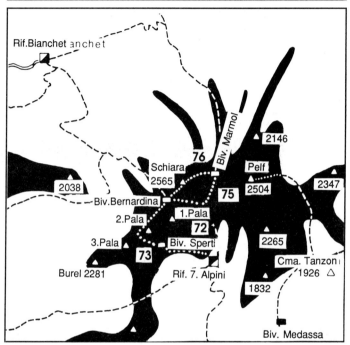

of June to the end of September. Accessible from all directions. The most convenient approach to the hut is the path through the Val d'Ardo from Bolzano-Bellunese via the Case Bortot (707m, car park and guest-house) in about 3hrs, waymarked No.501.

B) The Rif. Furio Bianchet owned by the Forestry Authority but managed by the Belluno Section of the CAI, 1245m, on the north of the Schiara Group, 36B, cosy guest-room. The hut was built on the previously abandoned 'Pian dei Gat' alm.

Approach from Val Cordevole on the wide forest-road from I Pinei or from the entrance to the Viscovà Valley at the 16km stone. Driving along the road is prohibited.

The Ugo Dalla Bernadina bivouac-box can be reached on Path No.503 in about 3hrs from the Furio Bianchet Hut, a continuation of the Luigi Zacchi Via Ferrata, No.72.

72.   Via Ferrata Zacchi
Schiara Group   (Group e)

This route (waymark 503) is perhaps the finest in the Schiara group and very impressive in its line. It begins at the Alpini Hut (1498m). At first it leads as a comfortable path over grass slopes with isolated beech trees to the start of the climb (about 1800m) on the right near the 'Porton', a great black break in the wall that looks from the hut like the entrance to a grotto, in the fall-line of the fore-summit. To here about ³/₄hr.

Ascent: From the start following the wire ropes about 10m obliquely up to the right, then with the help of two ladders, through a ravine on to a ledge. Follow this left to three ladders. Up these and along the wire rope that follows, into a deep chimney. Without protection, but without difficulty up in this (careful of loose stones), under and through a chock-stone and out left on good holds on to an earthy little path which leads up to a green platform. (Here the branch right to the Via Ferrata Marmòl, Route 75.)

The Via Zacchi soon leads to a vertical chimney, 15m high, which is surmounted energetically with the help of wire rope slings and a few rungs (hardest pitch of the lower section of the Via Zacchi). Then about 60m up over easy crag and walking terrain to a once more steeper belt of wall, which is climbed with a short ladder and subsequently with the help of rope and rungs. In this way one has reached a craggy ridge which leads up the right on to the Schiara South Wall and so to the start of greater difficulties. After a short protected section and a little ravine, there follows a sloping wall about 80m high, which is very well mastered without protection, but with the help of excellent hand- and footholds (Grade I). Soon afterwards one reaches a short traverse, made easier with a double series of iron rings (one of the airiest pitches of the Via Zacchi). Via a very exposed ladder-system one reaches the grassy Zacchi Ledge in the upper part of Schiara South Wall, which is followed at first, ascending to the left. It soon narrows to a small ledge over which the still good protection (iron rails and wire ropes) helps one comfortably along (breathtaking view down into the Pis Pilan high combe). Then up the ledge - broad once again - in a few minutes to the Ugo Dalla Bernadina bivouac-box, 2320m (sleeps 6) opposite the slender Gusela del Vescovà rock needle. From the hut to here 3¹/₂-4hrs.

Crossing to the Bianche Hut
Path No.503 leads past the bivouac hut into the gap, where it joins Path

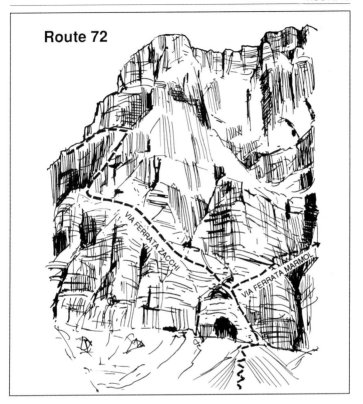

Route 72

VIA FERRATA ZACCHI

VIA FERRATA MARMOL

504 (Sperti Way, Route 73). One goes to the right, northwards, via scree-slopes on the big terrace under the Schiara north-west wall. A series of rock steps and scree ledges leads to a sudden descent which is made passable with 3 short ladders. The middle one was damaged by stonefall (1972). A fixed rope sling makes the pitch easier. So one gets down into the El Vajo combe which is surrounded by great rock walls. The north-west dièdre of the Schiara is especially imposing from here.

Keeping to the left, the combe is traversed, taking careful notice of the waymarks. The landscape becomes greener all the time and is broken up with groups of trees. The path goes on to the north-east precipices of the Cima Bramosa and follows these roughly in a north-west direction to an altitude of about 1600m. Here the waymarked path bends sharply east, traversing the vegetated slopes pretty horizontally at first, later descending into the stream-bed and turning north and north-west. Mostly along the stream-bed to the abandoned Pian del Gat alm, 1245m, where the Belluno Section has a new bivouac hut in use, the Rif. Furio Bianchet with 36 beds. From here a good motor road for forestry vehicles leads left towards the valley exit down through the Val di Vescovà to the Stelle Casa alla Vecchia in the Cordevole Valley, 454m, or, following the forestry road, to I Pinei.

From the Gusela gap to here about 4hrs.

73. Via Ferrata Sperti
Schiara Group (Group d)

This path (waymark 504) climbs up in the middle of the Pala chain and then follows the summit ridge to the right to the Forcella della Gusela where it meets the Zacchi (Route 72).

Approximately in the middle of the route at an altitude of about 2000m stands the Gianangelo Sperti bivouac-box; and at the end of the route, by the Gusela gap, the little Ugo Della Bernadina bivouac hut, 2320m. Both bivouacs sleep 6.

Approach: From the Alpini Hut follow Path No.502 (Forcella Oderz) for a short distance. Cross a stream; on the far side there is a fork where Path No.504 branches upwards to the right. It leads over grassy slopes with isolated bushes to a deep stream-bed. A taut wire rope makes the descent easier. On the other side a latschen slope. Via this slope one walks easily on a good path to the start of the climb at an altitude of about 1800m (1¼hrs).

Ascent: Immediately by the start into a shallow couloir with the help of iron rungs. This leads fairly straight up for a good way. Some little walls are easily surmounted with steps and rungs.

In this way one gets over the preliminary rocks easily. There follows a series of grooves with some small platforms. On the left some rock windows. Then follows a slope of crag and grass with trodden-out foot-marks which lead directly to the G. Sperti Bivouac-box (2000m). The little hut stands on its own and very finely on a grassy shoulder sticking out of the wall. Water is not available! From the bivouac-box one goes via grass ridges and a ramp, keeping to the left, into a ravine. Then comes a horizontal traverse left through a part of the south wall of Pala II. The wall is very steep, the ledge narrow, but well protected. This is the only exposed place on this path.

Then round a corner into the ravine which runs down from the Forcella Sperti. Now one follows the west edge of Pala II. Up over some steep steps to a short shut-in chimney, all well waymarked and protected. After creeping through, up over some places with artificial climbing aids into the Forcella Sperti (about 2250m) which is incut between Pala III and Pala II.

Through the gap, then at first down somewhat to the right, and then up again. The continuation winds through between the summits of the eastern Pala chain, via ledges and terraces, through grooves and gaps with and without protection between the summits of the eastern Pala chain, chiefly climbing somewhat, and tiring.

Pala II is circumvented on the north side, Pala I also, but Nason on the south side. Then via the terrace on whose southern rim the 40m high Gusela del Vescovà rock needle (2360m) stands. In the end a short descent into the Gusela gap (about 2300m) and one reaches Route 72 at its highest point. The Sperti Way is here at an end. About 5hrs from the Alpini Hut. The Bernadina Bivouac-box stands a few metres to the right. Round the corner there the Zacchi Way (Waymarked 503) leads down to the Alpini Hut.

(The crossing to the Bianche Hut leads from the gap left (north) down through the 'Van della Schiara' combe into the Vescovà Valley and further into the Cordevole Valley at I Pinei, little below the village of La Muda).

74. Via Ferrata Berti
Schiara Group   (Group e)

The Via Ferrata Berti (Waymark 504) which leads to the almost 250m higher summit of the Schiara, 2565m, begins a few metres right (south) of the Ugo Dalla Bernadina bivouac-box. The route is very beautiful, not as exposed as some of the pitches of the Zacchi Way, but fairly complicated in its line, so that it is advisable to pay close attention to the clear waymarking.

First straight up without protection, then obliquely left under huge overhangs to a short, overhanging ladder which leads into a gloomy cleft. Up without protection on the left bounding wall into a gap. A narrow gorge is crossed to the right and climbed with the help of protection on the rib which bounds it on the right (east). Then at the very top, at the mouth of the ravine, to the left again and to a steep ridge which is surmounted with the help of a ladder-system. To the left on the craggy, highest west ridge and without difficulties via it to the great Schiara summit cross.

Descent via the East Ridge of the Schiara to the Marmòl Bivouac-box:
From the Schiara summit immediately downwards via the narrow but easily practicable east ridge and on to the subsidiary summit (Anticima, 2506m). Leave this elevation to the left from the ridge via a short steep step (wire rope) and, via rubble-covered broken crag, reach a broad, green ridge, and follow this, always towards the Monte Pelf. Soon the red waymarking leads down to the left.

Down to the right at a fork in the path (sign: Alpini Hut; the path branching left leads to the Bianche Hut) and finally over a short steep rock step protected by wire rope to the Marmòl Bivouac-box. Continue the descent as for Route 75.

The traverse from the one bivouac-box to the other demands about 2$^{1/2}$hrs, and the whole mountain excursion back to the hut about 9hrs. When thunderstorms threaten the traverse is not to be recommended because there is no possibility of shelter on the whole stretch between the two bivouacs.

75. Via Ferrata Marmòl
Schiara Group (Group e)

Because the passage of the ice gorge below the Forcella Marmòl (2262m) is very dangerous (on account of the continuous stonefall from the friable west wall of Monte Pelf) the route which was indicated by waymark 514 and is still so marked on many maps, has been abandoned and replaced by the much better, protected climbing-path, the Via Ferrata Marmòl, likewise waymarked 514.

This path (completed in 1967) follows the old Sperti-Veil ascent route and is above all important for walkers who have done the Dolomite High-level Route No.1 and wish to descend through the Canale Marmòl high valley to the Alpini Hut after the ascent. For this reason this route is described in descent.

Route75

V.F. ZACCHI

On this route too, it is important (especially in mist) to pay close attention to the waymarking. This is duplicated (red spots and blue triangles) and therefore hard to miss.

The Marmòl bivouac-box stands at about 2280m in a south-west facing bay on the edge of the broad east ridge of the Schiara where this forms a kind of shoulder. Water is not available, but snow patches can usually be found in the neighbourhood. The bivouac-box is not visible from the Alpini Hut, only from the G. Sperti bivouac on the other side of the combe. There are sleeping-places for 9 persons in the Marmòl bivouac Hut.

Descent: From the Marmòl bivouac-box first obliquely downwards to the right on a clear path without difficulties. The terrain soon becomes steeper and after a short zone of broken crag, wire ropes lead very steeply down into a narrow gap. Now downwards to the right (in descent) and, always following the waymarks, through the sloping flank of scree and broken crag (wire ropes on some steeper descents) into the bottom of a gorge. Cross this and one reaches a ledge on the steep wall opposite which one follows to the left, via several very airy places where it is interrupted. Finally, ladders lead steeply down on to a grassy terrace.

Down to the left on tracks, then over rubble-covered crag on to a ledge that is followed without difficulty around several corners to its end. Here a ladder leads over a steep step on to a ledge in a gloomy ravine. On the opposite wall of the ravine airily left on a ledge interrupted in several places, and finally through a short chimney up on to the grassy platform where the Via Marmòl meets the Via Ferrata Zacchi. Continue on this down to the foot of the wall.

From here on a good path to the hut in $^1/_2$-$^3/_4$hr.

Suggestions for Outings Linking the Individual Schiara Routes Starting Point: Rifugio 7° Alpini

Pala - 'Passes' Route (Routes 72, 73) (Total time required about 8hrs.) The Zacchi way is taken in ascent as far as the Bivacco Ugo Dalla Bernadina ($3^1/_2$ to 4hrs). Descent into the Gusela gap and crossing left on to the Sperti way. Along this between Gusela and Nason, going around Pala 1 and II on the north side (right) via terraces and ledges up and down through gaps and grooves to the Forcella Sperti. Here left into the deeply indented ravine, via ladders and steps, through a shut-in chimney, on wire ropes always following the waymarking down to the traverse through the south wall of Pala II on a narrow ledge. After this one soon comes to the Biv. G. Sperti. From here it goes via the lower mass of the mountain, first over grass with footmarks, then again through grooves and via small walls with many rungs, short ladders and wire ropes down to the end of the climb at about 1800m ($3^1/_2$hrs).

From the end of the climb on a footpath down via a latschen-slope, crossing some deep streamcourses, to the hut (about 1hr).

Schiara Traverse (Route 72, 74, 75) Total time required about 9hrs.

The Zacchi way is taken in ascent as far as the highest point ($3^1/_2$-4hrs).

After a short rest in the Biv. Dalla Bernadina one goes a short way back to the signpost on the Zacchi ledge, from where one ascends left via the Berti Way to the summit of the Schiara. Further as described in the description of Route 75 to the Marmòl bivouac-box, about 2¹/₂hrs from the Ugo Dalla Bernadina biviouac-box. The red waymarking (No.514) and the blue-triangle waymarking of the Dolomite Long-distance Route together lead from here back to the hut (3hrs).

The Big Schiara Outings (Routes 72, 75, 74, 73)

Total time required about 10hrs. This outing traverses the Schiara from the Marmòl gap to the Gusela gap and then the Pala chain to the Sperti gap.

On the Zacchi and Marmòl Routes (72, 75) to the Marmòl Bivouac on the east ridge (2350m, 3-3¹/₂hrs).

There one goes up the broad scree ridge that leads up to the fore-summit of the Schiara (2506m). Our route leads in a westerly direction via the ridge, which becomes sharper, then over the fore-summit on to the main summit with its great summit cross, 2565m.

From the summit one goes further in a westerly direction on the Berti Way (Route 74, Waymark 504); first over scree, then further, more or less following the west ridge down - fairly difficult to follow (pay careful attention to the waymarks!). This part of the route is of extraordinary beauty: distant panoramas, splendid view of the Gusela, the Pala Chain and the deep combes to its left and right, the Cordevole Valley and the wild mountains of the Dolomite Nature Park. The Berti Way ends just on the left of the second bivouac-box (Dalla Bernadina) 2¹/₂hrs from the Marmòl.

From here one descends into the Gusela gap (2300m) and there - going further in a westerly direction - one comes upon the Sperti Way (Route 73, Waymarked 504). Going round the imposing Gusela del Vescova, this winds through between the summits of the eastern Pala chain to the Sperti gap (2250m). Descent through the gorge which opens to the south, past the Sperti Bivouac (2100m) to the end of the climb (1800m) and then back to the hut on a little path.

Taken as a whole this great mountain excursion demands a long day. If one has good weather for it, it becomes an unforgettable experience on account of the beauty of the scenery, the grandeur of the route (although one leaves out the most impressive part of the Zacchi Way).

The Brenta

The Brenta extends north from Lake Garda and west from Trento (Trient) and is separated from the Dolomites by the valley of the River Adige (German: Etschtal).

It is a rock range running north-south and having only very unimportant side ramifications. Only at the southern end of the central core, beginning about at the Cima Tosa, does the mountain range begin to split up into two longer branches enclosing the Val d'Ambièz, and then gradually slopes down in gentler mountain shapes from its original form, when it is still bold and on a dolomitic scale, to its southern boundary. In the north, on the other hand, a second, parallel ridge runs likewise in a north-south direction, separated from the main ridge by the extensive stony area round the Lago di Tovel.

In the Brenta Group there are still several small areas of glaciation, all lying on the west side of the main Brenta ridge. The heaviest glaciation is around the Cima d'Ambiez: Vedretta di Camosci, Vedretta di Vallagola, Vedretta Pratofiorito and Vedretta dei Dodici Apostoli. The Vedretta dei Sfulmini in the Sfulmini chain is also worth mentioning. The glaciers are harmless today but still show nevertheless all the typical glacial characteristics, such as moraines, ice-tongues, crevasses and 'mer de glace'.

At the height of the ice age the complete ice cover reached up to 2400m. The Brenta soared up out of the gigantic ocean of ice like a mighty reef, and for its part sent mighty hanging-glaciers down on to the ice-plain, which at that time flowed down as vast Adige and Sarca Glaciers.

There are almost no scree-slopes in the Brenta and therefore vast mountain cliffs. Around the Tuckett Hut cyclopean hands seem to have played dice with rock cubes weighing many tons.

Scenically the Brenta is one of the mightiest mountain areas in the whole of the Dolomites. Magnificently structured summits, bold rock towers and spires, splendid cliffs, wonderfully soaring arêtes and ridges characterise the mountain scene.

The orange colour of the rocks, which blend their tones variously under the influence of the sunlight, enhances the impression. The Brenta Group always leads a very individualistic existence and for a distance of

42km is a perfect example of dolomitic landscape, richly contrasted in form and colour, weight and lightness, and at the same time brim-full of optical stage-effects.

In spite of its grandeur it was comparatively late in being discovered by mountaineers. On 24th July 1864 John Ball inaugurated its opening-up to climbers with a visit to the Bocca di Brenta. This 'Mouth' (bocca) 2552m, embedded like a portal between Brenta Alta and Brenta Bassa, is today still the most important pass in a west-east direction from Madonna di Campiglio to Molveno.

Exactly a year later Giuseppe Loss from Primiero stood with six companions on Cima Tosa, 3173m, the highest elevation in the Brenta. All the important summits were subsequently climbed by British, German and local mountaineers, until in 1899 Ampferer and Berger, both from Innsbruck, wrote one of the most important chapters in Brenta history: they conquered the Campanile Basso - already intensively wooed by Garbari and Pooli from Trento.

Even in the 1930's people had begun to widen where necessary the horizontal rock ledges hewn out of the cliffs by wind and weather from the Bocca di Brenta to the Bocca degli Armi, and to equip them with pegs, ladders and wire ropes as a protected high-level route. The particular installations and connections became more and more exciting and diversified until the Sentiero delle Bocchette extended from the Dodici-Apostoli (Twelve Apostles) Hut in the south via the Tosa Refuge to the Tuckett Hut in the north. There is ample provision for variations on the high-level-way menu inside the figure-of-eight round the heart of the Brenta.

Today the Brenta is one of the most popular areas in the whole of the Alps. The bases in the central area - Tuckett, Brentei, Alimonta and Pedrotti (Tosa) Huts - are frankly taken by storm by tourists at weekends in the summer. Very few of them are qualified rock-climbers who want to gather their laurels on Brenta routes. Bocchette Way is the watchword on which the fame of the Brenta Group has been founded in recent decades, and which today more than ever draws mountineers of all grades of competence and from all over the world almost irresistibly under its spell.

In spite of all artificial climbing aids the Brenta even today can always, and dramatically, show the mountaineer the superior power of the mountain: a sudden drop in temperature, snowfall in high summer, or autumn icing can present even the most experienced and expert climber with very serious problems. The strongest warning must be given against thoughtlessness, especially when a thunderstorm is coming up. Even if the much-feared Brenta mist is not ground for turning back early, still one must be careful not to take a path whose route cannot be safely followed unambiguously even in the worst possibly visibility; when necessary you must distinguish inadequately marked sections with your own cairns; to lose the way in thick mist must be avoided in every case, as the terrain practically never allows of a pathless descent.

The Most Important Valley Centres

MALE, *721m,*
In the north on the Tonale Pass road in Val di Noce. Small mountain village, good guest houses. It can only be considered by the mountaineer as a starting-point for the Peller Hut, 2060m.

DIMARO, *767m,*
In the north on the Tonale Pass road. Small mountain village, church with fine frescoes. Starting-point for the Peller hut, 2060m.

MADONNA DI CAMPIGLIO, *1522m,*
Famous international hotel-village on a large scale, splendid situation at the very head of the Valle Rendena surrounded by diversified coniferous woods. All the important Brenta huts can easily be reached from Madonna di Campiglio on short ascent paths. Madonna di Campiglio is therefore the most convenient valley base for the Brenta Group.

Tourist Office (Azienda di Soggiorno) opens 9-12; 15-18.30: Phone 0465/4 10 26.

Cableways:
1. Cabin Cableway (Funivia) up Monte Spinale, 2093m. Valley station by small lake.
2. Grostè Cabin Cableway in two sections to Passo del Grostè, 2437m, built 1962. It makes it possible to get to the mountain ridge and the start of the Bocchette Way (Route 79) quickly and without effort. The valley station is on the main road 2km above (northwards) Madonna di Campiglio.
3. 5-Laghi (Five Lakes) Cableway (since 1977, replacing a chair-lift) into the Presanella Group. Valley Station in town centre on the main road.
4. Pradalgo Cabin Cableway into the Presanella Group.

Camping: Nearest campsite, 'Faé della Rendena' between San Antonio di Mavignola and Pinzolo, open summer and winter. Phone 0465/5 13 92.

Bus Routes: Frequent daily service to Trento; 4 times daily from 1.7 - 3.9 to Malè; once daily from 10.7 - 10.9 to Bolzano; once daily to Molveno (towards Trento, change at Ponte Arche).

VALLESINELLA HUT, *1522m*
South-east from Madonna di Campiglio, 4¹/₂km without ascent, can be reached on a minor road with own car or taxi (return journey for groups by owner's minibus also); on foot in 1hr; private, 30B & M, open and wardened 20.6 - 20.9. From there the shortest ascent to the Tuckett and Brentei Huts.

Shortly before it on the right at the middle waterfall, the Cascate-di-Mezzo Hut, 1480m.

SAN ANTONIO DI MAVIGNOLA, *1122m*
Very picturesquely situated on the Pinzolo-Madonna di Campiglio motor-road, starting point for the 'Twelve Apostles' Hut through the lower Val Brenta Alta and the Val d'Agola. Camp-site.

PINZOLO, *770m*
Pleasant mountain village at the entrance to the wild, romantic Val Genova. Church with fine bell-tower. Near the village and worth seeing - early Romanesque church with splendid frescoes inside and out. Always locked, but key available in Pinzolo.

Good guest houses, provision stores, doctor, chemist, guides. Alpine centre above all for the Adamello-Presanella Group; for the Brenta, of course, only the ascent to the 'Twelve Apostles' Hut, which is shortened by using the cableway and chair-lift to Dosso del Sabion, 2100m. Camp-site 3km to the north.

SAN LORENZO IN BANALE, *792m*
Pleasant mountain village at the mouth of the Val d'Ambièz (south side of the Brenta Group). Favourite summer holiday resort. Access to Agostini Hut, 2410m.

STENICO, *668m*
Mountain village to the south of the Brenta Group. Access by foot or car to the Val d'Algone (also from Tione in the south-west) to the Ghedina Hut,

1116m, and Malga Movlina, 1746m, as starting-point for an ascent to the Twelve Apostles hut, 2488m.

MOLVENO, *864m*

Picturesquely situated on a steep mountain slope at the northern end of Lake Molveno, a lake naturally dammed through a landslip. Summer holiday resort, numerous hotels, guest houses and pensions. Guides, Doctor, Chemist, chair-lifts in two sections up the Pradel (1600m), a broad green slope with a splendid view of the Brenta. Swimming bath at the warm Lake Molveno, very pretty lakeside campsite.

Because of its low situation only second-rate as base for climbing in the Brenta Group.

The most important approaches to the via ferrata system

I   From Madonna di Campiglio:
1. To the Passo del Grostè (start of the Bocchette Way system) by the Grostè Cableway (on foot 3hrs).
2. To the Tuckett Hut: A) first to the Vallesinella Hut, on foot 1hr, better with own car or by taxi; ascent from there 2hrs (3hrs altogether). B) From the Grostè Pass on Path No.316, 1¹/₂hrs.
3. To the Brentei Hut via the Vallesinella Hut, ascent from there 2hrs (3hrs altogether).
4. To the Alimonta Hut via the Brentei Hut, 1hr longer (4hrs altogether).
5. To the Pedrotti (Tosa) Hut via the Brentei Hut, 2hrs longer (5hrs altogether).
6. To the Twelve Apostles Hut: first to Lake Agola (2hrs on foot) better with own car or by taxi. Ascent from there 3hrs.

II   From Pinzolo:
7. To the Twelve Apostles Hut: first by cableway to the Dos del Sabion, 2101m. From there, descend to the Passo Bregn del'Ors, 1836m, and then ascend in 3hrs altogether.
8. To the Twelve Apostles Hut on foot, 5-6hrs altogether; on account of the great difference in altitude of 1700m, not to be recommended.

III   From Molveno:
9. To the Pedrotti (Tosa) Hut: from the middle station of the chair-lift on Path No.340 + 319 in 4hrs altogether. Altitude difference 1150m.

IV   From Stenico or Tione:
10. To the Twelve Apostles Hut: by car as far as Malga Movlina; from there on foot, 2¹/₂hrs altogether.

V   From San Lorenzo in Banale:
11. To the Agostini Hut: via the Rif. Cacciatori on foot, 5-6hrs altogether.

Huts in the Central Brenta and their most important approaches and links

If there is a goods-cableway or jeep-route, this indicates that the hut is well stocked with food and drink.

The huts in the central Brenta Group (Tuckett, Brentei, Alimonta. Agostini, Twelve Apostles and Pedrotti Huts) are regularly heavily over-filled in good weather in summer, especially in August, and above all at week-ends.

Graffer Hut (Rif, M.O. Giorgio Graffer) 2261m

CAI-SAT Trento Section, open and wardened from 20.6 - 30.9 and in winter, built in 1946 to replace the Stoppani Hut, burnt down in 1939, which stood immediately by the Grostè Cableway Terminus. 24B with bed-linen, 26B without bed-linen on the ground floor with poor ventilation. Phone 0465/4 13 58.

The hut is situated a little below the Passo del Grostè 2443m in a splendid position under the light-grey limestone walls of the Pietra Grande, with a wide open view of the whole central Brenta Ridge from the Passo del Grostè as far as the Cima Tosa. Ideal starting-point for the beginning of the Brenta traverse.

Principal Ascent Routes from Madonna di Campiglio

1. On well waymarked mountain way 384 through open natural forest, later over open alm country with widening all-round view to the height of the Monte Spinale, 2093m. Here a small private hut and cableway mountain station. Then on path No.331 over the broad alm country, past the little Lake Spinale to the Graffer Hut, 3hrs. Seldom used today because of the cableway from the valley.
2. Either using the chair-lift or the cabin cableway built alongside it quickly up to Monte Spinale, then on foot as for 1 to the Graffer Hut in 1hr: the usual ascent route today.
3. Using the Grostè cabin cableway to the terminus and from there on foot in 15-20mins to the Graffer Hut.

Tuckett Hut, 2268m, and by it the **Sella Hut, 2271m** belonging to it. Both CAI-SAT Trento Section. The Sella Hut was built by the SAT in 1900 and the Tuckett Hut by the DAV in 1906. Open 20.6.- 20.9. Tuckett Hut wardened. Goods cableway. 95B with bed-linen, 35B without bed-linen.

Winter room (without mattresses or covers). Phone 0465/4 12 26.

Fine situation at the foot of a bold, orange-coloured tower, the Castelletto Inferiore, 2595m an ideal climbing-mountain.

The Tuckett Hut lies in the middle section of the Brenta and also serves as a base for climbs.

Ascent from Madonna di Campiglio only

1. Although there is plenty of car parking space at the Rifugio Vallesinella, 1522m, nevertheless there is an excessive amount of traffic during the high season, especially at weekends. On the south side of the clearing Path 317 leads right through the middle of the former alm hut, first over the stream (Sacra di Vallesinella) and steeply, with many curves through the dark forest to the Casinei Hut, 1825m privately owned. From here continue, at first still through the forest, but soon through more open territory on a fine path with an interesting glimpse into the Val Vallesinella: so, directly to the Tuckett Hut. 2hrs from the Rif. Vallesinella.
2. From the Rif. Vallesinella there is a scenically even more attractive alternative way to the Casinei Hut: the Via degli Orsi. First, continue on the dirt road from the car park; after 3mins go left at the first crossing and climb leisurely through mature forest to the Malga Vallesinella di Sopra, 1678m. Here, well sign-posted, to the right across the stream and in big bends up the slope opposite to the Casinei hut. Continue as for ascent 1.
3. The path via the waterfalls ("Cascate") is even more beautiful. Start on the dirt road, as for alternative 2, but keep right after 200m and in 5mins you reach the bottom station of the goods cableway to the Casinei Hut. You now follow the very beautiful path by the steep rock steps of the waterfalls to the alm. Here you are joined by the path of alternative 2.
4. Up on the Grostè cableway to the top station and from there south on Path 316 in 2hrs to the Tuckett Hut.

Brentei Hut (Rifugio Alberto o Maria ai Brentèi) 2120m

CAI-SAT Monza Section. Built in 1932, enlarged several times. Open and wardened 20.6. - 20.9. Goods cableway. Cooking allowed in ante-room. 30B with bed linen, 35B with or without bed-linen, as desired, 25B without bed-linen in loft; two rooms also there with 20M altogether. Open winter-room (without mattresses or covers) with cooking facilities. Phone 0465/

4 12 44. The situation of the hut on an almost level, grassy, somewhat projecting spur immediately over the middle section of the Val Brenta Alta, one of the mightiest and grandest rock areas of the Brenta, is extraordinarily impressive. Near the hut there is an impressive mountain-chapel.

Ascents from Madonna di Campiglio only

1. Via the Malga Vallesinella to the Casinei Hut. Now follow the well planned and much used Sentiero Bogani, Path No.318, one of the finest mountain paths in the Brenta. At first it climbs steeply through natural forest, then crosses an open slope at a gentler gradient, and finally reaches the almost level final section to the Brentei Hut through an interesting natural rock tunnel. During the whole route a fine view of the mighty Crozzon and the green meadows and forest lands far below in the Val Brenta Alta.

    From Madonna di Campiglio 3hrs, from the Vallesinella Hut, 2hrs.

2. Via the Brenta Alms. From the minor road to the Vallesinella Hut branch off to the Cascata Vallesinella, a fine waterfall in the midst of the forest, where the Vallesinella stream falls raging and foaming over a 50m high rock wall. You should, if at all possible, make this short diversion, even if not ascending further. Nearby, the Cascata-di-Mezzo hut.

    Now through the spray on a bridge over the boiling water, then through fine natural forest to the Malga Brenta Bassa, 1268m, one of the most magnificent scenic areas of the Brenta: level tracts, green meadows, enclosed by crags and natural forest, and the gigantic pillar of the Crozzon soaring up vertically beyond. Now a good forest road, No.323, for a while, and then a path on the left (true left) of the valley, which leads up on the second terrace of the valley to Malga Brenta Alta, 1666m, on wide, almost level meadow-land, enclosed by isolated trees and framed in a broad semi-circle by a magnificent world of rock. The final long ascent to the Brentei Hut on an old but still quite good little path over craggy terrain follows from here.

    Today the route is hardly used but has value for those who want to experience an especially fine scenic picture. Duration of ascent, 5hrs.

Alimonta Hut, 2600m

Private, on the south side of the west shoulder of the Cima Molveno, at the foot of the two Gemelli Towers (The Twins). Open and wardened from 25.6 - 25.9. Goods cableway. 22B with bed-linen, 31B without bed-linen,

10M in loft. No telephone at hut. Proprietor: G.Alimonta, 1-38 084 Madonna di Campiglio, phone 0465/4 11 78.

The hut was completed in 1968 and enlarged in 1973. It stands on a wide, almost level ramp of limestone pavement, a former glacier-bed on the approach route 305 from the Brentei Hut to the central Bocchette Way in the direction of the Pedrotti Hut. Ascent from the Brentei Hut to the Alimonta Hut ¾hr. The Alimonta Hut forms an ideal base. It has the advantage for the walker on the Bocchette Way that he need not descend as far as to the Brentei Hut.

Pedrotti Hut, 2496m, and the little **Tosa Hut** below it.

CAI-SAT. Trento Section. 2 Huts which now belong together and are shown on signs as 'Rif. Tosa'. Pedrotti Hut built in 1912 by the DAV, enlarged in 1921 and 1963; Tosa Hut built in 1874 by SAT. Open from 20.6 - 20.9, Pedrotti Hut wardened. Goods cableway, 60B with bed-linen and 60B without bed-linen in the Tosa Hut, 20B without bed-linen and 20M in the loft; winter room. Phone 0461/4 73 16. The hut stands just below the Bocca di Brenta on a limestone pavement situated there in a fine, open situation, in the immediate neighbourhood of orange-coloured rock towers and walls, with a direct view of the double-coned Croz dell'Altissimo. Near the hut a beautiful little mountain chapel.

Ascents

1. From Madonna di Campiglio via the Vallesinella Hut to the Brentei Hut. From here on well waymarked Path 318 through the Val Brenta Alta, climbing steadily into the Bocca di Brenta, 2552m, which is visible from a distance and is a narrow gap between the Cima Brenta Bassa and the Cima Brenta Alta, which rises from here in a magnificent vertical ridge. The innermost section of the Val Brenta Alta - one of the finest rock areas of the Brenta - is traversed on this path. The path leads immediately at the foot of the Guglia into a snow-filled basin; here always a broad track trodden out to the craggy rocks. Over these with the help of wire ropes and via a second snow-field soon to the gap. From here the Pedrotti Hut is already visible; behind it the hut climbing-tower, Croz del Rifugio and beyond it again the broadly built massif of Monte Daino. The hut is reached in a few minutes from the gap. From Madonna di Campiglio, 4½-5hrs; from Brentei Hut 1½-2hrs.

2. From Molveno on a wide path 319 in 5-6hrs to the hut. Using chair-lift, 4-5hrs.

North-west on Path 319 into the Valle delle Seghe, into the furthest end of this high valley, left via a steep step and in many serpentine curves to the Selvata Hut, 1630m, a little mountain guest-house where it is possible to stay the night. From here, a magnificent view of the gigantic wall of the Croz dell'Altissimo. Up a steep section to the Baito Massodi, 1982m, a flat, grassy limestone pavement behind which the Sfulmini ridge now begins to rise up more and more impressively. The path leads from here into a rock valley which leads up towards the Bocca di Brenta, but keeps left on the craggy slope and reaches first the Tosa Hut and then the slightly higher Pedrotti Hut. The first section of the chair-lift from Molveno to the Pradèl makes the ascent route appreciably easier and shortens it by 1-2hrs. The fine footpath 340 leads almost horizontally in the Valley delle Seghe from the Pradel. After $^3/_4$hr you reach the Croz-del-Altissimo Hut, 1500m, at the foot of the giant south-west walls of the Croz-dell'Altissimo. From there 1hr to the Selvata Hut and a further 2hrs to the Pedrotti Hut.

Agostini Hut (Rif. Silvio Agostini), 2410m

CAI-SAT Trento Section (private until 1975/6). In the south of the Brenta, in the Val d'Ambièz. Built in 1937, enlarged in 1975. Open and wardened from 27.6 - 20.9. Provisioned by jeep since 1968. 51B with or without bed-linen as required, 22B in winter-room. Phone 0465/7 41 38.

The situation of the hut at the innermost end of the Val d'Ambièz is exceptionally impressive. By the hut a pretty mountain chapel. Ascent from San Lorenzo in Banale, 792m. On narrow motor-road (for jeep) 5-6hrs. Car-drivers can drive 2$^1/_2$km as far as the Gaststätte Dolomiti (car park). Luggage and passengers can be transported to the hut by jeep.

Ascent from San Lorenzo in Banale
Route 325 leads through the entire Val d'Ambièz, which rises in several steps. From the village up the d'Ambièz stream as far as the Ponte di Brocca, 1309m. After the first steep step you reach the Malga Prato di Sotto and after a further steep section, the Cacciatori hut. There a magnificent view opens out: the entire frame of the innermost Val d'Ambièz is spread out in a wide semi-circle with mighty walls and towers, and holds the green alm-land in its embrace. From the Cacciatori Hut the waymarked footpath 325 branches left, north-westwards from the jeep road and ends just before the hut.

Approach from the Pedrotti Hut to the Agostini Hut

The 'Sentiero Palmieri' is an easy, walkable, high-level way, which offers the shortest and most convenient connection between the two important bases in the south rock area of the Brenta; it is also usable in bad weather and therefore is a possible alternative to or way of evading the more demanding Sentiero Brentari.

At first follow the waymarking No.304 - the start of the Sentiero Brentari - from the Pedrotti Hut. Path 304 leads around the rock massif of the Cima Brenta Bassa and runs on the upper rim of the giant funnel of the Pozza Tramontana. Route 320 soon branches off to the left. It leads deep down on the rim of the funnel-hole, in order to climb steadily again into the gap of Forcolotta di Noghera, 2423m, quite steep at the end, with many curves. Here the path leads into a new mountain area, the innermost Val d'Ambièz, and runs under the rock walls of the Cima Ceda, 2757m. The Punta Dell'Ideale and the east wall of the Cima d'Ambièz come into view to dominate the scene, and soon the Agostini Hut is also reached.

Time: Pedrotti Hut - Agostini Hut, 3hrs.

Twelve Apostles Hut (German: Zwölf-Apostel Hütte; Italian: Rif. Dodici Apostoli, also Rif. Garbari) 2489m

CAI-SAT, Pinzolo Section, open from 20.6 - 20.9. Goods cableway (no transport for rucksacks). Built in 1908, enlarged in 1953. 12B with bed-linen, 12B without bed-linen, 24M in annexe. Phone 0465/5 13 09.

The hut stands boldly on a gigantic round boss of rock, polished by glacial ice, immediately before the wall plunges away. Splendid view of the Adamello-Presanella Group to the west. A small chapel is hewn out of the foot of the wall of Croz dei Dodici-Apostoli as a memorial to those killed in the mountains. A rock tunnel forms the entrance and a mighty cross struck out of the wall the end. Daylight enters the interior of this unique rock sanctuary - in which mountain Masses are often read - through four cruciform windows.

Ascents

1. From **Pinzolo** by cableway and chair-lift to Dos del Sabion, 2101m, one of the outlying mountains of the Brenta Group, from which one has an incomparable view of the panorama of the Brenta in the east and the Adamello-Presanella Group in the west. Mountain guest-house on the summit. Even from the summit of this you can see the Twelve

Apostles Hut and its entire mountain setting. Furthermore, you have a splendid view into the wild, rocky, Val di Nardis, through which the ascent to the hut leads. In $^{1}/_{2}$hr you descend to the Passo Bregn de l'Ors, 1830m (= 'Bears' Fodder-trough' in popular speech, and 'Brandalors' on the signs). Here a small, open chapel. From the pass a direct descent to the north across a pasture into the Val d'Agola is possible. Three minutes further east you reach a branch to the south, which leads into the Val d'Algone over another broad, outlying alm-saddle, the Passo del Gotro, without waymarking.

To the hut ($2^{1}/_{2}$hrs) a fine path (No.307) leads straight on, dropping gently through forest on to level, green terrain, the Pian di Nardis. From here a relatively good path leads on the left side of the valley through a scree-zone, then surmounts a steep step with many serpentine bends and wire rope in places, once more crosses an area of scree and reaches the firm limestone. Through the limestone grooves on to the massive slab of rock on which the hut stands.

2. From the north through the Val d'Agola, from **Pinzolo** or **Madonna di Campiglio.** In either case first drive on the motor-road towards San Antonio 1122m and on the forest road to Lago di Val d'Agola, 1595m, easily negotiable by motors. From here the path, always well waymarked with 324 leads, climbing steeply through open woodlands, into the Val Nardis and reaches Pian di Nardis where it joins path 307 coming from Pinzolo. Then on this as for Ascent 1.

   Duration of ascent from Lago d'Agola, $2^{1}/_{2}$-3hrs. So the route has advantages if you can use a car, otherwise not.

3. From the south a good forest-road leads from **Stenico** or **Tione** through the Val d'Algone as far as Malga Movlina, 1746m (car park). From here on an easy level path to the junction near Passo Bregn de l'Ors; from here as for ascent 1. $2^{1}/_{2}$hrs from Malga Molvena.

4. From the Brentei Hut via the Bocca dei Camosci, 2770m. The well waymarked path is one of the finest crossings in the Brenta and provides an abundance of the finest and most lasting impressions without special effort. From the Brentei Hut on path 327, southwards, down into the bottom of the Val Brenta Alta. On the other side of the valley path 327 leads steeply and in curves to just under the rocks of the Crozzon, continues comfortably under them for some time and then leads absolutely immediately under the steep mass of the splendid Crozzon arête into the Val dei Camosci; by the arête one of the most splendid viewpoints of the Sfulmini ridge.

The narrow path, waymarked and also marked with stone blocks, now leads steeply upwards directly under the west walls of the Crozzon, through an area of large, rough blocks on to the crown of a moraine and steeply up this. The rock ridge is now filled with the Vedretta dei Camosci, a small glacier, completely enclosed by vertical walls. Not until high up do you get on the harmless glacier, on level, permanent snow. You cross the snow-basin to the right directly up the Bocca dei Camosci, 2770m, which is already visible from a distance.

The Bocca dei Camosci is a striking point: you leave the rock basin through which you have been walking until now, but you have an overpowering view back from the gap to the orange-coloured walls of the Cima Tosa; after only a few metres this view disappears and a completely new area, totally hidden until now, lies there, wide open: the mountain area around the Twelve Apostles Hut, which itself is already to be seen. A splendid little path (No.304) leads steadily downhill. A fine little glacier, Vedretta d'Agola, accompanies it and offers fine, high-alpine scenes. Somewhat later two further small glaciers come fully into sight - the Vedrotta Patrofiorito and Vedretta dei Dodici Apostoli. The broad area of limestone at the foot of this glacier is crossed and the hospitable Twelve Apostles Hut is reached. Time 4hrs.

Casinei Hut, 1825m

Private, built in 1909, enlarged in 1970, open and wardened from 15.6 - 10.10. Goods cableway, 24B with bed-linen, 28B without bed-linen. Phone 0465/4 27 08. The hut lies about ¾hr above the Vallesinella Hut on the way to the Tuckett and Brentei Huts.

Survey of the Via Ferrata System

The Via Ferrata System is divided into the following sections:

NORTH-SOUTH

Sentiero Alfredo Benini (Route 76)

Passo de Grostè (Cableway mountain-station) - Bocca di Tuckett (Tuckett Hut).

Sentiero delle Bocchette Alte (Route 77)

1st section, Sentiero Enrico Pedrotti: Bocca di Tuckett - Bocca Bassa di Massodi (Alimonta Hut, Brentei Hut).

2nd Section, Sentiero Umberto Quintavalle: Bocca Bassa di Massodi -

Bocca degli Armi). Alternative to 2nd Section: Sentiero Oliva Detassis:
Bocca Bassa di Massodi - Alimonta Hut.
Sentiero delle Bocchette Centrale (formerly Via delle Bocchette) (Route
78):
Bocca degli Armi - Bocca di Brenta (Pedrotti/Tosa Hut).
Variations to Routes 77 and 82:
Via delle Bocchette (Sentiero SOSAT) (Route 79).
Tuckett Hut - Brentei Hut; from here to the Bocca degli Armi and via Route
82 to the Pedrotti/Tosa Hut; *or:* on path No.318 direct to the Pedrotti/
Tosa Hut (avoiding the main ridge on the west side).
Sentiero Osvaldo Orsi (Route 80)
Tuckett Hut - Pedrotti/Tosa Hut (avoiding the main ridge on the east side).

EAST-WEST
Sentiero Brentari and *Sentiero dell'Ideale* (Route 81)
Pedrotti/Tosa Hut - Sella di Tosa - Bocca d'Ambièz - Bocca dei Camosci
- Twelve Apostles Hut.
Alternative: Sentiero Ettore Castiglioni (Route 82)
Pedrotti/Tosa Hut - Sella di Tosa - Agostini Hut - Twelve Apostles Hut.

Summary of Hut-to-Hut Times

Grostè Cableway - Tuckett Hut	
on the Sentiero A. Benini, Route 76	4hrs
Tuckett Hut - Alimonta Hut	
on the Sentiero delle Bocchette Alte, Route 77	5hrs
Alimonta Hut - Pedrotti Hut	
on the Sentiero delle Bocchette Centrale, Route 78	3hrs
Pedrotti Hut - Twelve Apostles Hut	
on the Sentiero dell'Ideale, Route 81	4$^{1/2}$hrs
Pedrotti Hut - Agostini Hut	
on the Sentiero Brentari, Path No.304/358, Route 81	4hrs
Pedrotti Hut - Agostini Hut	
on the Sentiero Palmieri, Path No.304/320	3hrs
Agostini Hut - Twelve Apostles Hut	
on the Sentiero Ettore Castiglioni, Route 82	2$^{1/4}$hrs
Twelve Apostles Hut - Brentei Hut	
on Path No.304/327/392	3hrs
Brentei Hut - Tuckett Hut	
on the Sentiero SOSAT, Path No.305, Route 79	3hrs

Tuckett Hut - Grostè Cableway	
on Path No.316	2hrs
Brentei Hut - Pedrotti Hut	
on Path No.318	2hrs
Tuckett Hut - Pedrotti Hut	
on the Sentiero Orsi. Path No.303, Route 80	4hrs

Thus, starting at the Grostè Cableway one can cover the whole climbing-path system without hurrying in 5 to 6 days, and can return to the starting-point on lower paths within this space of time.

76. Sentiero Alfredo Benini
From the Grostè Pass to the Tuckett Pass (Group d)

The route laid out extends towards the north and is scenically fantastic, and takes a worthy place in the grand Brenta roundabout. Persevering 'ferrata' - enthusiasts have in addition the possibility - to be recommended - of continuing at the Tuckett Pass directly into the tracks of the Via delle Bocchette Alte (Route 77) without loss of height.

Even a lover of the Brenta with less alpine experience - but not the completely inexperienced! who is vertigo-free, can enjoy during $3^{1}/_{2}$ hours walking on the Sentiero Benini an overwhelming, rapidly changing panorama, which fascinates everyone without exception.

The most pleasant thing is to do the Benini as a day-tour from the Grostè Pass, which is reached by cableway from the Campo-Carlo-Magno Pass above Madonna di Campiglio.

The Route: At the Grostè Pass, 2443m, immediately outside the exit to the cableway station is a stone slab with the No.305 an the inscription 'Sentiero Alfredo Benini'. From here, following the continuous waymarking, first in a south-easterly direction over a small summit - on the right, the ski-tow station. Now the path climbs easily over broad, flat, limestone pavements with remarkable funnel-holes, and over slanting, polished slabs in the direction of the Cima Grostè, which is crossed on its northern foot. Before the traverse of the actual south-east flank of the rock ridge, after an hour's walking, is the bronze plaque, 'Sentiero Alfredo Benini' at an altitude of about 2600m. A distinct, narrow path continues upwards first of all going almost right round the Cima Grostè.

The view opens magnificently to the south over lower, weathered, narrow ridges, stretched out in front, with the Crossara di Fibion and Cima di Vallazza, together with the smoothly polished slabs and limestone pavements strewn with broken rock, which lie between them and which never fail to give the impression of a lunar landscape.

After the Bivacco del Mattino - a biggish rock niche - you pass the Bocca dei Camosci, 2770m, a narrow indentation with an exciting glimpse into the steep snow couloir on the far side, which reaches down to the Vedretta Vallesinella. A narrow ledge, protected with wire rope and exposed in places, leads along the Campaniletto and the Campanile dei Camosci. Always well marked, and protected with wire rope where necessary, the wall of the Cima Falkner is traversed, climbing imperceptibly. Then one is standing on the highest point of the route, about 2900m, before scrambling almost 100m down a well protected rock nose via grooves and shelves.

Via terraced ledges of the Campanile di Vallesinella one arrives near the Rocca delle Val Perse, about 2845m, a splendid resting-place and viewpoint. Now one changes over to the west side and is unexpectedly confronted with a completely new panorama. The view into the Val Perse and of the dark northern rocks of the 3150m high Cima Brenta lying opposite, with the narrowly constricted hanging glacier, is a climax hard to beat. (1¼hrs).

The route next goes down to the west over a fairly steep glacierfield, traversed by two short rock shelves, until the track turns distinctly to the left (to the south-west; post) to the rocks of the Dente di Sella.

Important Variation: If one stays on the right-hand track, one arrives (via a combe out of which the Castelletto Superiore, a rock tooth, springs up) at a broad block-and-scree couloir (well waymarked) which brings one steeply down to the broad crown of a moraine. From there in a few minutes to the path passing by below, on which one shortly afterwards reaches the Tuckett Hut. (1hr from Rocca del Perse). This descent is somewhat shorter but only to be recommended if the Tuckett Glacier is heavily iced in autumn during years when little snow has fallen.

The real Sentiero Benini first goes round the western summit massif of the Dente di Sella, then turns south, to end at the bergschrund of the Vedretta Tuckett after several scree-covered steep steps and a smooth chimney that demands some effort. A firm snow bridge and snow ridge join up with the Tuckett Pass, 2656m, an important junction. The path, which one follows to the Rifugio Tuckett (1¼hrs) is soon reached via the harmless glacier (good track) and moraine-scree.

Time Required: Mountain Station of the Grostè Cableway - Tuckett Hut 2¹/₂-3hrs.

Difficulty: Technically relatively free of problems. Sure-footedness and freedom from vertigo are taken for granted.

Descent, Return or Continuation:

1. *Return* to the Grostè Pass. After traversing the Sentiero Benini one can descend from the Bocca di Tuckett to the Tuckett Hut, and return northwards to one's starting point at the Grostè Pass in 1³/₄hrs via the very fine path No.316 along by the Castello di Vallesinella.

2. *Descent:* From the Tuckett Hut to Madonna di Campiglio, see under Tuckett Hut.

3. *Continuation:* When conditions on the route are normal one is strongly advised to continue the enjoyment of scrambling on the same day. The possibilities are:

A) From the Bocca di Tuckett one can start immediately on the route of the Sentiero delle Bocchette Alte and get as far as the Alimonta Hut, and if occasion arises and conditions are very good, even as far as the Pedrotti/Tosa Hut on the Sentiero delle Bocchette Centrale. (See Routes 77, 78.) (Warning! To reach the Pedrotti makes a long, hard day!)

B) An easier continuation to the Pedrotti/Tosa Hut is the Sentiero Orsi (see Route 80).

C) A continuation that is only fairly exposed and technically not difficult is the Sentiero SOSAT to the Brentei Hut or further to the Alimonta Hut (see Route 79).

Time Required: Top Station of the Grostè cableway - Tuckett Hut 2¹/₂-3hrs.

Difficulty: Technically relatively free of problems; sure-footedness and freedom from vertigo are assumed.

77.   Sentiero delle Bocchette Alte From the Bocca di Tuckett to the Bocca degli Armi (Group e)

This section of the Bocchette Way begins at the Tuckett Pass, pulls out all the stops of Brenta superlatives en route and ends at the Bocca degli Armi. Thanks are due to Bruno Detassis, for decades warden of the Brentei Hut, for opening up this splendid rock scenery: a unique climbing-path system of ropes and brackets leads over ledged walls, smooth monoliths and bizarre towers - a Dolomite world of coral, which was raised up out of the primeval central ocean 200 million years ago. One keeps going for five hours on this 'Sentiero' at an average altitude of 2750m. In spite of all the protection and waymarking one must never under-rate the high-alpine character of this route: a sudden change in the weather can bring winter conditions with it. The last section of this splendid main section was opened in 1969.

The Route: The Bocca di Tuckett, 2656m, is reached either via the Sentiero Benini (see Route 76) or from the Tuckett Hut (q.v.). From the hut one must climb for 1hr over the moraine and a track in the snow of the harmless Vedretta di Brenta Inferiore. Almost at the edge of the indentation, in the rocks on the right, is a bronze plaque 'Enrico Pedrotti - Coro del SAT' - the first section is dedicated to one of the founders of the SAT choir. Furnished with ladders and wire ropes, and also very well waymarked, the ferrata leads skywards, following at first the former somewhat complicated normal ascent route of the Cima Brenta. After the initial very airy upward swing, one reaches an obliquely falling scree-field (direction post) with a splendid view to Lake Molveno, which glitters aloft out of the hazy depths. After 1hr from the Tuckett Pass one reaches the well-known Garbari Ledge, the beginning of the section called Sentiero Carlo e Giuseppe Garbari. Comfortable, sufficiently wide, and protected, it cuts across the east wall of the Cima Brenta almost horizontally at the airy altitude of about 3,000m, and ends in easy, craggy terrain. The start of the ascent of the Cima Brenta (which in good conditions is unconditionally recommended to experienced climbers) is by a waymarking sign, almost at the Garbari Plaque (see route 85).

Around a rock corner one reaches a further, somewhat narrower and pretty exposed ledge, the Cengia Alta, from which a striking view downwards is obtained to the Orsiweg and to the green high-level valleys. Shortly afterwards one faces the most problematic place on the whole route - an exposed and steeply sloping snow couloir endangered by stonefall, which stretches down from the summit; a double rope protection helps one down the tricky passage - one along the rocks, the second snow-traverse - a rope with loops to hold, which one uses according to snow conditions. When the shady couloir is iced, steps must be cut with the ice-axe for the traverse, and weaker partners secured on a rope. This couloir is followed by a ledge that leads to a terrace-like viewpoint, the Spalla di Brenta, at 3020m the highest point on the route. The view of the jagged Dolomite groups in the east, the glaciated mountains in the west, of the Torre di Brenta and the Spigolo Castiglioni is unique. Here from July to October in 1968 and 1969 stood the yellow tent of the mountain guide Pietro Vidi, who completed a great part of the most difficult work of protection single-handed. Three times a day he made radio contact with the Brentei Hut, whose roof and helicopter pad can be seen from up there. Vidi carried out the necessary blasting entirely by night, so as not to endanger the tourists walking along the Orsiweg during the day.

The section which follows, the Sentiero Mario Coggiola is impressive because of a whole series of chimneys, little walls and little indentations: Via crag and a short ladder the route descends to the narrow Bocchette Alti de Massodi, 2950m, from which an airy ladder, the Scala degli Amici (Ladders of the Friends - it was financed by Dettassis' friends) goes up with its 67 rungs to immediately below the Spallone di Massodi, 2998m - a pleasant summit with a broad, flat top and offering fine views. In old guides it also appears as Cima Butler, a reminder of the Englishman who first climbed it.

Now the waymarking leads first further south to a little path only a few minutes' climbing below the summit, until wire ropes and ladders swing over crag and a narrow ledge towards the south-east. Then again in an arc to a scree-saddle situated to the west. One climbs down across the south wall via a long series of ladders - partly overhanging - to just above the Bocca Bassa di Massodi, 2790m, which is situated between the Spallone di Massodi and Cima Molveno. The two steep ice-couloirs which stretch up on each side intensify the strange, gloomy impression of the narrow gap. Here there are two very rewarding variations to the continuation of the route:

A) *Sentiero Umberto Quintavalle:* on the far side of the indentation in the ridge, ladders and wire ropes lead 100m upwards over the north flank to the scree-covered north shoulder of the Cima Molveno, 2890m. Now it goes down finally - again with the help of wire ropes and ladders - to the end of the route at the foot of the wall. There a plaque commemorates the patron Umberto Quintavilla. One crosses the Sfulmini glacier below the Cima Armi which follows, and reaches the Bocca degli Armi without effort.

B) *Sentiero Oliva Detassis:* At the Bocca di Massodi a sign, 'Rif. Alimonta 50min.' points to a small rock gendarme. A few steps to the west and a very narrow squeeze, and one is standing before a long very bold ladder-system with about 300 steps altogether, which leads down, in parts via

222

bulging rock, - very daring - the Scala degli Dei - Ladder of the Gods.

At the end of this boldly improbable ladder-system one now climbs down along the smooth, narrow ice-couloir via the yellowish-black wall to the edge of the Brentei Glacier, which is spread out in the shape of a fan.

Crossing the Brentei snow towards the left, one gets below the fissured 'Twins' and around these without loss of height to the limestone pavement with the Rifugio Alimonta. The Detassis Brothers have christened this extremely bold section of the route Sentiero Mamma Oliva, after their mother.

Time Required: Tuckett Hut to Alimonta Hut, 5½-6hrs.

Difficulty: High-alpine traverse, very exposed in places, couloirs with danger of stone-fall and icing, ice-axe and 25m rope strongly recommended. Weaker partners only accompanied by experienced alpinists.

Return, Descent or Continuation:
1. From the Alimonta Hut return to the Brentei Hut; from there further return via the Sentiero SOSAT or Sentiero Bogani to the Tuckett Hut; from here return to the mountain-station of the Grostè Cableway or descend via the Cassinei Hut to Madonna di Campiglio.
2. From the Brentei Hut, traverse to Agostini Hut or Twelve Apostles Hut.
3. Continuation of the climbing-paths from the Bocca degli Armi via the Sentiero delle Bocchette Centrale to the Pedrotti/Tosa Hut on the Bocca di Brenta. The whole route from the Tuckett Pass to the Bocca di Brenta amounts to more than 9km and demands 8-9hrs.

78. Sentiero delle Bocchette Centrale
From the Bocca degli Armi to the Bocca di Brenta
(Pedrotti/Tosa Hut)   (Group d)

On this high-level route built in 1936, one experiences the famous and therefore much over-used central piece of the classic Brenta climbing-path, whose individual sections also bear the names of celebrated Alpinists or deserving benefactors, and provide really overpowering impressions of beauty and power.

The Bocchette Way experience is most packed and intense between the Bocca degli Armi and the Bocca di Brenta and this section must be regarded as its absolute climax. Excellently waymarked, provided with

223

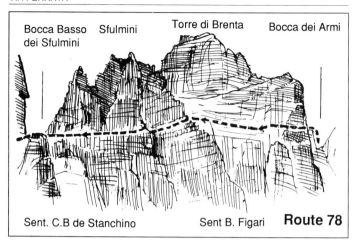

Bocca Basso dei Sfulmini Sfulmini Torre di Brenta Bocca dei Armi

Sent. C.B de Stanchino Sent B. Figari **Route 78**

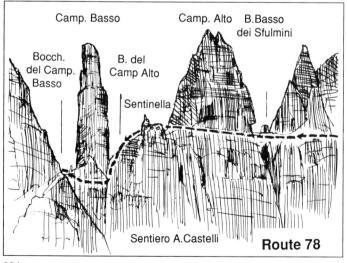

Camp. Basso Camp. Alto B.Basso dei Sfulmini

Bocch. del Camp. Basso B. del Camp Alto

Sentinella

Sentiero A.Castelli **Route 78**

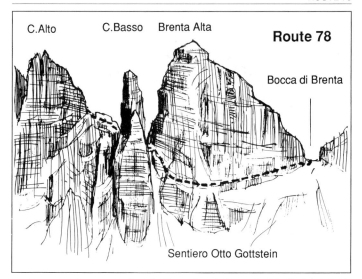

C.Alto   C.Basso   Brenta Alta

Route 78

Bocca di Brenta

Sentiero Otto Gottstein

continuous wire ropes, firm ladders, brackets and chiselled-out footholds, it is a section of path to be gazed upon, wondered at and enjoyed. In good weather anyone sufficiently free from vertigo experiences here, hours never to be forgotten. Formerly this section was called quite generally Via delle Bocchette and was considered as part of the path-system: Tuckett Hut - Sentiero SOSAT - Brentei Hut - Alimonta Hut - Bocca degli Armi - Pedrotti/Tosa Hut.

The Route: One reaches the Bocca degli Armi, 2749m, from the Alimonta Hut in ¹/₂hrs, first over scree-terrain, then via the harmless Vedretta di Sfulmini. The section Sentiero B. Figari starts from the permanent snow of the rocky indentation with a series of ladders which leads up to an airy ledge, the highest point of the route, and then leads across to the east shoulder of the Torre di Brenta. The Sentiero C.B. de Stanchino which follows, runs on a rock ledge on the east side of the Sfulmini Ridge, which comprises four sharp towers, to the Campanile Alto below the Bocca Bassa degli Sfulmini, up which, however, one does **not** climb.

The Sentiero A. Castelli runs along the east shoulder of the Campanile Alto as an almost horizontal rock stroll, until suddenly the Guglia rises up in all its slender elegance; now down to the foot of this celebrated rock

225

formation; about 150m lower down, one plunges into the bottom of the gloomy Guglia gap - a somewhat ticklish spot, this, if there is icing or hard snow - and reaches, via steps and rungs, the north-west side of the Brenta Alta, which rises up breathtakingly above the route. The last section, the Sentiero O. Gottstein, the finale of this magnificent route, begins with a rock ledge interrupted by two bridged ravines. A fascinating view of the Crozzon accompanies the walker on the concluding system of ledges, from which one finally descends via short ladders on to the snowfield; Path No.318 from the Brentei Hut comes up here. Now in a few minutes up to the Bocca di Brenta, where the Pedrotti and Tosa Huts are situated.

Time Required: Alimonta Hut - Pedrotti/Tosa Hut 4-5hrs.

Difficulty: High alpine traverse, very exposed in places, couloirs with danger of icing. Ice axe, crampons and rope advisable according to conditions.

Return, Descent or Continuation:
1.   Return on Path No.318 to the Brentei Hut, from here as occasion arises via the Casinei Hut to Madonna di Campiglio.
2.   Return to Bocca di Tuckett on the Sentiero Orsi (see Route 80).
3.   Continuation of the climbing-path expedition on the Sentiero Brentari and Sentiero Ideale (see Route 81).
4.   Over to the Agostini Hut on the Sentiero Palmieri (see under Agostini Hut).

79.   Via delle Bocchette (Sentiero SOSAT) From the Tuckett Hut to the Brentei Hut and via the Alimonta Hut to the Bocca degli Armi (Group d)

The first section of the route, the Sentiero SOSAT, built in 1961, is a well-protected rock path to the Brentei Hut and an easier variation than the high-alpine Sentiero delle Bocchette Alte. While it does not rival that unique route, it has nevertheless plenty of interesting sections with good views, and is a really enjoyable undertaking to be recommended even to ambitious climbing-path enthusiasts. By continuing on the Sentiero SOSAT one reaches the Alimonta Hut, and renews the connection with the high-alpine terrain at the Bocca degli Armi; here the Sentiero delle Bocchette Alte continues as the Sentiero delle Bocchette Centrale.

The Route: From the Tuckett Hut, first on the path to the Bocca di Tuckett to the east until below the glacier moraine. Before the tongue of the Vedretta di Brenta Inferiore the path turns south at the sign-post and leads out of the scree via the first short ladder into the craggy zone of the north side of the Punta Massari. First climbing westwards, by a spring, then gradually turning south into a land-slip area with gigantic boulders (watch the waymarking in mist!). An interesting traverse with ladders, brackets and ropes follows. An impressive 51 rung vertical ladder surmounts the deep rock ravine formed by the Punta di Campiglio, starting from a jammed boulder - very exposed. A cramped ledge follows. Soon the path turns a sharp corner - one is standing on a ledge high above the Val Brenta and is surprised by a view of the jagged Sfulmini Chain and the smooth Crozzon edge. At the end of the ledge one goes down through a short chimney on a ladder. Now either down to the Brentei Hut, which is already in sight, or, keeping to the right, up again on a good path to a flat limestone pavement on which the Alimonta Hut stands. Anyone wishing to continue via the Sentiero delle Bocchette Centrale, now climbs first via scree-terrain, then via the harmless Vedretta Sfulmini up to the narrow rock indentation - here on the Bocca degli Armi, 2749m, one is once more on the high-alpine central section of the climbing-path system between the Sentiero delle Bocchette Alte and the Sentiero delle Bocchette Centrale. For a description of the path on to the Pedrotti/Tosa Hut see Route 78.

Time Required: Tuckett Hut - Brentei Hut 2¹/₂-3hrs, Tuckett Hut - Alimonta Hut 2¹/₂hrs, from here to the Bocca degli Armi about another ¹/₂hr.

Difficulty: Technically relatively free of difficulty and without problems, but airy in places.

Return or Descent, Traverse or Continuation:
1.   Return to the Tuckett Hut: the **Sentiero Bogani,** Path No.328/318, is a fine, low-lying mountain footpath which offers a possible return route to aim at. A fine view of the Castelletto Inferiore can be seen from the high-level larch plantations; further on one crosses a rock-slip zone with impressive views of the rocky area around the Bocca di Tuckett.
2.   Descent to the Casinei Hut or to the Vallesinella Hut, at first once more on the Sentiero Bogani, but in the middle of the path down north-west on Path 328.
3.   Traverse to the Twelve Apostles Hut via the Bocca dei Camosci (see under Twelve Apostles Hut). No difficulty.
4.   Traverse to Agostini Hut via the Bocca d'Ambièz (see Route 81). No difficulty.

227

5.   Ascent to Bocca degli Armi and traverse of Sentiero delle Bocchette Centrale to the Pedrotti/Tosa Hut (see Route 78). Difficult.

80.   Sentiero Orsi From the Tuckett Hut to the Pedrotti/Tosa Hut   (Group b)

German mountaineers jokingly call the Bochette Way the 'Upper Cycle Track' in contrast with the Sentiero Osvaldo Orsi which they designate the 'Lower Cycle Track'. This exceptionally beautiful high-level route passes through the heart of the Brenta on its east side and offers an uninterrupted scenic spectacle of a series of really splendid walls, very bold towers and needles that seem to touch the sky. The greatest delight derived from about 4hrs of walking and looking at the views lies in the deeply hollowed combes from which rise the classic forms of the Guglia, Cima Molveno, Spallone di Massòdi, Cima Brenta etc. Even though this climbing-path variation is comparatively free of problems, it earns interest throughout because of its uniquely beautiful route.

The Route: First, from the Tuckett Hut over the harmless Tuckett Glacier, to the Tuckett Pass; here a fine view back to the weighty massif of the Cima Brenta and into the glaciated ravine that leads up to the summit. Then a steep descent into the uppermost part of the Val Perse. Keep to the left side: the first part of the route is well protected with a long wire rope. (Reports of rockfall damage to this path, 1986, 1987.) The Orsiweg begins as a good, well waymarked mountain path (303) branching to the right by a large block of rock. It runs along keeping just under the mighty east wall of the Cima Brenta, and allows the magnificent precipice of the Cima Roma, 2827m, to be seen across the Val Perse with particular impressiveness. The route begins to ascend steadily and reaches the striking Sega Alta, a broad rock ledge with wire rope protection along a wall falling vertically below a mighty overhang. A rock ridge follows immediately after with the Naso (Nose) 2527m at its end - the finest viewpoint on the whole route: the last sight of the Val Perse with its mighty enclosure of walls, and the first grand view into the upper Massòdi combes with its bold needles and tower: Spallone di Massòdi, 2999m, Cima Molveno, 2911m and Cima d'Armi, 2935m, enclose the wide rock corrie with magnificent walls. Going across under a pillar the route drops into the lower Massòdi combe. Here the showpiece of the Brenta, a classic rock formation of the Alps, towers up into the sky: the unimaginably bold, slim, elegant Campanile Basso (German: Nadel der Guglia) 2877m, accompanied by the mighty rock castles of Torre di Brenta, 3008m, Campanile Alto 2937m, and the grand phenomenon of the Cima Brenta Alta, 2969m. A rock realm of unusual impressiveness; a magnificent series of walls with orange rock-colouring surrounds the combe, which is filled with gigantic rubble from land-slips. After crossing this, is the descent into the rocky valley which runs down from the Bocca di Brenta. This is crossed; then the last short ascent to the Pedrotti Hut.

Time Required: Tuckett Hut - Pedrotti/Tosa Hut 4hrs.

Difficutly: Technically without problems.

Return, Descent or Continuation: Return from the Pedrotti/Tosa Hut back to the starting-point either

A) on the Sentiero delle Bocchette Centrale and the Sentiero delle Bocchette Alte (difficult), or

B) on the Sentiero delle Bocchette Centrale as far as the Bocca degli Armi, then down westwards and on the Sentiero SOSAT back to the Tuckett Hut (1st half difficult), or

C) on path No.318 to the Brentei Hut, from here on the Sentiero SOSAT back to the Tuckett Hut, comparatively free of problems.

Descents: Into the valley from the Brentei Hut on Path No.323/380 or, better, on Path No.318 (Sentiero Bogani) via the Casinei Hut.

Continuation of the climbing-path system via the Sentiero Brentari and Sentiero dell'Ideale or via the Sentiero Castiglione.

81. Sentiero Brentari and Sentiero dell'Ideale From the Pedrotti Hut to the Twelve Apostles Hut or From the Agostini Hut to the Twelve Apostles Hut (Group e)

These two sections of the route, completed in 1932, are the oldest parts of the climbing-path system of the Brenta. The high-alpine, glaciated traverse passes through its very heart; scenically it is one of the most magnificent mountain routes in the southern limestone Alps, and offers a superfluity of impressions of various kinds in rock and snow.

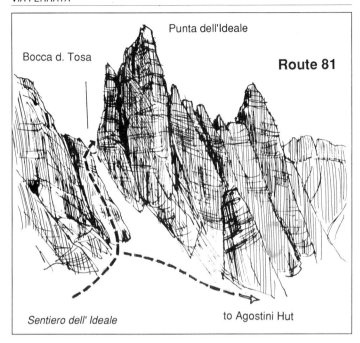

Bocca d. Tosa

Punta dell'Ideale

Route 81

Sentiero dell' Ideale

to Agostini Hut

The Route: From the Pedrotti/Tosa Hut Path 304 leads first around the base of the Cima Brenta Bassa, crosses the upper rim of a vast funnel-hole (the Pozza Tramontana) and turning southwards gets into a fascinating rock basin which is enclosed by the magnificent east wall of the Cima Tosa, the south wall of the Cima Margherita and the bold massif of the Cima Brenta Bassa. After another steep section the route leads into a small snow basin, from which the Guglia (Campanile Basso) can be very beautifully seen; the path climbs from here as far as the start of the normal ascent of the Cima Tosa (see Route 87) and crosses from there, climbing moderately, on to the rock ridge of the Sella di Tosa, 2860m, from where an impressive view of the smooth, bulging east wall of the Cima d'Ambièz opens up. The following section of the route, called the Sentiero Brentari, is a well protected climbing-path and leads pleasantly, with splendid scenic pictures, first to the Bocca di Tosa, the gap between the Tosa massif and the magnificent and striking peak of Punta d'Ideale, after which the next section of the route is named.

Iron ladders warped by lightning and winter snow-storms now lead up on the upper edge of the Vedretta d'Ambièz, over whose snow the track leads up from the Agostini hut, which is visible to the south, below, on the left (Path No.358). Now, according to conditions, first somewhat left to a short, steep, snow-couloir, whose start is often slippery and crevassed; one still climbs up most easily in the middle (footmarks usually). There are no safe snow-bridges over the bergschrund, which is surprisingly wide in warm summers, so one climbs up to the left between the Ambièz wall and snow, via snow-free rock steps and ledges to the Bocca d'Ambièz, 2871m, which joins the Cima Tosa and Cima d'Ambièz. From the saddle one climbs down via a short steep groove to the Vedretta dei Camosci, on a wire rope lying free on the snow, and one now crosses over to the left as high as possible; from the right, Path 327 comes up from the Brentei Hut (see under Twelve Aposltes Hut, ascents, No.4).

The magnificent Camosci basin is one of the surprising moments of this high-alpine traverse - it is enclosed on three sides by the rocks of the Crozzon, Tosa and Ambièz; opposite, the peak of the Fracinglo towers up and separates the two glaciers with its rock-foot like the bows of a ship. One now reaches the Bocca dei Camosci, 2770m, via the upper snowfield of the Camosci glacier; here there is rock rubble with waymarking. On the far side of this saddle an entirely new landscape opens up. A good path leads west down along the Vedretta d'Agola, via a last short ascent one finally reaches the hospitable Twelve-Apostles Hut on the glacier-polished limestone pavement.

*Time Required:*Pedrotti/Tosa Hut - Twelve Apostles Hut 4½-5hrs; Agostini Hut - Twelve Apostles Hut 4-4½hrs.

*Difficulty:*High-alpine, glaciated traverse, only for very safe climbing-path users with experience of high mountains. Crampons and ice-axe sometimes needed.

Return, Descent or Continuation:
A) Easier return to the Agostini Hut and to the Pedrotti/Tosa Hut via the Sentiero Castiglione (Route 82) and Sentiero Palmieri (see under 'Agostini Hut, ascent from San Lorenzo in Banale').
B) Traverse to the Brentei Hut (see under Twelve Apostles Hut, ascents, No.4).
C) Descent to Pinzolo (see under Twelve Apostles Hut, ascents, No.2).

82. Sentiero Ettore Castiglioni From the Agostini Hut to the Twelve Apostles Hut (Group d)

The Sentiero Ettore Castiglioni is an easier variation from the high-alpine, glaciated traverse via the Bocca d'Ambièz and the Bocca dei Camosci (Route 81). In the basin before the vertical wall the rock world of the Brenta is presented in impressive grandeur; on the wall one experiences a rock-route of extraordinary beauty and boldness. The descent to the Twelve Apostles Hut is one of the serener moments in the Brenta via ferrata circuit.

The Route: Anyone coming from the Tosa Hut, on the route already described (Route 81), crosses after the last ladders comfortably over the crevasse-free Vedretta d'Ambièz down on good tracks towards the foot of the Ambièz east wall, and meets the serpentine Path No.358 by a large cairn among the erratic boulders of the moraine; this leads directly to the nearby Agostini Hut ($^1/_2$hr from ladders). Shortly before the hut one comes across the notice Sentiero Ettore Castiglioni and the branch Path 321 to the right. Now left over a craggy zone into a small rock combe with a grand surround: Cima d'Ambièz, east wall of the Cima d'Agola and Cima Pratofiorita. The path leads imediately below a wall which is climbed vertically for about 200m on a splendid rock route: the ladders have about 300 rungs! Brackets as footholds, ladders and wire ropes solve the technical problems and make the climb pure pleasure. One crosses unexpectedly into a narrow rock gap, the Bocchette dei Due Denti, 2859m; here a splendid, open, all-round view opens up. The rock route ends here; the Twelve Apostles Hut can already be seen and the airily enjoyable climb is followed by an equally enjoyable downhill walk over the harmless Pratofiorito glacier. One either follows the waymarked path or, if the snow conditions allow, very steeply down without effort across the permanent snow; but down below one keeps to the right, where one meets the path again; on this one reaches the cosy, hospitable hut over the limestone pavement which stretches before one.

Time Required: Rif. Agostini - Rif. Dodici Apostoli 2hrs.

Difficulty: Technically not particularly demanding, but very airy on the wall.

Descent or Return:

A) Descent to Pinzolo (see under Twelve Apostles Hut, ascents, No.2).

B) Traverse to Rif. Brentei (see under Twelve Apostles Hut, ascents, No.4).

C) Return to the Agostini Hut on the Sentiero dell'Ideale (see Route 81).

Time Required: Rif. Agostini - Rif. Twelve Apostles 2hrs.

Difficulty: Not very demanding technically. (Cliff step very airy.)

SUMMIT ASCENTS REACHED FROM THE VIE FERRATE

Easily accessible summits, to be reached on prepared paths, such as the average mountaineer loves, do not exist at all in the Brenta. In its central area almost all tops can be climbed only on difficult/very difficult rock-climbing routes. The builders of the climbing-paths have here remained true to the original intention not to open up the summits themselves, but to protect only their principal approaches - natural systems of ledges, connecting ridges and traverses. Nevertheless, it is perfectly possible under good conditions for the more experienced climbing-path user to reach some of the most magnificent summits by their so-called 'normal routes' without having special climbing ability at his disposal. The selection given here is composed entirely of attractive goals; difficulty up to Grade II may be reached in places during the ascents, but not exceeded. Descent basically on the same route.

83. Cima del Grostè, 2897m
Reached from the Sentiero Benini

From the Gaffer Hut, 2261m, as starting point, or from the mountain-station of the Grostè cableway, 2437m, one goes at first on the Sentiero Benini (Route 76), which is followed, ascending easily in the direction of the Cima del Grostè over great stretches of limestone pavement until one comes to a boulder-filled couloir on the right. The boulder-couloir is ascended, to do which of course one sometimes has to use one's hands. Then on to the broad dome of the Cima del Grosté and here again on a good, narrow path to the nearby summit. From the mountain-station 2½hrs.

84. Cima Sella, 2911m
Reached from the Sentiero Benini

From the Tuckett Hut, 2268m, as a starting-point, first over the harmless Tuckett glacier to the Tuckett Pass. Here to the left, north via the ladders on the Sentiero Benini (see Route 76 in reverse). Into a wide combe at the foot of the Cima Brenta, which can already be seen from here, with broad ledges and built like a sloping roof. From the combe, to the right easily to a broad saddle between the rock tooth of the Castelletto Superiore, 2696m, and the Cima Sella, with a glorious view of the Cima Brenta. From the saddle up without difficulty over limestone pavement and crag until immediately by the summit massif of the Cima Sella. Path and waymarking until just under the summit massif, then pathless, with only very isolated cairns.

One now has to climb up continuously on short walls (6-10m high), and then to get as high as possible again on the broad ledges lying in between, from which the next wall obstructing the way must be surmounted, until one reaches the summit.

Mountaineering and rock-climbing experience are necessary; the difficulties are not great, but it doesn't go without rock-climbing, and therefore the inexperienced must be in the company of experienced companions. From the Tuckett Hut 3hrs.

85. Cima Brenta, 3150m
Reached from the Sentiero delle Bocchette Alte

The second highest summit of the Brenta is very frequently climbed from the Garbari Ledge; the ascent ridge lies at the end of this ledge, shortly before the Garbari sign (see Route 77). The route is unprotected and not waymarked, but clearly indicated by cairns, and leads up rock steps and shallow chimneys to a ledge. From here the best ascent is offered by the left (in ascent) branch of a double ravine. Following this it goes further up over steep rock steps (Grades I and II). Then one reaches a small rock summit, climbs down a few metres and crosses a level ridge of permanent snow about 30m long, from which a very steep ice couloir runs down to the permanent snow of the Tuckett glacier (on the left, vertical precipices and overhanging cornices). Perfect rope protection for the insecure partner is most strongly advised; for solo climbers, ice-axe and crampons are recommended as occasion arises. After crossing the snow ridge, over the craggy rock of the summit dome, and after a few minutes without further problems, to the broad summit with summit-book and a small iron summit-cross.

Some rock-climbing experience necessary. Inexperienced climbers only on an experienced leader's rope. Snow-ridge dangerous! From the Forest sign 1¼hrs, from the Tuckett Hut 4hrs.

86. Monte Daino, 2685m
Reached from the Pedrotti/Tosa Hut

Down from the Pedrotti/Tosa Hut on Path No.326 to the Passo di Ceda, until the path begins to descend steeply. Here one has already got round the rocky bulk of the Croz del Rifugio and finds oneself on a grassy area from which one can very easily ascend into the rocky combes of the Monte Daino which lie behind. One climbs up through these, keeping to the right all the time, and then the summit is reached via broad scree ledges and small walls. The ascent is worthwhile on account of the splendid view of the Brenta chain seen from the east.

The ascent is pathless and not waymarked, but without difficulty. From the Pedrotti/Tosa Hut 2-3hrs.

87. Cima Tosa, 3173m
Reached from the Sentiero Brentari

To climb the Cima Tosa, the highest Brenta summit, is the dream of many via ferrata users, and it is very frequently climbed.

From the Pedrotti/Tosa Hut one first follows Path No.304 as far as the start of the Tosa ascent. From here over intervening crags to the foot of the wall. On the right of a dark, vertical chimney, up over the well climbable wall pitch (Grade II. Abseil ring-piton above). This climbing-pitch is followed, surprisingly, by purely walking terrain; first along numerous rock cubes steeply up over crag to the summit snow. Over the extensive snow summit on a broad snow ridge and almost horizontally to the summit with splendid long-distance views. Recommended only to very experienced mountaineers on account of the climbing-pitch at the foot of the wall. From the Pedrotti/Tosa Hut 2½-3hrs.

88. Cima Pratofiorito, 2900m
Reached from the Sentiero Ettore Castiglione

From the Twelve Apostles Hut follow at first the Sentiero Ettore Castiglioni (Route 82) Path No.321, to the beginning of the small glacier, Vedretta Pratofiorito. Here to the right by a small glacier lake and directly on the permanent snow to the clearly visible Passo del Vallon, 2796m. The snow is very steep in the final part of the ascent. From the pass a very fine view into the upper basin of the very lonely Vallon (Busa di Vallon Alto, 2585m) surrounded by forest. From the Passo del Vallon the ascent continues up to the left via a craggy step on to a broad rock ridge, and up this quickly to the summit. Magnificent view of Cima d'Ambièz and Cima Tosa.

Ascent not difficult, but mountaineering experience and sure-footedness are needed. Inexperienced mountaineers are strongly advised against going without an experienced companion. Ice-axe recommended. No path, no waymarking. From the Twelve Apostles Hut 3hrs.

89.   Sentiero Gustavo Vidi - Sentiero Claudio Costanzi, Cima Sassara 2892m
Northern Brenta Group
From the Passo del Grostè to the Nuovo Rifugio Peller Or to the Passo Campo Carlo Magno (Giro della Pietra Grande)   (Group e)

The northern Brenta is considered to be hardly developed and in spite of the new waymarks between Paso del Grosté and the Nuovo Rifugio Peller, is hardly used. Anyone who takes this extraordinarily long and complex route, with its many exhausting re-ascents, certainly does not find any sensational alpine experiences such as may be found on the show-pieces of the Bocchette Paths, but in their stead a mountaineering experience of usually absolute solitude in a surprisingly untouched scenic setting. Anyone wishing to get back to his car in the evening without technical traffic problems is recommended to use the very full round-tour described here. Anyone who continues the walk from Sasso Rosso as far as the Nuovo Rif. Peller should provide in advance for the return journey along the long stretches of road. (Put one car at the start and another at the end of the walk!)

The Route: At the Grostè Pass a sign just at the exit to the cable-car station directs you to the 'Sentiero Gustavo Vidi' (Path No.390). In a few minutes you are standing on the level Grostè Pass, 2443m, and from there you can make out a big red sign on the rock face. Go a short distance north on the level, then in steep curves to the east flank and on a narrow ledge to the red sign. Five minutes on a level path over a scree-covered ledge below which the rock falls steeply away.

In front of a big scree-basin the path turns fairly steeply up again, leads through the scree- and grass-covered flank and finally reaches the friendly ridge. Further via a grassy ledge on to the now rising ridge. A narrow rock fissure is crossed at the first ropes. In the middle of the grassy hump-back of the ridge the path turns down on to the west flank. It follows a long horizontal traverse through a scree-covered flank interspersed with grass. In the morning it is really shady and cool here; only the topmost jagged peaks of ridge are bathed in morning sunlight. Below the path is a yawning abyss, so take care if it is damp, snow-covered or icy. The sole outlier of the ridge - with a bold rock-needle below the path - is got round with protection. A gentle series of ladders soon follows up an area of broken rock. The ledge - now continuously protected - leads on, somewhat higher. Down through a shallow, easy, well-protected chimney. Now the path leads further along the level, dropping down, too, in places, through a fairly steep flank of scree. Some places which tend to push you off require care. A section again follows for a short time which is sunny even in the morning and which leads to a broad, grassy outlier from the ridge. It is worthwhile taking a last look back from here at the unified panorama of the whole Brenta.

At the sign 'Sentiero G.V.1960', somewhat below this mountain meadow, the path forks. To the left it goes - adequately protected - over a steep rock step down again to Path No.336 and via the Rif. Giorgio Graffer to the top station of the cable-car. (This is the shortest variation of the Pietra Grande Circular; an easy half-day's outing, but not profoundly impressive.)

To continue you now go further on the shady west flank, cross a scree-corrie and get to a broad, sunny outlier of the ridge with an almost level alpine meadow. A ten-minute detour to the adjacent gentle, rounded top offers yet another incomparable view of the Brenta as a whole. Continue very leisurely over broad, green alpine meadows and user-friendly, gentle scree-slopes. From far below comes the tinkle of cowbells on the Malga Mondifra. The third outlier from the ridge opens up a new panorama. A big corrie lies on the west flank of Cima Vagliana; a gigantic, apparently key-hole-shaped rock-gate shines in the *contre-jour* lighting in the midst of the extremely wild ridge. Down into the corrie to a boulder with the inscription: 'Graffer 2 Std, Peller 7 Std' (Rif. Graffer 2hrs; Nuovo Rif. Peller 7hrs).

(Here there is a second opportunity to return through the Val Gelada to Path 336 and to the Rifugio Giorgio Graffer or directly to Malga Mondrifa - some sections at the beginning not waymarked, however.)

Now steeply through scree to the Passo Tre Sassi, named after the three jagged rock peaks which tower up like the stumps of rotten teeth out of the frayed col on the ridge, already crumbled into scree. Under the pass is a sign 'Sentiero Claudio Costanzi, 1974, Nr. 336' with the photo of the bearded giant after whom it is named. The Bocchetta Tre Sassi offers a fine view down into the Val delle Giare. Only an indistinct, unwaymarked path leads down from here to the east. Up steeply from the pass, through scree at first, then through broken rock to a little grassy spot near the ridge. Easily on a broad ledge and further on the level. The only rocky place is protected with a rope. Around a wide valley to the next pass. Here a waymarked path forks off down to the east (Malga Tuenno - Lago Tovel, Path No.380). Now, very steeply and laboriously at first through scree, then on a firm path to the base of some rock. A ladder and good, new steel bolts lead easily and securely over the short rock-step on the next user-friendly scree-ridge. Here ropes lead off the ridge again to the left onto a gravelled ledge. *(Warning:* At the start this is overhung by rock and only 1 metre high. High-packed rucksacks must be taken off here.) Down, with rope-protection to a little col in the ridge, and now further on the east side of the ridge to the scree-covered summit massif of Cima Sassara, 2892m, which you reach in a few minutes on a path over fine scree - a five-minute detour, really rewarding. A big iron cross (1977) crowns this summit.

Do not go back to the path, but go easily north over the well waymarked summit ridge to a helicopter pad and the *Bivacco Bonvecchio,* outwardly an aluminium box, but inside a clean and surprisingly cosy little hut with six immaculate little beds. From the dreary site of the bivouac on the scree-field on to an airy grassy ledge and - well protected - over a steep step of broken rock up to the ridge. Down to the right at a rock-barrier and on exciting, steep rock steps to the next ridge, with several clumps of edelweiss. A quiet walk follows, partly on the ridge, partly below it to the west. After the next big rounded rocky hillock down steeply with wire-rope protection; a tiring switchback among little summits and hummocks, grooves and wind-gaps.

A short chimney with no protection is very easy to descend (Grade II-), after which a leisurely stroll downhill relieves the tension. A new climax is soon provided, however. The waymarking leads round the whole of the following ridge with some really exciting sections. One short section is also very airy in ascent (Grade II-). Here it is essential to pay attention to the waymarking, which crosses a wild flank of grass and broken rock where nature is completely untouched. After half-an-hour you reach the ridge again. A deep cleft, on its right a big snow field, then again up and down over a hummock of broken rock. You climb only half-way up the next hump. *[The German guidebook calls this "Sasso Alto, 2804m", but this is clearly an error. Translator.]* Half way up, the route goes left again, west, on the flank. Now you reach a sign "Sentiero Claudio Costanzi" with the direction "Sasso Alto" pointing back the way you have come. A simple, level section of ridge follows, then the direction "Peller". Here go left, straight through a gentle flank of boulders and across level terrain of slabby rock in wide curves around a completely splintered little tower on the ridge. Now an unusually red mountain appears - Sasso Rosso, 2645m. At its foot on the south side, at the Passo di Pra Castron, 2503m, Paths 310 and 329 cross Path 336, which continues to the Nuovo Rifugio Peller (two direction signs: Peller, Sasso Alto). Path 336 contours the east flank of Sasso Rosso and climbs to reach the col on the north slope of this mountain. It leads down from here through the Pian della Nana, via the Baita (hut) di Nanno (Baito Nana), then on Path 306 over the Passo della Forcola, 2103m to Malga di Cles, 1885m and from here on Path 308 via two re-ascents finally to the Nuovo Rifugio Peller, 2022m. (Total time from the Passo del Grostè 7-9hrs.)

If you want to get back to your car on the same day without problems it is advisable to go down west into the Val del Vento *[ie. From Passo di Pra Castron, and NOT to continue to the Nuovo Rif. Peller. Translator.]. Descent:* You follow, therefore, the waymarks to the left *[ie. from Passo di Pra Castron. Path 329. Translator].* The sparse, bristly grass has as yet no trace of tracks, so you must pay careful attention to all waymarks. At a clear signpost Path No.329 turns south at a right-angle and leads down by the steep south wall *[Should not this read "north wall"? Translator]* of the upper Val del Vento. Now the path leads in big curves from one side of the valley to the other - splendid flora. Beware of taking tempting short cuts here, for the valley, especially in its highest, completely confused, belts of trees and shrubs, is cut through by a number of dangerous crags. After a gentle section of the path the first water splashes over an almost inaccessible rock wall. But only a minute later you come across a tiny spring between two rocky crags. Probably no one will ignore this first opportunity for refreshment after a good eight hours' walking. The path now leads on a soft carpet of spruce-needles down through the forest to the abandoned Magna Scale (alpine hut), 1562m. Now take care. Do not under any circumstances follow the two paths which lead further west.

Path 355 to Madonna di Campiglio is a nasty tractor-track which leads south directly up into the forest. A forestry road has destroyed the old path here. This road climbs, moderately at first, soon very steeply until you reach the first original tracks of the path with waymarks. After levelling out it soon goes down very steeply. A short stretch of forestry-track again follows the old path, which, however, soon joins a vehicular road which leads up to Malga Mondifra, 1636m. Once more you climb to the left up a steep bend in the road and reach the big alm by road. Down on the road to the valley station of the Grostè Cable-car.

Time Required: Funivia Grostè Top Station - Passo di Pra Castron - Funivia Grostè Valley Station (recommended Route) 10-12hrs. Funivia Grostè Top Station to Nuovo Rif. Peller about 9-10hrs. Shortest variation of the Round Tour of the Pietra Grande (descent immediately west of Pietra Grande, with return to the Top Station) about 3-4hrs. Middle variation with descent through the Val Gelada - either on Path 334 via the Malga Mondifra to the Valley Station or on Path 336 to the Top Station - either way 6-8hrs.

Difficulty: Apart from two short airy sections technically without difficulty, but because of its enormous length only recommended to walkers with great staying power. Under no circumstances set out in mist or snow conditions. In those conditions great danger of losing one's way, in spite of the good waymarking. Because it is so remote only those with appropriate experience are recommended to go alone.

Bases: Rif. Giorgio Graffer at the starting-point. About half-way the Bivacco Bonvecchio, unwardend; 6 beds; room for some emergency sleeping-places. At the end, if applicable, Nuovo Rif. Peller, 2022m, (Club Alpino Italiano/Società Alpinistico Tridentini) 56 beds, wardened from 15 June to 25 Sept.

Note: Do not spend the night in the bivouac except in case of emergency or if the weather is absolutely settled. A sudden fall in temperature and atmospheric pressure overnight with mist or snowfall can have unpleasant consequences for the bivouacker!

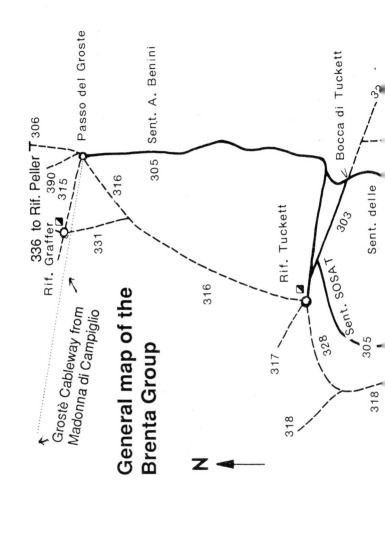

General map of the Brenta Group